The Economics of Michał Kalecki

The Economics of Michał Kalecki

MALCOLM C. SAWYER

M. E. SHARPE, Inc.
ARMONK, NEW YORK

First published in the United States of America in 1985
by M.E. Sharpe, Inc.

Library of Congress Cataloging in Publication Data
Sawyer, Malcolm C.
The economics of Michał Kalecki.
Bibliography: p.
1. Kalecki, Michał. 2. Economics. 3. Macroeconomics.
I. Title.
HB113.K28S28   1985   330.15′6   85–11777
ISBN 0–87332–352–1
ISBN 0–87332–353–X (pbk.)

Printed in Hong Kong

Contents

Preface and Acknowledgements

In writing this book, I have sought to satisfy four major objectives. The first one is to provide a systematic and sympathetic discussion of the work of Michał Kalecki, written to appeal to a wide audience including undergraduate students. There is a relatively small band of the *cognoscenti* who regard the work of Kalecki very highly (as discussed in the introduction to Chapter 1). For example, Harcourt (1977b) argues that 'Kalecki is a most important patron saint of the post-Keynesians'. This book seeks to extend the knowledge and enthusiasm of the *cognoscenti* to a much wider audience. In particular, I would argue that Kalecki has much to offer to the development of a macroeconomics which can help us to understand the crucial problems of unemployment, slow growth, inflation, etc.

The second objective is to consider Kalecki's work as a coherent whole. This involves consideration of Kalecki's macroeconomics of capitalist economies (Chapters 2 to 7 below) as a complete 'package'. It also involves a discussion of the extent to which his approach to capitalist economies can be seen to be consistent (in a broad sense) with his approach to socialist and developing economies.

The third objective is to begin an evaluation of Kalecki's place in the study of economics. This is reflected in a number of ways. I shall seek to indicate places where Kalecki's work can be seen as a (often unacknowledged) forerunner of the ideas of others. In Chapter 1 and at a number of other places scattered through the text, I contrast Kalecki's approach with the prevailing neo-classical orthodoxy. I seek also to place Kalecki within the broad Ricardian–Marxian tradition in Chapter 1, and this is followed up in Chapter 8 by a comparison between the work of Marx and that of Kalecki. One reason for making that comparison is that Kalecki was clearly strongly influenced by the work of Marx, and to some degree the work of Marx permeated that of Kalecki.

A number of ideas developed by Keynes in the 1930s were also developed independently by Kalecki at about the same time. In Chapter 9 I compare the work of Kalecki with Keynes's *General Theory*. This permits further discussion of the work of Kalecki within the general field of economic theory, as well as dealing with the question of the extent to which Kalecki could be said to have anticipated Keynes (and *vice versa*). This comparison also allows some indirect comparisons between Kalecki and conventional (Keynesian) macroeconomics.

The fourth purpose is to establish pointers for possible developments of a Kaleckian macroeconomics. In recent years, there has been a considerable interest in development of such a macroeconomics, after thirty years of substantial neglect. In Chapter 12, I seek to bring together a number of points raised in the earlier chapters which relate to refinements and extensions of Kalecki's approach to economics.

A comprehensive intellectual biography of Kalecki is already available in Feiwell (1975). Whilst sharing with Feiwell a high regard for the work of Kalecki, this book has rather different aims compared with Feiwell (1975). I have aimed the book specifically at a level suitable for undergraduates, and aimed for a more interpretative book, with more comparisons between Kalecki and other authors. I have limited the extent of biographical detail to the minimum I thought necessary, although in Chapter 9 I have used extensive notes to relate some points of interest on the intellectual relationship between Kalecki and Keynes.

In the references I have only listed those works of Kalecki which are actually referred to in the text. A comprehensive bibliography of Kalecki's work is given in Kowalik (1964) (for works before 1964) and in Feiwell (1975). A selective bibliography is provided in *Oxford Bulletin of Economics and Statistics*, vol. 39. The collected works of Kalecki are currently being published in Polish, and it is to be hoped that an English translation may soon be available. My research has inevitably been somewhat restricted by my lack of Polish which means that some of Kalecki's articles have not been consulted in the preparation of this book.

I am very grateful to many people who have helped with comment on drafts and with discussion on particular points. The interest which many have displayed in this book has been a considerable spur in its writing. I would like to thank Mrs Ada Kalecki for written information which is used in Chapter 9 with her permission. I was particularly fortunate that during the academic year 1983–4 when this book was being completed, Dr Jerzy Osiatyński was visiting the Institute of Development Studies, University of Sussex. As the editor of Kalecki's works and a former student of Kalecki, he was able to provide me with much valuable information. Dr Włodzimierz Brus (now of Wolfson College, Oxford), a former colleague of Kalecki, provided valuable background information, particularly on Kalecki's involvement with policy discussion in Poland. I am grateful to another colleague of Kalecki, Professor Kazimierz Łaski (now of University of Linz, Austria) for permission to refer to unpublished papers.

I would like to thank those whose comments on earlier drafts led to considerable improvements in style and content of this book. Philip Arestis (Thames Polytechnic) and Peter Reynolds (North Staffordshire Polytechnic) read through Chapters 1 to 7 of the first draft. George Catephores (University College London), Raja Junankar (University of Essex) and Keith Gibbard (Manchester Polytechnic) helped me with comments on Chapter 8, and discussions with Vicky Chick (University College London) have helped clarify points discussed in Chapter 9. Paul Hare (University of Stirling) and Jan Toporowski (Polytechnic of the South Bank) read Chapter 11 for me and Sheila Smith (University of Sussex) read Chapter 10. Whilst this book has benefited considerably from their comments and advice, it is still the case that those who have helped me do not necessarily agree with what I have written (indeed in some cases I know that they will not agree).

Dr Sam Aaronovitch responded enthusiastically to the idea of a book on Kalecki, and his comments (and our general discussions) have also improved the book.

I would finally like to thank participants in seminars given on the relationship between Kalecki and Keynes at the Universities of Dublin and Lancaster, Polytechnic of the South Bank (London), Manchester, Newcastle and Wolverhampton Polytechnics, and the joint seminar of North Staffordshire Polytechnic and Keele University for comments and stimulus to further thinking.

I am very grateful to Mrs Ada Kalecki for permission to quote extensively from the following books and article written by her husband: *Selected Essays on the Dynamics of the Capitalist Economy*; *Selected Essays on the Economic Growth of the Socialist and the Mixed Economy* (both published by Cambridge University Press); *Essays on the Developing Economies* (published by Harvester Press); 'Theories of Growth in Different Economic Systems', *Scientia*, nos 5–6 (1970). I am also grateful to Allen & Unwin for permission to quote from M. Kalecki, *Essays in the Theory of Economic Fluctuations* (1939).

University of York   Malcolm C. Sawyer
England
January 1985

1
An Introduction to Kalecki and His Ideas

Introduction

The widely varying evaluations of the work of Michał Kalecki made by economists tells us much about the state of economic thinking about capitalism. For some, Kalecki occupies a place amongst the greatest economists. *The Cambridge Journal of Economics*, for example, places Kalecki alongside Keynes and Marx as the three main sources of traditions which have 'much to contribute to the understanding and treatment of current economic and social issues'. The series of books, of which this book is one, cites Kalecki with Marx and Sraffa as providing a 'more fruitful point of departure' than the prevailing orthodoxy. Joan Robinson (Robinson, 1980, p. 122) as well as Eichner and Kregel (1975, fn. 1) acknowledge the contribution of Kalecki's ideas rather than those of Keynes, to the tradition which labels itself post-Keynesian.[1] Galbraith has acknowledged 'how much those of us the world around have owed to the intellectual capital you (Kalecki) have provided over these past decades' (quoted in Feiwell, 1975, p. 17 from a letter from Galbraith to Kalecki). Worswick (1977), until recently director of the National Institute of Economic and Social Research, London, has indicated that 'I thought him [Kalecki] the best [economist in the world] when I knew him in the war, and I still think so'. Harcourt (1975a) has described Kalecki as 'the most neglected of all great modern economists'.

Despite these acknowledgements to the stature of Kalecki and his ideas, it is probably the case that most students of economics in Britain and America (particularly the latter) would not have heard of Kalecki (nor Sraffa) and not have studied the work of Marx. When the work of Kalecki is deemed worthy of a mention in an economics degree course, it is likely to be a brief and dismissive discussion of a misinterpretation of his degree of monopoly theory of income distribution (see Chapter 2 below on this theory). Although it is difficult to separate microeconomic and macroeconomic aspects in Kalecki's work, nevertheless his main work on capitalist economies could be labelled macroeconomic. Yet a check of six leading macroeconomics texts failed to reveal one reference to Kalecki. The failure to consider Kalecki's work seriously is symptomatic of the dominance of neo-classical economic theory in the teaching of economics, and the manner in which alternatives to neo-classical economics are excluded from serious consideration. Textbooks on macroeconomics (and much discussion) centre attention on the relatively trivial disputes between Keynesians and monetarists, and thereby ignore the challenge to the Keynesian-monetarist orthodoxy presented by post-Keynesians, Kaleckians and Marxists.

The trite response to this virtual exclusion of consideration of the work of Kalecki and others is that it represents the considered judgement of the economics profession based on a thorough evaluation of their work and the evidence relating to it. The way in which Kalecki's degree of monopoly theory has been discussed (as shown on pp. 28–36 below) suggests that neither thorough evaluation nor considered judgement were used in that instance. The revival of interest in the work of Kalecki, Marx and Sraffa amongst a substantial minority of economists also indicates that the relative usefulness of their approaches and the neo-classical approach is far from settled. The purpose of this book is to set out in a systematic and sympathetic way the ideas of Kalecki and to indicate their relationship with other ideas in economic analysis so that readers can form their own views on his ideas and their usefulness. The book is largely theoretical, though we do briefly consider some aspects of empirical support for the approach of Kalecki (also considered in a slightly different context in Sawyer, 1982a, Chapter 7).

This book is mainly a presentation of the ideas of Kalecki on developed capitalist economies, but it would be a slur on the breadth of Kalecki's intellectual activities to ignore his work on developing economies and on planning under socialism. In Chapters 10 and 11 we consider Kalecki's ideas on the 'second' and 'third' worlds.

Whilst the writing of this book is motivated by a belief that

Kalecki's work has much to offer in the understanding of capitalist (and other) economies, this does not imply a belief that Kalecki has provided the last word or that there should be a search for what Kalecki really said or meant. Moreover, accepting Kalecki's own work as the final authority would contradict his own views in at least two ways. First, economies evolve and change and consequently an analysis appropriate for the 1930s, say, is not necessarily appropriate for the 1980s. Second, Kalecki displayed considerable scorn for those who slavishly followed the work of others in an unthinking and uncritical manner. Kalecki showed 'scorn for the "top pupil" – his own words. This is the man who studies according to instructions, memorises his lessons well, knows how to flatter his teachers, and so gets "top marks". But he is also the man who lacks true depth or understanding, originality or creativity' (Feiwell, 1975). In the concluding chapter, we discuss those areas and aspects of Kalecki's work which in our view are in need of some refinement. We follow this by discussing post-war developments which require the extension of the work of Kalecki.

A Brief Biography of Kalecki[2]

In this section, a brief outline of some major events in Kalecki's life is given. A major purpose is to sketch the background of Kalecki which is necessary to appreciate the development of Kalecki's ideas. In particular, his intellectual background of a self-education in economics, influenced by Marx and Rosa Luxemburg, his experience of the effects of unemployment and his early research in product market conditions are all reflected in his economic analysis.

Kalecki was born in 1899 into a Polish–Jewish family in Łódź (Poland), then occupied by Russia. He finished school in 1917, and then studied at the Polytechnic of Warsaw (1917–19) and at the Polytechnic of Gdansk (1921–3). His studies were interrupted by military service and were brought to an end by his father's unemployment, when Kalecki was forced to find work in order to support his family. Kalecki's studies were in engineering, which meant that his mathematical knowledge was considerable (and he undertook research in mathematics much later in the 1960s). He was also interested in economic problems, and read, *inter alia*, the works of Luxemburg and Turan-Baranovski (whose ideas Kalecki discussed in Kalecki, 1971a, Chapter 13).[3] He was also influenced by the work of Marx. Thus Kalecki's background in economics was rather different from that of most American and British economists, and also from that of many Polish economists of the time under the influence of Walras and the general equilibrium approach. One consequence of this difference in background was that Kalecki was not concerned with the type of questions which concerned neo-classical economists, such as whether unemployment equilibrium was possible since he did not think in terms of equilibrium and took the existence of substantial unemployment as a general experience under capitalism.

Kalecki's employment during the 1920s covered a range of jobs from making credit ratings of firms applying for loans to undertaking market research and economic journalism. With this background, he obtained a job with the Research Institute of Business Cycles and Prices in Warsaw in late 1929. Much of his early work at the Institute was concerned with reports on specific industries, often those which involved monopoly or cartels. The Institute took a generally anti-monopoly stance, in a period when cartelisation was extensive. Zweig (1944) indicated that by 1929 there were 100 cartels controlling nearly 40 per cent of industrial production, and the number rose to 266 by the end of 1936. A major project at the Institute with which Kalecki was involved was the pioneering preparation of estimates of national income and its components.

Much of this work laid the foundations for future work. Kalecki's work is characterised by the interplay between theoretical ideas and economic statistics. The importance of monopoly in price determination, and the impact of the availability of credit on investment and the size of firms will become clear. It will also be seen that Kalecki's first major excursion into economic theory (Kalecki, 1935a; 1935b) was concerned with the explanation of business cycles, arising out of his work at the Institute.

During this period, Kalecki contributed many articles to the two periodicals which had previously published his work, and also some more general articles under the *nom de plume* of Henry Braun in the *Socialist Review*, which was a short-lived journal founded by a group of socialist intellectuals. Kalecki was 'closely connected with the leftist socialist movement' (Kowalik, 1964).

From the prespective of this book, the most important feature of his work in the early 1930s was his pursuit of theoretical studies of prices and the business cycle, leading up to the publication of an 'Outline of a Theory of the Business Cycle' (Kalecki, 1933). In that paper, he presented the basic idea of the importance of investment as the generator of business cycles.

Kalecki's ideas on the generation of business cycles were presented before a wider audience at the conference of the Econometric Society in 1933 held in Leyden, Holland.[4] There was some attention paid to this paper amongst the relatively small group of mathematically-inclined economists interested in business cycles, but little outside of that circle. Shortly afterwards, Keynes published his *General Theory* (Keynes, 1936) and all (macroeconomic) eyes were focused on that.[5]

A Rockefeller Foundation Fellowship for a year had enabled Kalecki to travel from Poland in 1936, first to Sweden to make contact with economists such as Ohlin, Myrdal and Lindahl who had also been seeking answers to the causes of unemployment. Whilst in Stockholm, Kalecki was sent a copy of Keynes's *General Theory*. He realised the significance of Keynes's ideas for his own research and writing plans, leading to a delay on developing his ideas into a book.[6]

In Chapter 9, we discuss in some detail the similarities and differences between the macroeconomics of Kalecki and Keynes. It is sufficient here to indicate that we will argue there that the ideas of Kalecki and Keynes are sufficiently different for it to be misleading to bracket their ideas together, notwithstanding that they both stressed the importance of the level of effective demand for employment and output. In respect of the principle of effective demand, a number of economists (e.g. Robinson, 1964; Klein, 1951, 1975; Johansen, 1978) have argued that Kalecki could claim priority of publication over Keynes by some three years (Kalecki, 1933) compared with (Keynes, 1936), and this question is also examined in Chapter 9.

In April 1936 he travelled on to England, and spent much time at the London School of Economics and at Cambridge, where he made contact with Keynes and others (notably Joan Robinson). During his stay in England, two of his closest associates at the Institute of Business Cycles and Prices in Warsaw were discharged in response to government pressure, following a report written by them on Poland's economic position. Kalecki resigned from the Institute in protest at this political interference.

Kalecki was based mainly in England from this time until 1945. He visited France for several months in 1937 to observe the experience of the Popular Front government of Blum (see Kalecki, 1938b). During the late 1930s Kalecki was without a permanent job, and an attempt by Keynes to set up a research project which would have provided a job for Kalecki failed. In this period Kalecki worked on his book of *Essays on the Theory of Economic Fluctuations*, which appeared in 1939 (Kalecki, 1939). During this period he also published two important papers on the principle of increasing risk (Kalecki, 1937c) and on the degree of monopoly and the distribution of income (Kalecki, 1938a), both of which are included in revised form in Kalecki (1971a) as Chapters 9 and 6 respectively. The ideas in these papers form important parts of Kalecki's general approach, and are fully discussed below (Chapters 5 and 2 respectively). These papers are important for laying the foundations for a macroeconomics built upon the general view that capitalism is not characterised by perfect competition but rather is characterised by imperfect competition, oligopoly and monopoly. The oligopolistic nature of industries becomes important in the explanation of key variables such as investment, the distribution of income and employment.

For most of the war years, Kalecki was employed at the Oxford University Institute of Statistics. Many of those working there were also effectively refugees from continental Europe because they were Jewish or because of their political beliefs, and many were destined to become well known economists. The Oxford Institute represented the major independent critic of British government economic policy, and published a bulletin every three weeks with commentary on current economic problems and policies.[7] Kalecki contributed frequently to these bulletins, particularly on budgetary policy, rationing, inflation, distribution of income, the money supply and the Beveridge report. His articles published in the *Bulletin of the Oxford Institute* illustrate his general concerns and the combination of detailed statistical work within a broad theoretical framework. Kalecki also gave thought to the post-war possibilities for full employment in a series of articles. These include a contribution to the Oxford University Institute of Statistics (1944) where he examined the technical difficulties of achieving full employment, and in Kalecki (1943b) he examined the political-social difficulties, which he rated to be much more of an obstacle to full employment than economic difficulties. These and other contributions are discussed in Chapter 7 below.

The years 1945 and 1946 saw Kalecki working in France, Canada and then back in Poland on a number of assignments mainly connected with post-war reconstruction. At the end of 1946 he was appointed, with the approval of the Polish authorities, as deputy director of a section of the economics department of the United Nations secretariat in New York. An important part of this work was the preparation of world economic reports, with Kalecki particularly involved with dealing with employment and inflation questions.[8] His stay in the UN ended with his resignation at the end of 1954. This resignation was the culmination of restrictions placed on Kalecki and the members of the UN secretariat in general by the wave of McCarthyism which swept the United States in the early 1950s. A reorganisation which would have had the effect of reducing Kalecki's influence and role in writing reports was the final straw leading to Kalecki's resignation.

From the beginning of 1955 to his death, Kalecki's home was Poland. In the first part of that period (up to about 1960), he was actively involved in public affairs, including three years as Chairman of the Commission of Perspective Planning. At the Commission, Kalecki and his staff were particularly involved in working out a fifteen-year perspective plan for Poland covering the years 1961 to 1975. The perspective plan was strongly attacked on the grounds of being too pessimistic. After that Kalecki's influence declined and by 1960 he had effectively withdrawn from public affairs. During this period he continued his academic work with research into contemporary capitalism with a group at the Polish Academy of Science.

After 1959, Kalecki's academic work was heavily involved with problems of development. He was heavily involved with seminars organised at the Academy of Sciences, Warsaw University and at the Central School for Planning and Statistics. By 1968, the political climate in Poland had changed considerably for the worse from the climate of relatively free discussion in the late 1950s. Kalecki's outspokenness and disagreement with the heavy industry investment programme (cf. pp. 230–2 below) brought him into disfavour. Many of his followers were purged from office and employment (and many eventually leaving Poland). Kalecki's 'name' saved him from the full rigour of the moves against his followers. He died in April 1970.

Kalecki and Conventional Economics

Reading Kalecki can come as something of a shock and present difficulties to those steeped in conventional economics. The first reason for this is the apparently trivial one of Kalecki's style of writing, although that style does reflect something of his general approach. His writing style has often been described as terse and laconic, and he did not express his ideas at length and generally did not repeat them for emphasis. Johansen (1978) commented that Kalecki in 'his writing . . . is terse and to the point. He is near to the optimum from the point of view of communicating his ideas clearly and efficiently'. In further contrast to much writing in the field of economics, Kalecki made few references to the work of others, whether by way of justification for what he was saying or as the object of criticism. In general, Kalecki was concerned with getting to the heart of the problem at hand and making assumptions which allowed a clear analysis of the central issues. In the words of Joan Robinson (Robinson, 1976a, p. 9) '(i)n every case, he could diagnose the main problems in terms of his clear and penetrating scheme of ideas'. The terseness of his style is reflected in the fact that his collection of selected essays on capitalist economies (1971a) containing many important ideas takes up less than 200 pages (Kalecki, 1971a).

The second reason, which also helps to explain the hostility of many economists to the degree of monopoly theory and the ignoring of his macroeconomics, is that Kalecki's approach contrasts sharply with the conventional neo-classical approach. The full nature of Kalecki's approach will become apparent below, and his underlying methodology is further discussed in comparing his work with that of Marx (Chapter 8) and with Keynes (Chapter 9). Here, we can highlight three broad aspects of Kalecki's work which contrast with the neo-classical orthodoxy.

First, Kalecki consistently viewed the capitalist economies as 'semi-monopolistic and monopolistic' in his terminology (which we will call oligopolistic) and regarded perfect competition 'as a most unrealistic assumption' which 'when its actual status of a handy model is forgotten becomes a dangerous myth' (Kalecki, 1971a, p. 158). The consequences of the rejection of a perfectly competitive view of the world will become apparent below, when (output) prices (Chapter 2), wages (Chapter 6) and finance (Chapter 5) are discussed. Briefly, we can say that from the output price side, price is seen as a mark-up over costs, leading to the view that the share of profits in output depends on the mark-up, which in turn is determined by the market power of the firms involved, summarised by Kalecki in the term the 'degree of monopoly'. In the labour market, the relative power of trade unions is seen as relevant, rather than the interaction of demand and supply of labour. In the finance market, firms are limited in their ability to obtain funds, without pushing up the interest charges which they face to unacceptable levels. Further, the available funds for a firm are closely linked to profits, whether directly through profits providing the funds or indirectly through enhancing the credit-ranking of the firm. In sum, the whole 'vision' of the economy and its operation is changed.

Second, Kalecki made little use of (and indeed was hostile to) that major tool of analysis in neo-classical economics, namely equilibrium analysis. '"Equilibrium" is a term that is rarely, if ever, found in Kalecki's writings' (Asimakopulos, 1977). The notion of equilibrium is used, albeit in a rather different way, in the Ricardian–Marxian tradition, and we consider the relationship between Kalecki and that tradition later in this chapter, and return to this theme in part of Chapter 8.

In neo-classical economics, equilibrium (whether at the individual market or economy level) is a situation of rest where there are no internal forces generating change. In general, equilibrium is regarded as a position to which the individual, market or economy quickly tends.[9] Thus, the position of equilibrium is designed to tell us something about what will actually happen in the real world. Indeed, a theory whose predictions are derived from an equilibrium position (which is usually the case in neo-classical economics) can only be tested if it is assumed that the real world is in or near equilibrium. In contrast, Kalecki regarded equilibrium positions as hypothetical ones which would not be reached, and that there was a danger in confusing possible equilibrium positions with what actually happens.

The approach of Kalecki is generally concerned with the evolution of an economic system through time, without imposing any view that the system would reach some ultimate equilibrium position or that it would grow at some balanced equilibrium rate of growth. It is noteworthy that the titles of Kalecki's books contain words such as cycles, dynamic, fluctuations which are suggestive of a non-equilibrium concern. Indeed Kalecki viewed the capitalist economy as inherently cyclical. This is suggested by observation of those economies, and is to be understood partly in terms of the links between changes in economic activity and investment in an accelerator type of mechanism (see Chapter 3 below). Further, as the economy fluctuates over time, the long-term path of the economy is gradually built up from the short term events in that economy of which the level of investment would be particularly important. 'In fact, the long term trend is but a slowly changing component of a chain of short-period situations; it has no independent entity . . .' (Kalecki, 1971a, p. 165). Thus, for Kalecki, there is no short run equilibrium position to be analysed nor is there any underlying long-run equilibrium to which the economy will tend.

Much conventional economics, following the Marshallian tradition, draws on the distinction between the short run and the long run. It is usual to analyse short run equilibrium holding long run factors constant, and separately to analyse the long run equilibrium. There are some problems with this approach, particularly over the extent to which the short run can be analysed whilst the long run is held constant, and also to know which factors are to be allocated to the short run category and which to the long run one. Kalecki viewed firms as operating in a short term always, although making decisions on prices and investment, and the long run is built up from a series of short runs.

There are a few places where it might appear that Kalecki is using an equilibrium approach, notably in Kalecki (1937a) where he uses the term equilibrium.[10] This related particularly to the use of the equality between savings and investment (in a closed private economy). Kalecki did not treat that equality as an equilibrium condition between *ex ante* savings and *ex ante* investment. He concentrated on investment decisions, and largely assumed that decisions led to expenditure. Further, savings in any particular period were forced to adjust to the level of investment expenditure. In a subsequent period, firms make different investment decisions (which will be influenced by the previous level of savings). Thus the focus is on the accounting identity between savings and investment, and on the way in which the volume of investment changes over time. These brief comments are filled out below (see pp. 48–54 and pp. 72–7).

Third, Kalecki made virtually no use of those standard tools of neo-classical economics – the utility function and the production function. He never used the concept of utility (or anything similar) and only used a function rather like a production function in the analysis of growth in a socialist economy (discussed below on pp. 253–6). On the production side, Kalecki usually made the working assumption that in the short-term when capital equipment is not easily varied, the amount of labour and material inputs are basically determined by the level of output. Thus Kalecki paid little attention to lags of actual employment of labour behind output changes, but much more importantly the composition and level of inputs do not depend on any relative prices. In general, Kalecki took the relationship at a particular moment of time between inputs and output are given within the analysis. However, the relationship between inputs (notably labour) and output is not to be seen as technologically determined from a production function, but rather would depend, *inter alia*, on the degree of control exercised by the firm over its labour force. Kalecki also generally assumed (drawing on substantial evidence in its favour) that unit direct costs were constant with respect to output up to full capacity. Thus, in comparison with neo-classical economics, Kalecki rejected the notion of a technologically determined production function, the U-shaped cost curve and the impact of relative prices on the demand for inputs.

The neo-classical approach with its emphasis on equilibrium is heavily imbued with the idea that there is a harmony of interests between different individuals. In contrast, the Ricardian–Marxian approach stresses the importance of conflict of interest between social classes. In the work of Kalecki, as will be seen below, this conflict is exhibited through the degree of monopoly in the sense that a rise in the degree of monopoly adds to profits and detracts from real wages (see pp. 108–15 below).

Kalecki undertook his analysis at the level of social classes rather than the level of individuals. In neo-classical economics the utility maximising individual is, in principle, the starting point of the analysis, often followed by some aggregation into groups of individuals. The particular grouping used would depend on the purpose. The use of social classes as the basis of the analysis has two important consequences. First, there is no role for utility analysis, which must operate at the level of the individual. Second, it recognises that social classes have an existence which is not merely as a grouping of individuals.

In this respect, and others, Kalecki was in the Ricardian–Marxian tradition rather than the neo-classical one, and we now turn to a discussion of the Ricardian–Marxian tradition.

Kalecki and the Ricardian–Marxian Tradition

There is a broad tradition in economics, which has been variously labelled the Ricardian–Marxian or the classical tradition or the surplus approach (e.g. Dobb, 1973; Harris, 1978; Meek, 1977 especially Chapter 8).[11] This tradition is a broad one, and can be characterised in a number of different ways. But its important features include the following. There is, first, an emphasis on the distribution of income between classes (in Ricardo's words 'the principal problem in political economy') and on the accumulation of capital and on growth and development. From this brief and bald statement, some important consequences flow, which can be contrasted with the neo-classical approach. Harris (1978) (p. 19) described one set of consequences as:

'[i]n general, the central feature of neo-classical analysis is that the problem of distribution, conceived in terms of a society of atomistic individuals, is solved entirely within the sphere of exchange as related both to exchange of fact or services and to exchange of products. Underlying this analysis is the conception of a society *without* classes, defined either in terms of appropriation of the product according to divisions in property ownership, as in classical economical analysis, or in terms of a social-production relation (the capital–labor relation) based on control of labor in production, as in Marxian theory. In this respect, there is a fundamental division between the substance of neo-classical theory on the one hand and that of classical and Marxian theory on the other.

There also an the emphasis on growth. At a minimum this leads to concern over the determinants of the rate of growth, and factors which would raise the rate of growth rather than concern over the efficiency of the allocation of resources at each point in time.[12] The stress on accumulation points to the link between investment and growth.

A second aspect of the Ricardian–Marxian tradition is the concept that in a capitalist society, profits are linked with some notion of a surplus. This has two sides to it. First, that on the income side, profits rest on the ability of firms to extract a surplus of price over costs. The source of that ability varies, which Marx placing the source in the process of production and capitalists control over production, whilst Kalecki can be seen as placing the source in the market power of firms (these differences are discussed further in Chapter 8). Second, profits are seen as largely saved, and savings out of profits form the bulk of savings with workers saving little or nothing. In a simple closed private sector economy, savings and investment are equal, and investment is the difference between output and current consumption. Thus investment requires the surplus of output over consumption.

In Chapter 8, we will discuss in some detail the similarities between Kalecki and Marx. In this section, we briefly indicate how the work of Kalecki fits into this broad framework. It has already been stated above that Kalecki's analysis was at the level of classes rather than individuals, where the classes were workers and capitalists. He generally made what is often termed the classical savings assumption – that workers do not save, and most or all profits are saved. This stemmed from the idea that wages were often close to some notion of a 'subsistence' level, leading to all wages being spent. Profits play a different role from wages, and as part of the competitive struggle firms are required to plough back profits. In turn, profits share is closely linked with the degree of monopoly (a broad indicator of market power), and thus with firms' ability to charge prices in excess of profits. Whilst there are some differences on the source of nature of profits between Kalecki and Marx which we explore below, nevertheless they share the common view of profits as a surplus, and do not relate profits to neo-classical concepts of marginal productivity (of capital) and abstinence from consumption.

The level and rate of change of profits are central to Kalecki's theory of investment, and in turn the level of investment is central to the determination of the level of profits. Thus, as will be seen below, investment and profits are crucial to Kalecki's approach. Investment is seen as a key element in the determination of the level of demand (and hence of output), and of the rate of growth.

The attention to growth, income distribution, accumulation

(investment) and social classes places Kalecki firmly in the classical tradition. One of Kalecki's major contributions to that tradition can be seen in terms of his 'theory of effective demand in a Marxian setting [providing] an account of the realisation of surplus value, which Marx left rather vague' (Robinson, 1980).

The Ricardian–Marxian tradition makes some use of equilibrium analysis, although usually for rather different purposes from those of the neo-classical tradition. Within the Ricardian–Marxian tradition, equilibrium analysis is often used to ease the analysis and to understand certain central tendencies, rather than seeing equilibrium as a position which is reached.[13] Equilibrium is often viewed in terms of the equalisation of the rate of profit across industries and the implications which that has for the relationship between prices, wages and profits.

Kalecki, as noted above, did not make use of equilibrium analysis. In particular, he did not make use of any notion of equilibrium prices (or natural prices, prices of production), and always dealt with actual market prices. This point is expanded in our discussion in Chapter 8.

A Brief Outline of Kalecki's Macroeconomics

In the next five chapters, discussion focuses on elements of Kalecki's macroeconomics, and in this section we provide a brief overview of that. In Chapter 7, Kalecki's views on the possibility of full employment are considered, including his views on the political and social constraints on the achievement of full employment through government macroeconomic policy. In Chapter 8, some comparisons between the work of Kalecki and Marx are made, whilst in Chapter 9, the comparisons are between Kalecki and Keynes. The subsequent two chapters outline Kalecki's writings and views on development and on socialist planning and growth. In these chapters, we are interested in how his views in these areas can be seen as forming a coherent approach with his views on capitalist economies. Finally, in the concluding chapter, we discuss some difficulties and problems with Kalecki's work, and also look forward to ways in which Kalecki's ideas could be extended and developed.

The ideas of Kalecki should be seen as forming a coherent approach, and as such there is always a problem of selecting the starting point for any discussion of those ideas. Our choice is to begin with pricing and the distribution of income (Chapter 2). In oligopolistic markets price can be viewed as a mark-up over costs, where the mark-up depends on the market power of the firms, summarised in Kalecki's work by the phrase degree of monopoly. The effective degree of monopoly depends on factors such as the level of industrial concentration, degree of collusion, extent of advertising and sales promotion. From this, it follows that the share of profits in value added (or gross output) depends upon the degree of monopoly.

This approach means, *inter alia*, that prices change in response to changes in the degree of monopoly and in costs, rather than through the interplay of demand and supply curves. The general conditions of demand and of supply may influence the degree of monopoly and cost conditions, but it is these general conditions rather than the specific notion of *ex ante* demand and supply functions of relative prices only. In particular, relative prices will change only through changes in the degree of monopoly or costs. One important 'relative price' is the real wage, and, as will be shown below (pp. 108–15) this depends upon the degree of monopoly and is effectively determined in the product market, rather than the labour market. Thus adjustment of real wages, which is often seen in conventional economics as a cure for unemployment, would depend on a change in the degree of monopoly. But in the Kalecki approach, employment depends mainly on the level of demand and output and not on the real wage. Further, an important determinant of the level of demand is the level of real wages, and falls in the real wage can easily lead to falls in the level of demand, and hence in output and employment.

Profits are largely saved and wages are largely spent. Focusing on the former, Kalecki argued that profitability of a firm is a strong influence on its ability to raise finance. Profits are a direct source of internal finance for a firm, and also enhance a firm's ability to borrow money from banks and the capital market. Internal finance is advantageous for a firm as a relative cheap source of funds and a source which does not lead to a dilution of control by existing shareholders. Kalecki viewed the finance markets as inherently imperfect in the sense that finance is not available in unlimited quantities to a firm at a constant price. For reasons explored in Chapter 5, a firm would find that interest and other charges would increase as it sought to expand its borrowing and eventually become so high as to be virtually unobtainable. This view of the capital market enforces the role of profits in the generation of finance for a firm.

In order to emphasise the point under discussion, we take the case where there is no savings out of wages, and the economy is closed without a government. Then the savings equal investment condition becomes $S_P = I$, where S_P is savings out of profits and I investment. The level of investment is then seen as the determining factor on the level of savings out of profits, and thereby the level of profits (given the propensity of savings out of profits). Thus the degree of monopoly is seen as shaping the share of profits in national income and the level of investment the level of profits (and income as well).

Kalecki worked with the condition that savings equals investment as an identity, fulfilled by the effective investment demand leading by and large to actual investment and the level of savings adjusting to the level of investment. He did not incorporate any notions of planned savings, solely that actual savings had to adjust to investment. By effective investment demand, we mean that demand which is backed by purchasing power (i.e. money). There are lags between the decision to invest and that investment taking place (for a variety of reasons), and the focus is on when the investment takes place, rather than when the decision is taken. Thus Kalecki viewed investment as the driving force, to which savings adjust. This leads to two major points. First, it is necessary to construct a theory of investment decisions ('the central problem of the political economy of capitalism' (Kalecki, 1971a, p. 148), which Kalecki regarded must be linked to the level and rate of change of economic activity. It is from this linkage of investment with the rate of change of economic activity which reinforces cyclical tendencies within capitalist economies. Second, if investment is the active force and savings a passive response, how is investment financed? An important, though much neglected, contribution of Kalecki was his early recognition that decisions to have a higher level of investment expenditure can only be effected if there is an expansion in lending by banks (and in borrowing by firms) which generates the finance for the increased investment, since the previous level of savings would not be adequate for this purpose. His description of the process involved (Kalecki, 1971a, p. 29) and discussion below (pp. 91–6) illustrates the importance he attached to the creation of money.

The creation of money and the terms under which it is created are seen as crucial to the actual expansion of investment and of output. In Kalecki's approach, the working assumption is made that banks are not generally effectively constrained in their lending, and thus are able to meet the demands for loans. Money is thus easily expanded in response to increased plans for expenditure (particularly that on investment) and the associated increased demand for loans). Further, money is seen as largely credit money, i.e. money which consists of deposits with banks (and not, e.g., government-issued cash or gold). This means that whilst money is an asset for the non-banking public, it is a liability of the banks and thus money does not constitute net wealth for the private sector.

The rate of interest is seen as a monetary phenomenon, and is largely determined by the interaction of the banks' willingness to supply money and the non-banking public's demand for money. The level of demand (in money terms) is determined by investment demand, government and foreign demand, with consumer demand passively adjusting to the level of wages.

We now turn to a detailed development of Kalecki's macroeconomics.

Notes to Chapter 1

1. The term post-Keynesian is used here to signify the school of thought which labels itself post-Keynesian, and is associated with the *Journal of Post-Keynesian Economics*; see Eichner and Kregel (1975), and Eichner (1979), Davidson (1981).
2. This brief biography draws upon the following, to which the reader is referred for further information: Kowalik (1964), Feiwel (1975), Symposium in *Oxford Bulletin of Economics and Statistics*, February, 1977.
3. Rosa Luxemburg (1870–1919) was born in Poland and was one of the founders of the Social Democratic Party of Poland and Lithuania. She was forced to flee abroad as a result of the general political and religious oppression in Poland. She settled in Germany where she was acknowledged as leader of the left-wing German Social Democratic Party, and became a co-founder of the German Communist Party in 1918. She was assassinated whilst under arrest in 1919. Her famous book was *The Accumulation of Capital* published first in 1913, in which she developed the idea of lack of purchasing power as a cause of crisis, which led to a competitive search by capitalists for markets overseas. She stressed the role of imperialism and armaments expenditure as ways in which capitalism seeks to maintain demand.

Mikhail Tugan-Baranovski (1865–1919) was born in the Ukraine, and elected to a Chair of Political Economy and Statistics in 1913 but the Russian government refused to endorse the election. He initially took an unorthodox approach to Marxism (sometimes labelled a 'revisionist' approach), but in the early years of the twentieth century abandoned Marxism (which he had never fully accepted), though continued to call himself a socialist. He rejected the concept of class struggle and was involved in the promotion of co-operatives. His main theoretical contribution was the development of the disproportionality theory of crises, whereby crises arise through some sectors expanding out of proportion with others because of the incorrect allocation of investment between sectors.

For further details see, *inter alia, International Encyclopaedia of Social Sciences.*

4. For a summary of discussion on Kalecki's paper and the environment within which it was presented see *Econometrica*, vol. 2, pp. 187–203. Kalecki's paper was published as Kalecki (1935b). Frisch and Holme (1935) presents critical comments on Kalecki's paper, which is also commented on in Tinbergen's survey of business cycle theory (Tinbergen, 1935).

5. Kalecki's review of Keynes (1936) was first published in Polish in 1936, and has now been translated into English in Targetti and Kinda-Hass (1982). A partial translation is given in Feiwel (1975), pp. 62–6.

6. There are differing accounts of Kalecki's reaction to his reading of the *General Theory*. These vary from that he gave up work on a book when he learnt of the *General Theory* (Kowalik, 1964) through to believing that the *General Theory* was the book which he intended to write, and that his reaction was to lie in bed for three days (Robinson, 1976b, 1977a). We discuss this point further in Chapter 9.

7. A selection of articles from the bulletin and other papers published by members of the Oxford University Institute of Statistics were published in *Oxford University Institute of Statistics* (1947).

8. For a full discussion of Kalecki's work at the United Nations, see Dell (1977).

9. Hahn (1973), however, advocates the use of general equilibrium analysis in a rather different way. He argues that general equilibrium is not meant as a representation of the real world, but rather designed to show what at most the price mechanism can do. If, for example, the price mechanism is general equilibrium cannot deal with externalities, then it will not be able to do so under conditions of disequilibrium.

10. Most of the occasions on which Kalecki used terms such as equilibrium, equilibrium position appear to be in articles published in the late 1930s. It has been noted that in the volume of selected articles on the capitalist economy (Kalecki, 1971a) the term equilibrium does not appear (see Nuti, 1977). This selection was made by Kalecki on the basis of his most important papers. In many areas Kalecki continued to work and refine his ideas, and hence it is particularly relevant that in the final version of his ideas that the concept of equilibrium is not used.

11. Cameron *et al.* (1983) make a three-way division of economic thought into neo-classical, costs of production and value theory approaches. Broadly speaking, our discussion here covers the latter two approaches.
12. This links with Robbins' (1932) famous definition of economics as the subject which deals with the allocation of scarce means between alternative ends.
13. For further discussion on this aspect, see, for example, Kregel (1973), pp. 38–45.

2
Prices, Profits and the Degree of Monopoly

Introduction

A central and crucial feature of Kalecki's analysis is the view that developed capitalist economies are characterised by oligopoly, imperfect competition and monopoly, particularly in product markets. He regarded the widely adopted assumption of perfect competition as 'a most unrealistic not only for the present phase of capitalism but even for the so called competitive capitalist economy of past centuries: surely this competition was always in general very imperfect' (Kalecki, 1971a, p. 158). It could be said that throughout his work, Kalecki stressed the monopolistic nature of modern capitalism, and perhaps neglected the rivalrous aspects. This point is developed in Chapter 8 when we compare the works of Kalecki with those of Marx.

The oligopolistic nature of industries led Kalecki to the view that the mark-up of price over costs was determined by the degree of monopoly, which is a shorthand expression for a variety of oligopolistic and monopolistic factors (such as collusion, sales promotion). In this chapter, we will explore the factors which influence the degree of monopoly the significance of viewing prices as a mark-up over costs, and the implications for the determination of profits. We will also consider some of the criticisms directed at the degree of monopoly approach.

Kalecki made a basic distinction between prices whose changes are largely determined by changes in the costs of production and those prices whose changes are determined largely by changes in demand (cf. Kalecki, 1971a, pp. 43–4). Kalecki focused on the former group which he took to be the prices of finished goods (excluding agricultural products). The supply of finished goods is seen as being elastic (with respect to demand) as a result of existing reserves of productive capacity, and with costs roughly constant with respect to output changes. This means that 'when demand increases it is mainly by an increase in the volume of production while prices tend to remain stable'. The prices of finished goods can be affected by demand-induced changes in the cost of raw materials, but 'it is through the channel of *costs* that this influence is transmitted to the prices of finished goods' (Kalecki, 1971a, p. 43). These finished goods industries are also characterised by oligopoly, and the mark-up of price over costs depends on the extent of oligopoly power, summarised in the term degree of monopoly, which is explored in detail below.

The products whose price-changes are demand-determined consist mainly of raw materials and primary foodstuffs. In inter-war Poland these sectors accounted for around two-thirds of employment and the 'disparity between these prices (between industrial goods prices and agricultural prices) was one of the greatest pre-occupations in the economic problems of Poland, and caused a vast amount of trouble in the economic, social and political spheres' (Zweig, 1944, p. 56). However, in developed capitalist countries, the importance of agriculture and primary products is much reduced, and the use of agricultural price support programmes, for example, may have reduced further the relevance of demand-determined price changes.

For demand-determined prices, a rise in demand would lead to a rise in price since there would be inelastic supply, especially in the short-run. Kalecki indicated that in the 'sector of basic raw materials [conform] in their price formation to that of perfect competition' (Kalecki, 1971a, p. 161). However, Kalecki focused on the effects of changes in demand whereas in conventional economics the emphasis is on the level of excess demand leading to price changes.

In light of Kalecki's focus in his work on the oligopolistic sector of finished goods, it would be argued that his analysis only to oligopolistic sectors where production is subject to approximately constant variable costs. The analysis can be extended to other sectors of, for example, primary products provided that both oligopoly and constant costs conditions hold. Alternatively, for many Western economies (e.g. UK and Japan) most primary goods are imported, with prices determined by world trade conditions, and domestically produced primary goods (especially foods) sold at prices determined or influenced by governments.

There is a degree of correspondence between the distinction made by Kalecki between cost-determined and demand-determined prices (and price changes) and the fix-price/flexi-price distinction widely used in macroeconomics, and popularised by Hicks and others. In the words of Joan Robinson, 'Kalecki drew attention to the fact that there are two distinct systems of price formation in the modern worlds, one dominated by supply and demand and one by costs plus profits. This distinction has recently been rediscovered by Hicks' (Robinson, 1977b). Okun (1981) has built extensively on this distinction. However, there is rather more to the distinction used by Kalecki than solely the fix-price/flexi-price distinction. In the latter distinction, the market structure is not usually specified, and in the reappraisal of Keynesian economics literature (e.g. Clower, 1965; Barro and Grossman, 1971) atomistic competition is assumed. The fix-price/flexi-price distinction is then solely between speed of price adjustment within a competitive framework. For Kalecki the distinction is *not* to do with speeds of adjustment, but rather is based on differences in industrial structure and in cost conditions.

The idea that prices are based on a mark-up over costs leads to the view that cost changes are closely linked with price changes, particularly when the mark-up is thought to be fairly insensitive to demand levels or changes. Numerous other authors have advanced ideas in a similar vein, though usually they have confined their attention to price formation without drawing out the wider implications for macroeconomics. Hall and Hitch (1939) were amongst the first to focus their attention on the mark-up of prices over costs, and the factors which influenced that mark-up, including the question of whether the mark-up was related to the level of demand. For a survey of this material, the reader is referred to Silberston (1970), and Hay and Morris (1979), Chapter 4. Means (1935) provoked a related debate over the so-called administered price thesis, and of relevance here is the idea that oligopolistic industries differ in their price behaviour from that of competitive industries, and in particular the former maintain prices in the face of falling demand. Finally, in a modified form, studies of price change such as those of Neild (1963), Godley and Nordhaus (1972), Coutts *et al.* (1978), Sawyer

(1983) have emphasised the importance of cost changes in the determination of price changes.

Although there is some similarity between Kalecki's approach and full cost pricing under which firms determined price by adding a standard mark-up to average direct costs calculated for some normal level of output (originating with Hall and Hitch, 1939), nevertheless there are important differences as well. Kalecki (1943a, p. 27) pointed to the indeterminacy of the mark-up which is applied. Kalecki (1971a, p. 51) argued that the impact of overheads (in relation to prime costs) and the influences of the prices of other firms on the price charged by a firm were the important differences between his theory and that of full cost pricing. A further difference explored below is the possibility of the influence of trade union activity on the mark-up in Kalecki's approach.

The constant costs assumption was often made by Kalecki as a useful first approximation, which partly allowed considerable simplification of the analysis. Many studies of cost conditions in the short-run (which is the one relevant to Kalecki's approach) have come to a similar conclusion, surveyed by, for example, Johnston (1960), Koutsoyiannis (1980) and Wiles (1961). In our discussion below of criticisms directed against the degree of monopoly approach we will come back to the constant costs assumption.

The Degree of Monopoly Theory

The starting point for Kalecki's analysis of price determination and thereby of the shares of profits in national income, is the view that firms (outside primary product sector) typically operate in conditions of imperfect competition and at levels of output below practical capacity with average prime costs (materials and manual labour), approximately constant. Firms are primarily interested in profits, though 'in view of the uncertainties faced in the process of price fixing it will not be assumed that the firm attempts to maximise its profits in any precise sort of manner' (Kalecki, 1971a, p. 44).

The two factors which are the major influences on the firm's price decision are its average prime costs and the prices of other firms producing similar products. Clearly, firms have to pay regard to the prices charged by rivals and limit the extent to which their own price

becomes out of line with rivals' prices. On the other hand, the firm
pays regard to its profit margin and wants to ensure that prices are
not too low relative to average prime costs. Kalecki summarised
these arguments in the equation:

$$p = mu + n\bar{p} \tag{2.1}$$

where p is price charged by firm in question, u unit prime costs and $\bar{p}$
is the weighted average price charged by all firms (where the weights
used are the output of the firms), and where m and n are positive
coefficients.

Summing over all the firms in an industry, we obtain the following:

$$\bar{p} = (m/1 - n).\bar{u} \tag{2.2}$$

where $\bar{u}$ is the weighted average of unit prime costs, and m, n are now
the weighted averages of the corresponding firm-level concepts.[1]

The straightforward interpretation of equation (2.2) is that prices
in an industry are higher relative to prime costs as m and n are higher
(with n subject to an upper limit of 1). 'The coefficients m and n
characterising the price fixing policy of the firm reflect what may be
called the degree of monopoly of a firm's position' (Kalecki, 1971a,
p. 45).[2]

It should be noted that direct costs include material costs and
wages of manual workers, but not salaries of non-manual workers.
Kalecki gives little justification for this, other than to say when
applying the theory to the distribution of income that 'from the
social point of view it would be more interesting to consider the
share of labour as a whole: but it is the relative share of *manual*
labour which is suitable for theoretical analysis' (Kalecki, 1939,
p. 13). A distinguishing characteristic between manual labour and
non-manual labour within Kalecki's approach is that the employment of manual labour is easily changed by firms whereas the
employment of non-manual labour is approximately constant with
respect to the level of output. We discuss whether this division of
labour payments into wages (as part of direct costs) and salaries (as
part of overheads) is a useful one in Chapter 12.

In terms of factors which would lead to a change in the degree of
monopoly (and thereby to a change in the mark-up of price over
costs) Kalecki focused on the process of concentration and on sales
promotion. The former is relevant because larger firms know that

their prices have a large impact on the average price $\bar{p}$, and that other firms will react to their prices. Further, there may be tacit agreement amongst firms which is easier to maintain the less firms there are. Thus, the fewer the firms are in number and the larger they are in size the higher will be n.

Advertising and sales promotion are relevant in that they tend to diminish price competition (thereby raising the mark-up) and tend to protect existing firms' positions enabling them to charge a higher price.

The above style of formulation is not widely used in economic theory, but the relationship between Kalecki's degree of monopoly theory and other theories of oligopoly can be shown. Following the general ideas expressed in Cowling (1982), Chapter 2, applied to a model of oligopoly with firms producing differentiated products, we have the following. The profit function for firm i is:

$$\pi_i = p_i.q_i(p_i, p) - C_i(q_i)$$

where p_i is price of output of firm i, p the price index of rivals' output, q_i output of firm i and C_i its variable costs. The first-order profit maximisation condition, using price as the decision variable is:

$$\frac{\delta \pi_i}{\delta p_i} = q_i + p_i \left(\frac{\delta q_i}{\delta p_i} + \frac{\delta q_i}{\delta p}.\frac{\delta p}{\delta p_i} \right) - \frac{\delta C}{\delta p_i} \left(\frac{\delta q_i}{\delta p_i} + \frac{\delta q_i}{\delta 0}.\frac{\delta p}{\delta p_i} \right) = 0$$

which yields:

$$p_i = \frac{\delta C}{\delta q_i} (e_i - a_i e)/(e_i - a_i e - 1)$$

where e_i is $-(p_i/q_i)(\delta q_i/\delta p_i)$, e is $(p/q_i)(\delta q_i/\delta p)$ and a_i is $(p_i/p)(\delta p/\delta p_i)$. The key factors determining the mark-up of price over marginal costs are seen to be the two elasticities of demand and the interdependence of prices between firms (reflected in the a_i-term). Further, it could be expected that collusion and the level of concentration would strongly influence a_i whilst advertising and sales promotion would influence the elasticities of demand.

This formal model can be usefully compared with the discussion in Kalecki (1940) on the supply curve under imperfect competition. In that paper, Kalecki began by taking the case, which he labelled as pure imperfect competition, of an industry of a large number of firms producing differentiated products but without any recognised interdependence in their pricing decisions. The state of market imperfection in that context is described by the function $e_k(p_k/p)$

which is the elasticity function facing firm k, and the degree of market imperfection is said to rise when e_k declines. Under pure imperfect competition, the relationship between price and marginal cost is given by $p_k = m_k(e_k/e_k - 1)$, from the usual profit-maximising conditions, where e_k is the (point) elasticity of demand for firm k when it assumes that other firms do not respond to its price change. Kalecki then portrayed price under oligopolistic situation as $p = a_k . m_k(e_k/e_k - 1)$ where a_k is greater than 1. The coefficient a_k is seen as reflecting the degree of monopoly, and the ability of the oligopolist is to raise price over the corresponding pure imperfect competition case. The value of a_k is such that the firm k feels that raising or lowering price would reduce profits, and this is based on firm k's view of how other firms would respond to its price change.

There is a correspondence between the oligopoly model outlined above and this approach by Kalecki. First, we can see that in both instance, the 'pure imperfect competition' case will have a mark-up of $(e_k/e_k - 1)$. Second, the extent to which the oligopoly mark-up is above that 'bench mark' margin depends on oligopolistic interdependence reflected in the $a_i e$ term in our formal presentations and in the term a_k in Kalecki's presentation.

Kalecki noted that the relevant elasticity of demand for the firm's calculations would be the perceived elasticity of demand, and that elasticity might diverge substantially from the actual elasticity. Further, there may be lack of precise information on marginal costs and how those costs would change as the firm changes its output level. This may lead a firm to focus on a

> crude notion such as the average cost of manual labour and raw materials at the 'normal' level of output. It is obvious that for the purposes of the preceding argument we must attribute to the marginal cost m not its actual value but what the entrepreneur considers it to be; and that in consequence the relevant marginal cost curve is often horizontal up to the point of the full use of equipment (Kalecki, 1940).

In this treatment the factors determining the mark-up of price over marginal cost are seen to be those connected with the state of market imperfection, which would include the extent of product differentiation, advertising and sales promotion and those connected with degrees of rivalry and competition between firms.

Kalecki introduced two other factors of importance in the determination of the degree of monopoly, namely the level of overheads and the power of trade unions. Both of these are further discussed below, with the level of overheads later in Chapter 12 (pp. 275–6) and the power of unions in Chapter 6. Briefly here we can indicate that Kalecki considered that the level of overheads would tend to raise the degree of monopoly, whilst the power of unions would tend to reduce it.

At the industry level, we write equation (2.2) as:

$$p = k.u \qquad (2.2')$$

where we have dropped the bars for convenience, p is industry average price, u average direct costs and $k(=(m/1-n))$ is determined by the degree of monopoly. Total receipts of the firms are $p.Q$ (where Q is total output) can be divided into π (profits), O (overheads, including salaries), W (wages) and M (materials), and the term $u.Q$ is $W + M$. Then we have:

$$\pi + O + W + M = k(W + M) \qquad (2.3)$$

and hence

$$\pi + O = (k - 1).(W + M) \qquad (2.4)$$

The share of profits in value added $(= \pi + O + W)$ becomes, with $M = j.W$:

$$\pi/Y = ((k - 1)(j + 1) - O/W)/((k - 1)(j + 1) + 1) \qquad (2.5)$$

and of wages:

$$w = W/Y = 1/((k - 1)(j + 1) + 1) \qquad (2.6)$$

These two equations contain some important implications. First, a rise in overheads (O) detracts from profits. Indeed, from equation (2.3), it can be seen that there is one-for-one effect of a rise in overheads on falls in profits. Second, a rise in materials costs relative to wage costs (i.e. a rise in j) leads, *ceteris paribus*, to a rise in profits share in value added and a diminution in the wage share. The mechanism is that output costs are marked-up and generate profits. A rise in input costs leads to a rise in price and in profits whilst wages remained unchanged.

These conclusions relate to the industry level. We discuss the move from industry level to economy level below. Kalecki's degree of monopoly approach can be seen as one of many theories of the firm, ranging over monopoly, oligopoly, managerial and behavioural theories (i.e. effectively all theories of the firm apart from perfect competition) which view firms as determining prices relative to costs in pursuit of their objectives. In each theory, price can be viewed as a mark-up over costs, with the theories differeing over what factors determine the mark-up and exactly which types of costs are marked-up. We have argued this view at much greater length elsewhere (Sawyer, 1983, Chapter 2), and do not repeat the details of the argument. The important points are that Kalecki's degree of monopoly approach is a *theory* of price determination (and of income shares) and that it is within the broad stream of theories of the firm in which firms are considered as price makers.

At a number of places, Kalecki argued that the theory of perfect competition was unrealistic and inappropriate for modern capitalist economies. He was well aware of the existence of oligopolies and cartels, so that the structural elements of perfect competition were often absent. He further argued that the evidence did not support the presence of perfect competition. He pointed to the requirement within the theory of perfect competition for a U-shaped cost curve (so that the size of the firm is thereby constrained) and contrasted this with evidence of approximately constant costs (discussed further below; see Kalecki, 1939, pp. 23–4). Perfect competition indicates that firms will generally operate at or above capacity, where capacity is defined as the output level where average variable and marginal costs are equal. The experience of firms generally operating with spare capacity contradict this view. As firms under perfect competition are seen as operating on the rising portion of the marginal cost curve (and correspondingly the declining portion of the marginal product of labour curve), so that real wages are expected to move in the opposite direction to employment and output. Kalecki argued that a number of places (e.g. Kalecki, 1943a, pp. 25–6) that the evidence did not support this contention. The relationships between real wages and the levels of output and employment are more fully discussed below in Chapter 6.

Criticisms of the Degree of Monopoly Theory

The degree of monopoly approach has been subject to many

criticisms, and in this section we examine six charges. These are that the degree of monopoly is a tautology (i.e. merely true by definition), untestable, empirically false, the degree of monopoly is solely determined by the elasticity of demand, the theory does not include perfect competition as a limiting case and that it is a temporary disequilibrium phenomenon. It is clear that some of these charges cannot be simultaneously true (e.g. untestable and empirically false) though some authors (e.g. Ferguson, 1969, Mitra, 1980) have made the charge against the degree of monopoly theory both that it is a tautology and that its predictions are empirically falsified.

We begin our examination of the criticisms made of the degree of monopoly approach by considering the tautology charge, which is made by, *inter alia*, Kaldor (1955), Ferguson (1969) and Bauer (1942).[3] Before examining the charge in detail, we must note that the degree of monopoly approach was gradually evolved by Kalecki in papers stretching from 1938 (Kalecki, 1938a) to 1971 (Kalecki, 1971b). But there is a sharp break between the early versions and those published in 1943 (Kalecki, 1943a) and after. The source of the tautology charge is the earlier version, though those making the charge have generally failed to consider the later versions even though those later versions were available before their criticisms were made.

There are two ways of interpreting an approach summarised by the block of equations (2.2′), (2.3), (2.4), (2.5) and (2.6) given above. The way, which corresponds to Kalecki's later versions, is to regard k as determined by the degree of monopoly (factors such as concentration, collusion, etc.). It is then clear that the main part of the theory is the view that the mark-up is determined by the degree of monopoly, followed by the important implications drawn out in equations (2.5) and (2.6) for the distribution of income. Indeed, a significant contribution of Kalecki could be seen as pointing out that pricing decisions have income distribution consequences.

The other interpretation is to treat equation (2.2′) as defining k. In Kalecki's presentation (e.g. Kalecki, 1939), he defines the degree of monopoly (following Lerner, 1934) as $\mu = (p - m)/p$ (i.e. $\mu = (k - 1)/k$), where m is marginal cost (i.e. u in (2.2′)). He did, however, note that when marginal cost equals marginal revenue, μ is equal to the inverse of the elasticity of demand, and did remark that the increasing concentration of industry tends to raise the degree of monopoly. Thus, whilst there are elements of a theory (in terms of what factors influence μ), it is relatively easy to interpret the presentation as a tautology. This is reinforced by the interpretation of the evidence where Kalecki observed that broadly the share of wages in national income had been roughly constant between 1913 and 1935 in the UK, whilst the equivalent of *j* had fallen so that 'the degree of monopoly *must* have substantially increased in this period'. (Kalecki, 1939, p. 33, italics added).[4]

Some of the confusion as to whether Kalecki's degree of monopoly approach is a theory or a tautology results from different usages of the term 'degree of monopoly'. Sometimes it is used to mean price–cost margin itself, whilst on other occasions as the forces, such as industrial concentration, determining the mark-up. Our usage will be the latter, to ensure that there is no doubt that Kalecki's approach is a theory and not a tautology. It is perhaps regrettable that Kalecki did not maintain the approach used in Kalecki (1941c) and (1943a) where he discussed the determination of the mark-up in terms of 'the degree of market imperfection and oligopoly and the bottlenecks in available capacities, [and] also . . . the rates of prime sellings costs' (Kalecki, 1943a). For there it is quite clear that Kalecki's approach was a theory and not a tautology.

The second charge is that the degree of monopoly approach is untestable, Reder (1959), for example, argued that 'my only objection is that no theory has ever been offered that relates, *in a testable way*, either factor prices or profit margins to such forces as bargaining power, oligopoly agreements etc.'. This line of argument clearly intends to judge a theory by the validity of its testable predictions alone, whereas we would argue that other criteria such as explanatory power, degree of insight are also relevant. It is also clear that concepts such as bargaining power and extent of oligopolistic agreements may be difficult to measure, but that does not mean they do not exist.

The major response to this line of criticism is that there have been many attempts to measure bargaining power and oligopoly power over the past thirty years. Indeed, a central preoccupation of industrial economists has been precisely that problem. Starting with Bain (1951), there have been numerous articles investigating the links between industrial structure and price-cost margins (or equivalently profit-sales ratios). Surveys of work in this area are given by Weiss (1971), Sawyer (1981, Chapter 6). This point can be seen most clearly from Reynolds (1984) in which he specifically tests the Kalecki degree of monopoly approach, with the mark-up of price over prime costs related to measures of industrial concentration, advertising intensity, barriers to entry and union power. It is also notable that three of the variables which crop up in most studies are the level of concentration, advertising intensity, and capital intensity which are close approximations to the first three factors listed by Kalecki as determining the degree of monopoly. The fourth factor (trade union activity) has made only limited appearances, though Cowling and Molho (1982) have incorporated this aspect.

Whilst measures used in many of these studies may be only loose proxies for the variables, and some crucial variables are generally omitted (e.g. extent of collusion not directly related to concentration, the elasticity of demand), these studies have often provided support for the Kaleckian view. In other words, concentration, advertising intensity and (to a lesser extent) capital intensity have often been shown to influence in cross-sectional studies the price--cost margin. It should also be noted that many of these studies have made the assumption that unit costs are constant with respect to output.

This discussion on the testability of the degree of monopoly approach also serves to overthrow the tautology charge. It also serves to dislodge some of the third line of criticism – that the theory is empirically false. This charge may be related to the assumptions of the theory (Ferguson, 1969) or to the predictions of the theory. The studies referred to above provide support for the view that Kalecki's degree of monopoly theory performs reasonably well on the 'prediction' criteria. On the assumptions, it is the linked assumptions of constant unit cost and of general excess capacity which are challenged. We can first note that whilst Kalecki took excess capacity as the normal state of affairs, he did not rule out cases where there would be full capacity utilisation (though he thought this only likely in wartime or during post-war developments). Indeed, he stated that when 'the utilization of equipment may reach the point of practical capacity and thus, under the pressure of demand, prices may exceed the level indicated by these formulae' (the equivalent of (2.1) and (2.2)) (Kalecki, 1971a, p. 54). The constancy of unit costs (with respect to output) was seen as a simplifying assumption for ease of analysis (cf. Kalecki, 1971a, p. 44).

The criticisms of Ferguson clearly relate to assumptions rather than predictions, although Ferguson did not cite any evidence to support his contentions on costs and on excess capacity. In the case of costs, we can note that in industrial economics it is often assumed as a working approximation (particularly in structure-profitability studies) that average direct costs are constant with respect to output. The justification for this assumption is the finding of studies such as Johnston (1960) who summarising fourteen studies on short-run cost functions concluded that 'the first (major impression) is that the various short-run studies more often than not indicate constant marginal cost and declining average cost as the pattern that best seems to describe the data that have been analysed'. The measurement of capacity utilisation is difficult, and it often proceeds by some comparisons of current output with peak or trend output. This presents the problem here of knowing how far the peak output could be said to correspond to full capacity utilisation. Thus the evidence which we cite may tend to understate actual under-utilisation if the peak does not in fact correspond to full capacity utilisation. Drawing on the figures for capacity utilisation reported in National Institute of Economic and Social Research (1981) for UK manufacturing industry, the average capacity utilisation over the period 1960 to 1980 was 91, when the utilisation in 1973 is taken as 100. In CBI surveys, the question is posed on 'is your present level of output below capacity (i.e. are you working below a satisfactory level of operation)?'. On average over the same period, 43 per cent of respondents answered no to that question, presumably leaving, on average 57 per cent with an unsatisfactory level of output. In view of the ambiguity of the question, and that a satisfactory level of output may still allow for expansion of output at around constant unit costs, this provides some support for the excess capacity position. Steindl (1952), Chapter 2 provides further evidence on excess capacity relating to the inter-war period, and also discussion on why firms might choose to operate with general excess capacity.

A loosely related criticism made by Ferguson (1969) is that 'even if mark-up pricing is a suitable approximation of the pricing process in manufacturing industry, it is not a suitable description in other sectors, notably agriculture, government, finance and services'. The opening paragraphs of this chapter show that Kalecki made a clear distinction between cost-determined and demand-determined prices, and his approach only applied to the former. It was clearly not intended to apply to government, and it would be surprising if any economic theory (especially the marginal productivity theory favoured by Ferguson) would apply in that area. A mark-up approach to pricing may well be appropriate in distribution and services. Silberston (1970) in his survey of pricing behaviour notes that in the wholesale and retail trades '(t)he common method of pricing is to add a gross margin to the purchase price to arrive at the selling price'. Cyert and March (1963) apply their behavioural theory to a case study of a retail department store, and postulate a pricing rule for 'standard items' as 'divide each cost by 0.6 (1-mark-up) and move the result to the nearest .95'. Hence here again a form of mark-up pricing applies.

The fourth criticism which we examine is the idea that the degree of monopoly is *solely* determined by the elasticity of demand (e.g. Johnson, 1973). For a profit-maximising monopolist, it is easily shown that price $p = (1 - 1/e)u$, and from comparison with (2.2') $k = (e - 1)/e$.

We make three comments on this line of argument. First, although it is called a degree of monopoly theory, it would be more accurate to call it a degree of oligopoly theory, which Kalecki did on occasions. A simple monopoly case (in the sense of a single firm) can be considered as a special case of more general oligopoly situations, when the number of firms dwindles to one and hence there is no interdependence to consider. The formalised approach given above, as well as the list of factors which Kalecki gave as influencing the degree of monopoly, indicate that the degree of monopoly encompasses more than just the elasticity of demand. Second, in a simple monopoly model the degree of monopoly is indeed only determined by the 'technical' data of the elasticity of demand, provided that it is assumed that a monopoly firm accepts as a datum the elasticity of demand which it faces and does not attempt to manipulate it by means of advertising, product innovation, etc. Third, if the world were one of simple monopolies, then the elasticity of demand would be the determining factor as far as income distribution is concerned, which again would contrast with the notion tht income distribution is determined by marginal productivity considerations. It can be seen from above that Kalecki recognised the possible links between the mark-up and the elasticity of demand.

The outcome of the pursuit of profits by firms depends upon the environment within which that pursuit of profit is conducted. Within conventional oligopoly theories, important aspects of the environment are the interdependences between firms and how firms react (conjectural variations). The approach of Kalecki is broader than that bringing the general environmental factors such as trade union power, and political and social attitudes towards collusion (Reynolds, 1983).

A fifth criticism which is made is that the model does not tend to a perfectly competitive outcome as the degree of monopoly tends to zero. Bronfrenbrenner (1971) argued that

> [t]he labor share is not equal to unity under free competition ... Nor is it sufficient answer to doubt in purist fashion for the existence of perfect competition on the model of a perfect vacuum or absolute zero: the labor share shows no sign of approaching unity in sectors with small degrees of monopoly.

The first response is that the analogy between free competition and a perfect vacuum or absolute zero may not be a good one, in that free competition may not be the limit towards which industrial structure tends as the number of firms increase. Monopolistic competition, or in Kalecki's terminology 'pure imperfect competition', can be seen as the limiting case. In that case, the mark-up of price over marginal cost does not tend to unity but to $(e_k - 1)/e_k$, where e_k is kth firm's own price elasticity of demand. Further, in industries where the degree of monopoly is so low that the rate of return on capital is unacceptably low, then firms would tend to move out of such industries, with the consequence that industries with high wage and low profit shares may tend to disappear.

The second response is that the theory of perfect competition is inapplicable in the circumstances taken as typical by Kalecki, namely that average variable costs are constant (with respect to output). When marginal costs and average variable costs are constant then output may be zero (if price is below marginal cost), indeterminate (if price is equal to marginal cost) or infinite (if price is above marginal cost). In the usual presentation of perfect competition, the profit margin is equal to the difference (at the prevailing level of output) between marginal costs and average variable costs, so that if that difference is zero so will the profit margin. This line of argument illustrates a severe problem in the theory of perfect competition rather than in the degree of monopoly theory. For whilst, as shown in note 1, the degree of monopoly theory can easily be extended to cover the case of average variable costs which are not constant, the theory of perfect competition cannot be amended to allow for constant average variable costs.

A third response is that the mark-up is not expected to tend to zero as the degree of monopoly tends to zero. Kalecki argued that there was an influence of overhead costs (including capital costs) on the mark-up (a point to which we return below). But it is a clear prediction of Kalecki's theory that the share of manual labour in value added will decline as the degree of monopoly increases (cf. equation (2.6) above), and indeed this is a proposition which has been tested by Cowling and Molho (1982).

Kalecki anticipated this line of attack. His response (Kalecki, 1939, pp. 23–4) was that the prediction of perfect competition was for firms to be producing where marginal costs are rising and marginal costs above average variable costs. 'In the real world an enterprise is seldom employed beyond the "practical capacity", a fact which is therefore a demonstration of general market imperfection and widespread monopolies or oligopolies. Our formula though quite realistic is not applicable in the case of free competition' (Kalecki, 1939, pp. 23–4).

A sixth criticism was made by Whitman (1942), to which Kalecki (1942b) was a reply. Whitman observed that the same degree of monopoly (leading to the same profit–output ratio) would lead to different rates of profit on capital when capital intensity differed between industries.

Kalecki's response can be usefully discussed in terms of the identity $\pi/K = (\pi/Y)\ (Y/Y^*)\ (Y^*/K)$, where Y^* is a measure of capacity-output. It is clear that where there is full capacity working (i.e. $Y/Y^* = 1$), then for the same rate of profit on capital, a more capital-intensive industry requires a higher degree of monopoly. In the absence of that higher degree of monopoly, the firms will not get the equalised rate of profit and in that sense the source of profits is seen as being the possession of monopoly power. Further, the mechanism by which rates of profits would be equalised whilst maintaining equal degrees of monopoly would be through the extension of capacity in high profit-rate industries. This development would lead to a fall in the rate of profit (as the capital stock rose) and a rise in the extent of excess capacity. The techniques of production do not change in response to profit rates, so that there is no change in the degree of capital intensity, but rather capacity utilisation changes. The degree of monopoly determines the first term on the right-hand side of the formula above. Then, according to Kalecki, equalised rates of profit can be consistent with different degrees of monopoly and different capital-intensities reflected in Y^*/K by variations in capacity utilisation (i.e. Y/Y^*).[5]

Further Aspects of the Degree of Monopoly

It is clear from our discussion above that the degree of monopoly theory is built on firm level behaviour to provide an industry-level view on the relationship between price, cost, profits and sales. This has two sets of implications which we explore here.

The first is that there are cross-section implications from the theory. We have hinted at some of these above in our discussion of evidence relating to the degree of monopoly theory. The degree of monopoly theory indicates that profits arise from monopoly power, and hence that more profits accrue to firms with more monopoly power. Kalecki argued (cf. Kalecki, 1971a, pp. 51–2) that the degree of monopoly was of importance for both the distribution of income between workers and capitalists and for the distribution within the capitalist class. A rise in the degree of monopoly caused by the growth of large firms would result in the shift of profits from small businesses to big businesses.

The second set of implications arise from the need to aggregate up from the industry level. Kalecki indicates the outcome for the share of wages in value added as:

$$w' = 1/(1 + (k' - 1)(j' + 1)) \qquad (2.7)$$

which is comparable with the formula at the industry level (cf. equation (2.6)). In this formula, the degree of monopoly in manufacturing determines the value of k'. The prices of materials for manufacturing industry depend upon prices of primary products, and by labour costs and the degree of monopoly at those stages of production which produce inputs for manufacturing. Thus j', which is the ratio of the unit costs of materials to unit wage costs, depend approximately on the ratio of primary product prices to unit wage costs and by the degree of monopoly in manufacturing. Kalecki noted that this is a rough generalisation 'based on two simplifying assumptions: (a) that unit costs of materials change proportionately with prices of materials, i.e. changing efficiency in the utilization of materials is not taken into account; and (b) that unit wage costs at the lower stages of production very proportionately with unit wage costs at higher stages' (Kalecki, 1971a, pp. 62–3).

At the aggregate level (which could be the economy or the industrialised sector to which the degree of monopoly theory is intended to relate), the materials will be imports into the sector. As can be seen above Kalecki identifies imported materials with primary products. But equation (2.7) can be interpreted more generally with j' relating to the relative price of imported inputs to wages. It can then be seen that the wage share is predicted to depend upon the relationship between imported input prices and domestic prices (or wages).

There are numerous interdependences between different sectors of the economy (e.g. two sectors may buy and sell to each other, whether directly or indirectly via a third sector), which in principle need to be taken into account through perhaps an input–output table. Here we illustrate by means of a two sector set-up in which the output of sector 2 is an input into sector 1. Writing S as 'surplus' (equal to profits plus overheads), for sector 1 we have:

$$S_1 = (k_1 - 1)(W_1 + M_1 + R_1) \tag{2.8}$$

where M_1 is imported inputs used in sector 1 and R_1 is inputs used by sector 1 and produced by sector 2. For sector 2, we have:

$$S_2 = (k_2 - 1)(W_2 + M_2) \tag{2.9}$$

and by definition

$$R_1 = k_2(W_2 + M_2) \tag{2.10}$$

The total 'surplus' is $S = S_1 + S_2$ is given by

$$
\begin{aligned}
S &= (k_1 - 1)(W_1 + M_1 + R_1) + (k_2 - 1)(W_2 + M_2) \\
&= (k_1 - 1)(W_1 + M_1) + (k_1 - 1)k_2(W_2 + M_2) + (k_2 - 1)(W_2 + M_2) \\
&= ((k_1 - 1)\lambda_1 + (k_1 k_2 - 1)\lambda_2)W + ((k_1 - 1)\lambda_1 j_1 + (k_1 k_2 - 1)\lambda_2 j_2)W \\
&= (k' - 1)W + (k' - 1)j'W = (k' - 1)(j' + 1)W
\end{aligned}
$$

where
$$W_i = \lambda_i W, \qquad M_i = j_i W_i = j_i \lambda_i W \qquad (i = 1, 2)$$
$$k' = k_1\lambda_1 + k_1 k_2\lambda_2, \quad j' = ((k_1 - 1)\lambda_1 j_1 + (k_1 k_2 - 1)\lambda_2 j_2)/k' - 1.$$

Thus the relationship between the surplus and the wage bill will depend on the industrial composition of output.

One reaction to Kalecki's degree of monopoly approach as a theory of income distribution is to query the use of a pricing decision to explain long-run movements in the share of wages and of profits in national income. In particular, it is often argued that there will be changes in the capital stock which will lead to the rate of profit on capital being equalised across industries and/or the overall rate of profit moving into equality with the rate of interest.

There are three points to be made here drawn from Kalecki's writings. The first is the general point that the long-run is merely a collection of short-runs. Thus the economy is always operating in some short-run, and in that sense short-run factors determine the outcome whether of employment, income distribution or whatever. However, there are changes through time such that the short-run factors change, and as they do so the outcomes change as well. Hence, in this particular case as the degree of monopoly changes so the share of profits in value added will change.

This general point is clearly expressed in the first two paragraphs of Kalecki (1941c). In those paragraphs, he argued that the question of income distribution was usually approached on the basis of analysis of long-run equilibrium positions. Although he did not explicitly mention it, it would seem that it was the neo-classical marginal productivity theory which Kalecki had in mind here. He argued that such an approach 'might be considered correct if our economy were quasi-stationary', that is fluctuated around a stationary level of activity. The modification of the analysis to permit a uniform growth rate was dismissed on the ground that the 'secular trend is at least as complex a dynamic process as the business cycle, and no simplifications representing it as a "natural growth" etc., will do'.[6] Further, he argued here as elsewhere that the portrayal of economies as being in equilibrium was unrealistic. One particular conclusion from that point (and arose also in Kalecki, 1941a) is that long run analysis should *not* incorporate any presumption of full employment.

The second general point is that even if, for example, the rate of profit were brought into equality with some rate of interest through capitalists continuing to invest until that equality occurred, nevertheless that should be seen as the combination of three effects. The first is that the degree of monopoly influences the share of profits in value added. The second is that current investment expenditure and capitalists' consumption determine the level of income and profits.

The third is that continuing investment decisions determine the capital stock and thereby the ratio of value added to the capital stock. However it must also be stressed that Kalecki considered that the rate of profit would generally be higher than the rate of interest (see, for example, Kalecki, 1943a, pp. 54–8). It should also be noted that if the rate of profit did fall to the level of the rate of interest, then the incentive to invest would be small. Consequently, since investment expenditure is a key element in the determination of the level of profits (see pp. 79–83 below), then low investment would entail low profits.

The third general point is that Kalecki (1941c) specifically dealt with this line of argument. Drawing on the first point made above, it is necessary to analyse long-run distribution of income in terms of short-run behaviour. Kalecki (1941c) focused on the share of wages in value-added, postulated to be a function of:

(i)   The degree of market imperfection, degree of oligopoly and the rate of prime selling costs, which we will put under the general heading of the degree of monopoly;[7]

(ii)   The ratio of wages to material costs;

(iii)   The rate of capacity utilisation.

The first two elements will be familiar from the previous discussion. The rate of capacity utilisation enters to reflect the relationship between average and marginal costs. Thus this presentation allows for average direct costs not being constant. Then the evolution of the wage share over time depends upon the evolution of the degree of monopoly, ratio of wages to material costs and the rate of capacity utilisation. Kalecki indicated that in the early development of capitalist economies the factors included under the heading of degree of monopoly would show different tendencies, but in later stages these factors are likely to rise, thereby depressing the share of wages. He looked at the changes in ratio of wages to material costs in terms of the relative requirements in production of labour and material inputs which could change under the impact of, e.g. technical change. He thought that the impact of changes in capacity utilisation would be small since the impact of changes in utilisation on the relationship between average costs and marginal costs would be small (i.e. average costs did not depart significantly from being constant).

There are some loose ends from the degree of monopoly approach. This category would include the question of how costs are divided into prime costs which are marked up and overheads which are not marked up, the impact of the level of overheads on the mark-up, and the problems of aggregation from the industry level, to the economy level. We discuss these problems in Chapter 12.

Prices and Costs Over the Business Cycle

The view implicit in Kalecki's degree of monopoly approach that price is a mark-up over unit costs, where the mark-up and unit costs do not vary substantially with the level of output, has been influential in many respects in Keynesian economics. We have seen above (p. 23) that Kalecki took as a good first approximation that average prime costs were constant with respect to output upto the limits of physical capacity. The factors which influence the degree of monopoly and thereby the mark-up are not likely to vary substantially with respect to demand and output changes.

Kalecki argued that 'there is a tendency for the degree of monopoly to rise in the slump, a tendency which is reversed in the boom' (Kalecki, 1971a, p. 51). In a footnote on that sentence, he notes that 'this is a basic tendency; however, in some instances the opposite process of cut-throat competition may develop in a depression'. In Kalecki's view the basic mechanism was that during a recession, overheads fell by much less than the fall in prime costs (related to the fall in output) which would mean a disproportionate fall in profits. Thus the protection of profits (both absolutely and relatively to value added) requires that the degree of monopoly rises.[8]

It follows from the above line of argument that the major effect of a general expansion of demand is predicted to normally be that output is increased with relatively little effect on prices. There may be occasions when it is not easily expanded through capacity constraints, but these occasions are seen as relatively infrequent. Further, if unit costs and/or the degree of monopoly have a tendency to decline with higher levels of output, then prices may decline in response to an increase in demand. The importance of this line of argument for economic policy discussions on the consequence of reflation are clear.

Notes to Chapter 2

1. If unit costs vary with output, then we have to distinguish between average and marginal costs. Assuming firms relate price to marginal costs (i.e. follow a profit maximisation course) then interpreting u as marginal costs, and putting a as average costs, we have profits plus overheads $= S = p.Q - a.Q = k.u.Q - a.Q$, and $S/pQ = (1 - a/ku)$. Hence the ratio of surplus to sales depends on the ratio of average costs to marginal costs as well as the degree of monopoly k. The ratio of a/u may vary with the level of output, so the main complication introduced is the dependence of the surplus to sales ratio on the level of output. Hence in order to arrive at the distribution of income, the level of output would need to be known.

2. Another version, which did not use the term degree of monopoly is given in Kalecki (1971b) (reprinted as Kalecki (1971a) Chapter 14). In this Kalecki argued that '(e)ach firm in an industry arrives at the price of its products p by marking up its direct cost u consisting of average costs of wages *plus* raw materials in order to cover overheads and achieve profits. But this mark-up is dependent upon 'competition' i.e. on the relation of the ensuring price p to the weighted average price of this product $\bar{p}$ for the industry as a whole. Or:

$$\frac{p-u}{p} = f\left(\frac{\bar{p}}{p}\right)$$

where f is an increasing function: the lower is p in relation to $\bar{p}$, the higher will be fixed the mark up'. However, as Reynolds (1979) notes, 'Kalecki does not provide any explanation as to why he introduces this new form of pricing equation'. There is a similarity between Kalecki's two approaches if the $(m/1 - n)$ in the text is taken to correspond with $(1 + f(\bar{p}/p))$ in this version. It could also be noted that Kalecki used a similar formulation in Kalecki (1941c) to that used in Kalecki (1971b) in which he wrote $u/p = g(p/\bar{p})$ (with a slight change of notation to ensure consistency), where the shape of g depends upon the 'degree of market imperfection, the degree of oligopoly, and the rate of prime selling costs'. In turn Kalecki (1941c) makes reference to Kalecki (1940) which we discussed in the text on pp. 25–6.

3. The argument of Ferguson is rather muddled. He argued that 'Kalecki's theory is entirely tautological. . . . There is one technological assumption (excess plant capacity) and one postulated behavioral relation (mark-up pricing). Beyond this, Kalecki's theory follows entirely from the *defined* break down of income' (Ferguson, 1969). Two points on this. First, the behavioural relation ensures that Kalecki's approach is a theory and not a tautology. Second, most economic theories are of the form of combining technological assumptions (e.g. production functions of a specific type) with behavioural assumptions (e.g. profit maximisation). Specifically Ferguson's preferred theory of marginal productivity fits into this pattern.

4. For further discussion on this point, see Reynolds (1983).
5. Riach (1971) in an article entitled 'Kalecki's "Degree of Monopoly" Reconsidered' argues that over the long-term, barriers to entry, concentration, etc., serve to protect the rate of profit on capital and not the share of profits. Whatever the merits of this line of argument, it is not Kalecki's line of argument.
6. This rather tersely expressed argument can be filled out. In a static equilibrium, one of the equilibrium conditions is the equality between the marginal product of capital and the rate of interest. This conclusion continues to hold in the context of neo-classical growth models, provided that the rate of (neutral) technical progress is exogenously determined. Full employment of labour results in this model from the assumed flexibility of real wages and the possibilities of substitution between labour and capital.
7. Note, however, that Kalecki did not himself use the term degree of monopoly in the article under discussion. But the list of factors under item (i) in the text is close to the list of factors influencing the degree of monopoly which Kalecki often gave.
8. Cowling (1983) presents evidence relevant to this issue. He concludes that

> in the case of oligopolistic industries the onset of a cutback in the demand for their output may initially lead to price cutting behaviour but this will be only a temporary effect and will be replaced by an underlying tendency to raise the degree of collusion in the face of mutual adversity. Thus unplanned excess capacity will tend eventually to raise the degree of monopoly, rather than reduce it, as many observers appear to believe. Evidence from the Great Depression and from the current slump is presented and seems broadly in line with these conclusions.

3
Investment, Business Cycles and Growth

Introduction

Throughout his career as an economist, Kalecki saw investment as a subject of great importance. The links between investment and the business cycle were the subject of his first major papers published in English (Kalecki, 1935b) and in French (Kalecki, 1935a) and of one of his last (Kalecki, 1968b), and 'there is a continuous search for new solutions in the theory of investment decisions' (Kalecki, 1971a, p. viii). He regarded the 'determination of investment decisions by, broadly speaking, the level and the rate of change of economic activity ... (as) the central *pièce de résistance* of economics' (Kalecki, 1971a, p. 165). His writings on socialist planning also generally concentrated on investment and growth (as indicated in Chapter 11 below).

In this chapter, we consider a variety of aspects of Kalecki's writings on investment. In this introductory section we place Kalecki's work on investment into context, and in the next section we deal with Kalecki's views on the determinants of the decision to invest and the lags between decision and implementation. In the following section, the equation for investment expenditure is used as part of the derivation of theories of the business cycle. This is followed by a consideration of factors which lead to a positive level of net investment, mainly technical innovation and of the relationship between investment and growth. Finally Kalecki's views on the theories of growth are examined.

In the early days of macroeconomics as a distinct part of economics, a central role was ascribed to investment. Investment expenditures were seen as the major determinant, via the multiplier, of the level of output and employment. Economists such as Samuelson (1939), Hicks (1950), Harrod (1936), developed simple models in which fluctuations in output resulted from the interaction of an accelerator investment function and the multiplier. Kalecki was part of the general approach, although as will be seen below his approach to investment was rather different from others.

In the development of mainstream economics over the past thirty years, the analysis of investment has gradually shifted from centre stage to side-stage, if not into the wings. In most macroeconomic theories there is still a variable labelled investment, but its only distinctive feature is as a component of aggregate demand which depends on the rate of interest. In some cases, for purposes of generality, both consumer expenditure and investment expenditure are taken as functions of income (or output) and the rate of interest. In this case, all significant differences between consumer expenditure and investment are removed and the effect of investment on the capital stock and the rate of profit are ignored.

Consideration of the business cycle has been largely dropped in macroeconomic theory, with attention focusing on equilibrium outcomes. This was perhaps in the belief that the business cycles are now of limited importance (as reflected in the title of Bronfrenbrenner (1969) – *Is the Business Cycle Obsolete?*). However, some neo-classical economists have recognised the persistence of elements of a business cycle. But their major concern has been with explaining how output and prices move together over the course of the cycle. This has been largely accepted as a 'stylised fact' in the need of explanation. The search for an explanation within the confines of neo-classical economics and continuous market-clearing has led to the 'surprise supply' function literature (e.g. Lucas and Rapping, 1969; Sargent, 1979). The main explanatory notion behind the 'surprise supply' function is that mistaken expectations are a major force behind cycles in output and prices. However, this approach does not appear to be capable of generating cycles autonomously, and the difference between actual and expected prices has to be taken as both given and self-generating.[1]

The approach of Kalecki to the explanation of business cycles was based on the view that it is fluctuations in investment expenditures which are the major force generating macroeconomic fluctuations. Indeed, it can be seen from many of his papers on the business cycle (e.g. Kalecki, 1935b; 1968b) that it was cycles in investment expenditure which were the focus of attention. However, the fluctuations in investment have to be analysed within the context of a growing economy. For growth in an economy arises from investment adding to the capital stock, and the prospect of growth generates the demand for net investment.

The analysis of business cycles and growth simultaneously is, however, likely to be very complex, and so for the purposes of analysis simplifications are sought. In his early work on cycles (e.g. Kalecki, 1939, Chapter 6), Kalecki worked with the case of no secular trend (i.e. on average zero growth) in order to focus on the cyclical elements and to make the analysis manageable. But the no secular trend case was used only as an analytically convenient simplification of the case with a secular trend. An economy which was actually subject to no secular trend would be rather different from one with a secular trend. Net investment is closely linked with growth and the expectation of growth, and a 'no secular trend' economy would have zero (on average) net investment and (on average) gross investment equal to depreciation of the existing capital stock. In those circumstances, cycles in investment would mainly arise from cycles in gross investment matching the depreciation of a capital stock with an uneven age structure (so that depreciation varies over time). With, on average, zero net investment there would also be zero net savings. Further, 'the net saving of salary earners and rentiers on the one hand and that of entrepreneurs on the other must each be equal to zero. For otherwise a shift of capital from entrepreneurs to salary earners and rentiers would take place, which would change the economic situation quite appreciably ...' (Kalecki, 1939, p. 122). The reason for this is that when savings are made by salary earners and rentiers it has to be passed back, via the capital market, to the entrepreneurs for financing of investment. This means that entrepreneurs have to use external finance more than otherwise, and for reasons explored below (pp. 101–6) this tends to depress the entrepreneur's investment plans.

In the model of the business cycle which we outline below, Kalecki first derived an equation involving cycles and growth, and then derives an equation for a 'pure' cycle by subtracting out the trend elements from the original equation. The trend itself is determined within the model by imposing certain conditions on the equation for cycles with growth. Thus the trend is established by the model rather than being exogenously imposed. The contrast can be drawn between this approach and the general neo-classical approach where the equilibrium rate of growth (the 'natural' rate of growth) is predetermined by the sum of growth of labour force and productivity (e.g. Hacche, 1979, Chapter 7).

However, the separation of cycle and trend relies on the equation for cycles-with-growth being linear and the coefficients of that equation not changing over time. Suppose, for example, that the variable of interest in period $t+1$ (labelled y_{t+1}) is related to its previous value in time $t(y_t)$ and to variable X_t which gradually changes over time by the formula $y_{t+1} = f(y_t, X_t)$. Denote the trend value of y by y' and that also satisfies the equation $y'_{t+1} = f(y'_t, X_t)$. The equation for pure cycles in the equation for the de-trended value of y, i.e. $y - y'$. This equation in general is $y_{t+1} - y'_{t+1} = f(y_t, X_t) - f(y'_t, X_t)$. If (and only if) the function f is linear can the de-trended value of y in period $t+1$ be directly related to the de-trended value of y in period t, permitting thereby the clear separation between short-run (cyclical factors) and long-run (trend factors).[2]

In his last paper on business cycles (Kalecki, 1968b), he admitted that he had approached business cycles in

> a manner which now I do not consider entirely satisfactory: I started from developing a theory of the 'pure business cycles' in a stationary economy, and at a later stage I modified the respective equations to get the trend into the picture. By this separation of the short-period and long-period influences I missed certain repercussions of technical progress which affect the dynamic process as a whole.

The final version of Kalecki's approach to business cycles and growth is considered below (pp. 60–3). We find in this area, as in a number of others, that Kalecki retained certain central ideas throughout his career but sought to improve his understanding.

Much theorising on investment, especially within the neo-classical tradition (e.g. Jorgenson, 1967; Nickell, 1978), has the following structure. Theorising at the individual firm level, with the firm postulated to be pursuing some objective (usually profits in some sense) in a situation where the supply of investment goods and of finance are readily available to the firm at the currently prevailing prices. This generates investment decisions by the firm, which led quickly to investment expenditure (indeed no distinction is usually drawn between decisions and expenditures). Strictly speaking, all this approach provides is a theory of the demand for investment goods at the individual firm level. But problems of how far the demand can be satisfied (and how quickly) and of moving from the individual firm to the aggregate level are largely overlooked.[3] Kalecki's aproach to investment is quite different, and can be seen to some extent by reference to Kalecki's review of Keynes (1936) in which he was particularly critical of Keynes's theory of investment, and the criticisms made there by Kalecki are largely repeated in Kalecki (1937a).

The major differences between Kalecki's approach and the neo-classical approach (and in this regard Keynes's approach is not dissimilar) would include the following points.[4] First, Kalecki drew a sharp distinction between investment decisions and actual investment expenditures. This distinction allows for a time difference between investment decisions and investment expenditures. Thus some allowance can be made for the fact that many investment goods are not immediately available. Second, Kalecki's analysis is undertaken at the aggregate level and incorporates conditions (such as investment expenditure equal to savings) which apply only at the aggregate level and not at the firm level. Constraints on the availability of finance and supply of investment goods are also incorporated, partly through the clear separation of investment decisions and investment expenditures.

Third, in Keynes's approach investment is undertaken up to the point where the marginal efficiency of capital is equal to the prevailing rate of interest, and in the neo-classical approach up to the point where marginal productivity of investment goods is equal to the cost of capital (relative to the price of consumption goods). Kalecki criticised two particular aspects of this approach in the case of Keynes, and these critcisms would also apply to the neo-classical approach. The first aspect of this criticism is that the marginal efficiency of capital depends on the general level of demand, which in turn depends on investment expenditure. If firms plan to invest more in a future period than they are currently doing, then in that future period demand (and hence profits) will be higher, because of the higher investment. The marginal efficiency of capital will then have risen, and firms will again plan to increase investment. This cumulative aspect of investment was omitted from Keynes (and is omitted from the neo-classical approach). The second and linked aspect is that the condition of marginal efficiency of capital equal rate of interest describes an equilibrium condition on the size of the capital stock. It does not indicate how fast the firm will strive to reach that position, i.e. it does not indicate the rate of investment.

Investment Decisions

Kalecki began his analysis with the basic distinction between investment decisions (D) and actual fixed capital investment (F), where the lag between the two arises because of period of construction of machinery, etc., delivery time and so on. The length of the lag between decision and implementation will clearly vary between different types of equipment. For some types the delay may be very short (e.g. purchase of cars), whilst for others the delay may be very extensive (e.g. specialised factories built to order). With τ as the average lag, there is the relationship:

$$F_{t+\tau} = D_t \tag{3.1}$$

This is taken as a useful first approximation, under the assumption that investment decisions which are firm enough to lead to the placing of orders for investment goods lead to actual investment expenditure. The cancellation of orders is seen as possible but costly and hence not often done by firms.

In each period, Kalecki argued, firms plan to expand their investment up to the point where further investment would not be profitable. The limits to further investment may arise from a limited market for that firm's products or from limitations of the capital market and the increasing risk of further finance (cf. p. 102 below). It can also be noted that firms are expected to have taken into account possible delays in the supply of investment goods. Thus firms have temporarily reached the limit on investment. But, in the next period, market may have grown and profits will have accrued, and these events lead to further investment. This line of argument does not imply that firms are in equilibrium in the sense of having the capital stock which matches the demand which they face or that the rate of profit is equal to some notion of the rate of interest. For firms are usually locked into the capital equipment which they have purchased in the past, which may not match their current requirements. Further, the expansion of the firm in a given period is held back by the availability of finance.

There are three broad categories of changes in economic circumstance of firms which, in Kalecki's view, generate investment. The first is the change in available finance which occurs as firms make gross savings out of profits. The second is the change in profits and the third the change in the capital stock. It is noticeable that the first of these occurs automatically through the passage of time, whilst the third occurs provided that non-zero net investment is proceeding.

In this discussion, following Kalecki, it will be assumed that investment decisions are made in real terms, being plans for a particular amount of extra physical capacity. These investment decisions are intended to be implemented at some stage in the future, and the actual expenditure depends on the course of prices in the intervening period (and on the nature of the contract for the investment goods, e.g. whether fixed in nominal price terms). A factor which could lead to a dislocation between decisions and implementation would be unexpected inflation. The mechanism here would be that firms make decisions in real terms (e.g. in terms of so much of a specified type of machinery), which needs to be translated into money terms in order to determine the need for finance. If it turns out that the prices of investment goods are unexpectedly high, then adequate finance may be not forthcoming. This could happen particularly when internal finance was to be used for the investment expenditure since it is profits from one period which are to help finance investment in a subsequent period when prices are higher.

Savings out of profits influence the availability of finance for a firm, both directly as a pool of finance and indirectly as enabling borrowing in the finance market. The reasons for this are elaborated in the next chapter (pp. 171–2). Further, the cost of finance to a firm depends on the extent to which it can use internal finance. Thus the financial constraints on firms' investment decisions depend upon the savings made by those firms. Kalecki also argued that there would be close relation between total savings and the savings out of profits by firms. In the formulation given below this influence on investment decisions is summarised by the term aS, where S is total savings. The value of a was expected by Kalecki to be less than 1. Indeed, if a were equal to or greater than 1, then investment plans would be up with or run ahead of savings, and hence the problem of investment expenditure lagging behind potential savings would not arise.

The value of *a* would be expected to depend on, *inter alia*, the extent to which savings are made outside of firms by, for example, salary earners and rentiers. The greater are those 'outside' savings, the more firms will have to resort to external finance. External finance is generally more expensive than internal finance, and places firms at some risk in that the interest payments on external finance, have to be serviced out of profits. This point is further developed below (pp. 101–6).

The second factors is the increase in the level of profits per unit of time. The argument here is simply that a rise in profits will make some capital investment projects appear to be profitable which previously were not so considered.

Kalecki focused on the effects of changes in profits and argued that changes in interest rates would have little effect on investment decisions. In part, this is derived from Kalecki's argument that the long-term rate of interest is the one most likely to be relevant to long-term investment decisions, but the long-term rate of interest changes little (cf. Kalecki, 1954, p. 88, 99). Further, interest rates regarded as the cost of external finance are of less significance in Kalecki's approach, when internal financing out of profits is seen as crucial. It is also implicit (and sometimes explicit as in Kalecki (1943a) that the rate of profit is much above the rate of interest which could be obtained by lending out funds and hence comparisons of the rate of profit with the lending rate of interest (regarded as opportunity cost) is not usually of much significance. Finally, Kalecki argued that movements in interest rates would be much like movements in profit rates (i.e. rising in the boom, falling in the slump), so that the effects of movements in interest rates can be incorporated with the effects of movements in profit rates.

Kalecki (1939) (pp. 102–5) argued that 'so long as constant returns prevail and we abstract the influence of imperfect competition the change in the rate of interest does not affect the method of production chosen by the entrepreneur, but only the size of the investment planned'. This conclusion arose through the limitation on a firm's investment arising from a rising cost of finance with a constant marginal rate of profit. A shift in the supply curve of finance then leads to increased size. However, under conditions of imperfect competition 'the decline in the rate of interest exerts some

influence towards more capitalistic methods of production in investment plan' (Kalecki, 1939, p. 105 fn).

The third factor is the net increase of capital equipment, which is
expected adversely to affect the rate of investment. As the volume of
capital equipment increases then, *ceteris paribus*, the rate of profit
falls, and some of the previous investment demands will have been
met. Thus increases in capital equipment tend to reduce the plans for
future investment. We can see that Kalecki incorporated the effect of
changes in the capital stock into his analysis of investment decisions.
This stands in contrast to most conventional macroeconomics where
the short-period analysis is carried through under the assumption
that additions to the capital stock from net investment is insignifi-
cant within the short-period.

A linear approximation of the above lines of arguments provides:

$$D = aS + b \, \mathrm{d}P/\mathrm{d}t - c \, \mathrm{d}K/\mathrm{d}t + d \qquad (3.2)$$

where D is the rate of investment decisions, S gross savings, $\mathrm{d}P/\mathrm{d}t$
rate of change of aggregate profits and $\mathrm{d}K/\mathrm{d}t$ the rate of change of
capital stock and d is taken as constant for the analysis of investment, even though it may change over the long run as the rate of
technical progress changes. Combining equations (3.1) and (3.2)
provides the investment in fixed capital equation:

$$F_{t+\tau} = aS_t + b \, \mathrm{d}P/\mathrm{d}t - c\mathrm{d}K/\mathrm{d}t + d \qquad (3.3)$$

This equation and other similar ones developed by Kalecki are
sometimes seen as sharing common features with the accelerator
model of investment. This arises partly through a common feature
of a role for changes in economic activity on investment, which in
Kalecki's approach are reflected in changes in profits. In order to
indicate the contrast between Kalecki's approach and the usual
accelerator approach, we first write down two simple versions of an
accelerator approach:

$$I_t = v(Y_{t-i} - Y_{t-i-1}) \qquad (3.4)$$
$$I_t = b(v.Y_t^a - K_{t-1}) \qquad (3.5)$$

In (3.4) investment is related to changes in output in the current
period ($i = 0$) or some past period ($i > 0$), whereas in (3.5) investment
is seen as a partial adjustment (indicated by the coefficient b) of the
actual capital stock (K_{t-1}) to the desired capital stock ($= vY_t^a$).
Particularly in (3.4), the importance of changes in output is clearly

seen. Kalecki's approach brings in a role for the *level* of economic activity (reflected in S_t in (3.3)) and *changes* in economic activity (reflected in dP/dt in (3.3)). But it is the impact of economic activity in terms of profits rather than output which is relevant in Kalecki's approach. Over the course of the business cycle, output and profits tend to move together. However, there are differences in the underlying rationale; in the accelerator theory, investment is undertaken to be able to meet actual or expected increases in demand whereas in Kalecki investment is undertaken for reasons of profit. Further, in ideological terms, there is a considerable difference between attributing a downturn in investment to a slow-down in output rather than to a slow-down in profits.

The roles of savings and finance are clearly visible in Kalecki's approach. This helps overcome the criticism often levelled at the accelerator approach that it ignored cost of finance or financing constraints. In Kalecki's approach a greater volume of profits (and hence savings) lowers the cost of finance for the typical firm (since more internal finance is available) and generally increases the availability of funds. Further, Kalecki usually assumed that any shortfall of available savings behind investment expenditure plans would be met by an increase in loans from banks and thereby an increase in the money supply (cf. pp. 91–6 below). There may be times when planned increases in expenditure are frustrated by a failure of loans to be forthcoming and for the money supply to expand (e.g. when monetarist policies of control and restriction over the money supply are operating effectively).

Kalecki also acknowledged through the inclusion of the *d*-term, the importance of long term factors, specifically technical change, on investment. Most presentations of the accelerator mechanism do not mention technical change, and we return to this point below.

The accelerator approach to investment is concerned only with the demand for investment goods, and actual investment may diverge from the demand if the supply is not forthcoming. Kalecki incorporates some supply effects in his investment equation. He recognised that there are lags between investment decisions and implementation, and that part of the lag was attributable to the production time of investment goods. Further, Kalecki adopted a general view of excess capacity as applying also to investment goods industries, so that many investment goods can be easily supplied as demanded (though even so extra production does take time to bring into effect). But since many investment goods are made to specific requirements and not purchased 'off the shelf', demand for investment goods may only lead to actual investment with the supply of the investment goods much later. Under these circumstances, it is important to give some recognition of the lag between decisions and implementation as Kalecki did. For the purpose of analaysis, Kalecki incorporated an average lag between decision and implementation. Clearly, a more empirical-based approach would need to take account of different lags in different circumstances.

Kalecki argued (Kalecki, 1939, p. 66; 1954, pp. 100–2) that his approach was superior to the accelerator approach. His argument was based on three differences. First, he argued, that the accelerator approach concentrated solely on changes in output, and omitted reference to other factors. This will be apparent from the above discussion. Second, during most of the business cycle there was spare capacity, and changes in output arise largely from changes in capacity utilisation. Hence, there is little reason for firms to invest in new capacity to meet increases in demand when there is spare capacity. Third, he argued that the accelerator approach was not consistent with observed movements in output and investment. The basis of his argument was that changes in output are highest at the midpoint of an expansion (i.e. half-way roughly between the bottom and the top of the cycle), whilst the level of investment reaches a peak at roughly the top of the cycle. Thus there is a lag between changes in output and investment of approximately one-quarter of a cycle. Investment decision would be at their height at the mid-point of the expansion, since they are based on changes in output in the accelerator approach. This implies a lag between investment decisions and actual investment expenditures of approximately one-quarter of a cycle. In the inter-war period (and before), the length of the business cycle averaged around eight years, and hence an implied lag between investment decisions and expenditures of around two years. '(I)t is difficult to assume that the time lag between investment decisions and actual investment would be more than one year' (Kalecki, 1954, p. 100), for which some evidence was brought forward (p. 109). On those grounds, Kalecki argued that the accelerator approach was inadequate. It can be noted that in the postwar period the length of the business cycle has shortened to around four years.

To reach the final version of the investment equation, two

amendments to (3.3) are required. First, investment in inventories has to be added to (3.3) which related only to fixed investment. Here, Kalecki took the very simple view that inventory investment would depend on changes in output (to keep the level of inventories in line with the level of output). Second the change in the capital stock (dK/dt) is equal to gross investment minus depreciation (i.e. $F - Dp$, where Dp is depreciation). Thus taking account of this second point the revised form of (3.3) becomes:

$$F_{t+\tau} = a\, S_t + b\, \frac{\Delta P_t}{\Delta t} - c\, (F_t - Dp) + d \tag{3.6}$$

This can be rewritten as:

$$\frac{F_{t+\tau} + cF_t}{1+c} = \frac{aS_t}{1+c} + \frac{b}{1+c}\, \frac{\Delta P_t}{\Delta t} + \frac{cDp + d'}{1+c} \tag{3.7}$$

which Kalecki approximated by:

$$F_{t+\theta} = \frac{a}{1+c}\, S_t + b'\, \frac{\Delta P_t}{\Delta t} + c'Dp + d' \tag{3.8}$$

The first point means that total investment (I) is equal to fixed investment (F) plus inventory investment equal to $e\, \Delta Qy/\Delta t$ where Q is output. Adding in this element leads to:

$$I_{t+\theta} = \frac{a}{1+c} . S_t + b'\, \frac{\Delta P_t}{\Delta t} + c'Dp + d' + e\, \frac{\Delta Q_t}{\Delta t} \tag{3.9}$$

It can be seen that to arrive at (3.9) many approximations have been made. The extent to which those approximations do not hold would mean that empirical work would need to be modified accordingly. The purpose of equations such as (3.9) is to focus on what are believed to be the key aspects of investment. In this case, it is clear that previous savings, changes in profits, depreciation, rate of technical advance and changes in output are seen as the key factors influencing investment.

Investment and Business Cycles

There are a number of alternative models on the business cycle presented by Kalecki (e.g. Kalecki, 1935b; 1943a). They contain the common theme that the level of investment expenditure depends on prior levels of changes in profits or output (cf. equation (3.3) above) and that the level of effective demand (and hence output) depends on the current level of investment. In this section, we draw on the approach to the business cycle first published in Kalecki (1943a), amended in Kalecki (1954) (reprinted as Kalecki, 1971a, Chapter 11). Here, as elsewhere, Kalecki made 'drastic simplifications to concentrate the attention of the reader on the most essential issues without, however, throwing out the baby along with the bath-water' (Kalecki, 1971a, p. 167). In this context, these drastic simplifications include the use of a closed private economy in which workers' savings are zero.

In building up the equation for the business cycle, Kalecki began with the idea that capitalists' consumption (CC) adjusts slowly to profits (P) expressed as:

$$CC_t = q.P_{t-h} + A \tag{3.10}$$

Workers make no savings, and wages are immediately spent. In the next chapter (p. 73), it will be shown that in these circumstances the equality between savings and investment becomes profits equal to investment plus capitalists consumption, with the later items determining profits. Thus:

$$P_t = I_t + CC_t \tag{3.11}$$

Substituting (3.10) into (3.11) yields:

$$P_t = I_t + qP_{t-h} + A \tag{3.12}$$

Successive substitutions leads to:

$$P_t = I_t + qI_{t-h} + q^2 I_{t-2h} + \ldots + A + qA + q^2 A + \ldots \tag{3.13}$$

Kalecki asserted that the first expressions of the right-hand side can be approximated by $I_{t-w}/(1-q)$, i.e. there is a lag of w such that I_{t-w} in each period, t, $t-h$, $t-2h$ etc. would lead to the same total. Accepting that, we then move to:

$$P_t = (I_{t-w} + A_t)/(1-q) \tag{3.14}$$

The relationship between output and profits is given by:

$$Q_t = \frac{P_t + B_t}{1-a} + E_t \tag{3.15}$$

where Q_t is output, B_t unmarked up costs and E_t indirect taxes, and a is related to the degree of monopoly.

In order to separate out the cyclical fluctuations from long-run trend, Kalecki imposed restrictions on the coefficients of the above equations. Specifically the parameters A, B and E from equations (3.12) and (3.15) and the term d' in equation (3.9) are taken as constant. Clearly, in the long-term these parameters would be expected to increase, and growth in A and d' would be the driving force behind expansion of demand. A further condition on d' is derived below.

With these conditions, we can derive from equations (3.14) and (3.15) the following:

$$\Delta P_t/\Delta t = (1/1 - q)\,(\Delta I_{t-w}/\Delta t) \tag{3.14'}$$
$$\Delta Q/\Delta t = (1/1 - a)\,(\Delta P_t/\Delta t) \tag{3.15'}$$

and combining these together yields:

$$\Delta Q/\Delta t = \Delta I_{t-w}/\Delta t \left(\frac{1}{(1-q)\,(1-a)} \right) \tag{3.16}$$

To the equation for investment (equation (3.9)), we add the condition that actual investment and actual savings are equal (in a private closed economy), and substitute in equations (3.14') and (3.15') and (3.16) to get:

$$I_{t+\theta} = \left(\frac{a}{1+c}\right) I_t + \left(\frac{1}{1-q}\right)\left(b' + \frac{e}{1-a}\right)\frac{\Delta I_{t-w}}{\Delta t} + c'\,Dp + d' \tag{3.17}$$

For this equation for a static system to be capable of being at rest it is necessary when at rest (so that $\Delta I/\Delta t = 0$), that there is zero net investment, so that gross investment (I) would equal depreciation (Dp). Inserting these conditions into equation (3.17) yields a condition on d', namely $d' = Dp(1 + c - a)/(1 + c)$.

An equation for net investment J can be obtained with $J = I - Dp$:

$$J_{t+\theta} = \frac{a}{1+c} J_t + \mu \frac{\Delta J_{t-w}}{\Delta t} \tag{3.18}$$

where

$$\mu = \frac{1}{1-q}\left(b' + \frac{e}{1-a}\right).$$

It is noteworthy that this equation for the business cycle is expressed in terms of investment rather than output, indicating the key role ascribed to investment by Kalecki. It is, of course, the case that the path of output would follow the path of investment via a multiplier relationship. The other feature of equation (3.18) of some note is that it is a mixed difference-differential equation, and this was featured in all Kalecki's business cycle models.

A crucial problem which arises with any theory of the business cycle is whether the model derived is capable of continuously generating cycles. It is generally assumed that there has been no strong tendency over time for business cycles in capitalist economies either to become much greater in amplitude (i.e. the cycle to explode) or to become much smaller in amplitude (i.e. for the cycle to die away). Thus the search is for an explanation of cycles which tend to persist through time. Within the context of models such as those presented by Kalecki, Goodwin (1982), Samuelson (1939), Hicks (1950), etc. there have been four routes to seeking to overcome this problem.

The first route, is to assert that the values of the parameters (in the case of equation (3.18) a, c, μ, θ, w) are such that the solution to the equation describing the time path of output or investment is a stable cycle. But this usually requires a rather precise relationship between the empirical values of the parameters, and the chances of that relationship holding are rather remote. Kalecki (1935b) initially adopted this approach, but was severally criticised for doing so by Frisch and Holme (1935) and in later versions dropped the idea.

The second route, which was taken by Hicks (1950), is to argue that the solution of the business cycle equation left to itself would be explosive, but is subject to limits usually labelled 'ceilings' and 'floors'. Then, for example, when output is rising it continues so to do until the 'ceiling' on output is reached, after which output growth slows down and then falls. The 'ceiling' is usually seen as set by full capacity or full employment, whilst the 'floor' is set by lower levels of investment and autonomous expenditure. Kalecki rejected this approach for the simple reason that 'there is no confirmation for the theory that the "ceiling" is usually reached in the boom' (Kalecki, 1954, p. 139).

The third route is to argue that the solution of the business cycle equation is damped but the cycle is kept going by various exogenous shocks. This clearly involves the unsatisfactory feature that the theory of the business cycle is left incomplete in the sense that appeal has to be made to these exogenous factors. This third route can be further subdivided. It can be argued that the major exogenous shock is the discovery of major new ideas (e.g. discovery of steam combustion and the development of the railways), which triggers off an investment boom. This approach can be linked with the ideas of Schumpeter (e.g. Schumpeter, 1939).

The route taken by Kalecki was to argue that there are numerous random shocks operating on the economy, and these are sufficient to maintain a constant business cycle, even when the underlying equation (such as (3.18)) left to itself would have a damped solution so that the business cycle would die away. This approach builds on ideas advanced by Frisch (1933). In Kalecki (1954) Chapter 13, he argued by means of elementary simulations that random shocks acting on his business cycles equation could generate a roughly constant cycle. There is the difficulty with this approach, which Kalecki recognised, that if the shocks are in some sense large then the time path of output and investment is largely determined by the shocks rather than by the underlying business cycle equation.

Kalecki did not give a formal mathematical proof for equation (3.18) generating a damped cycle. But the basis of his argument in that the term $a/1 + c$ will be less than unity. We have seen above (p. 49) that Kalecki thought that a would generally be less than unity, and with the term c expected to be positive leads to the conclusioon that $a/1 + c$ will be less than unity. When the term $a/1 + c$ is less than unity then, for example, upswings in investment would gradually die away as the impact of past investment on current investment is 'scaled down' by the factor $a/1 + c$.

The fourth route, advocated particularly by Goodwin (1982), is to develop non-linear equations, which are much more likely to generate roughly constant business cycles. This was not a route pursued by Kalecki, but it should not be difficult to introduce various nonlinearities into Kalecki's approach without destroying its essential ingredients.

The Long-run Trend and the Business Cycle

The discussion in the previous section can be relatively easily amended to move from a static into a growing economy. Effectively Kalecki's method was to allow for growth in many of the parameters which he held constant for the purpose of static analysis. In terms of

(3.14) and (3.15) this means allowing A_t, B_t and E_t to change over time. This then leads to the amended version of (3.17) as follows:

$$I_{t+\theta} = \frac{a}{1+c}I_t + \mu\frac{\Delta I_{t-w}}{\Delta t} + L_t + d'_t \tag{3.20}$$

where

$$L_i = \mu\frac{\Delta A_t}{\Delta t} + \frac{e}{1-a}\frac{\Delta B_t}{\Delta t} + e\frac{\Delta E_t}{\Delta t}$$

The term $L_t + d'_t$ is subject to changes as a result of the long-run trend in investment, where these changes in turn help to perpetuate the trend in investment.

Kalecki argued that L_t varies with the rate of change of the long-run level of investment. He reached that conclusion in the following manner. The first term in the expression for L_t given above relates to changes in A_t, which is the component of capitalists' consumption taken to be stable in the short-run analysis. In the longer term, it is argued that since profits follow investment (through equation (3.14) above), the consumption out of profits will evolve alongside profits and, thereby, investment. The second and third items involve changes in overhead costs (B) and in indirect taxes (E). Kalecki argued that in the long-term overhead costs and indirect taxes follow output as a first approximation, and output itself follows investment. Putting those all together gives the conclusion that L_t varies with the rate of change of investment.

The long-term trend in d'_t is derived by reference to the static case. There it was seen that from the condition for the system to be at rest $d' = Dp(1+c-a)/(1+c)$. In an economy with growth the volume of depreciation will change over time, and Kalecki relates depreciation simply to the level of the capital stock, i.e. $Dp = \delta K$ Then $d = ((1+c-A)/(1+c))\delta K$.

Kalecki further argued that there will be a stimulus to investment arising from factors such as technical innovation which raises d' above what it would be in a static economy. This, he relates, to the size of the capital stock to give:

$$d'_t = ((1+c-a)/(1+c)) . \delta K_t + \gamma K_t,$$

where γ is positive and measures the intensity of the 'development factors' which stimulate investment.

Thus equation (3.2) indicates that the level of investment depends upon previous investment, changes in investment, changes in the long-term trend of investment (operating through L_t), the level of the capital stock and 'development factors'. These 'development factors' are particularly important in that it is those factors which 'prevent the system from settling to a static position and engender a long-run upward trend' (Kalecki, 1954). We now leave this discussion to consider Kalecki's last approach to the business cycle, which also provides a clear indication of the relevance of these 'development factors'.

Kalecki's Final Version

In one of his last papers (Kalecki, 1968b), Kalecki introduced a number of novel ideas in his discussion of business cycle and the long-term trend. There are two particular differences between this article and his earlier work. First, although his views on the factors influencing investment remained much the same in the sense of stressing the relevance of the level and rate of change of economic activity, the route by which these conclusions were reached was different. Second, in this article, Kalecki sought to provide a much closer integration of the business cycle and the long-run trend than he had achieved before.

The abstractions adopted were similar to those used above – closed economy, no government, no workers' savings. One difference was that he now disregarded any lag between profits and capitalists' consumption. He also abstracted from overhead labour and assumed that all labour receipts were prime costs. He also dropped any reference to taxes, so that he could write $Q = P/1 - a$ (in terms of the notation used above).

The major novel part of Kalecki's discussion of investment decisions here is the idea of looking at the parts of profits which are 'captured' by new investment. Thus, at the aggregate level, there is some rearrangement of profits between firms and some changes in the level of profits (particularly due to innovations). Kalecki then related the level of investment in a particular year to the rate of profit generated on that investment. A function is postulated relating investment (I) to the rate of profit (π), expressed as $I(\pi)$ with the first derivative of I being negative. The nature of this function is that it relates the level of investment to the rate of profit which that investment yields. The direction of causation built into this function is from level of investment to the rate of profit, and *not* from the prospective rate of profits to investment decisions. The view that the higher the level of investment, the lower, *ceteris paribus*, will be the rate of profit gained by that investment (i.e. I' negative) reflects the competition between firms in the market.

Kalecki argued that there are two determinants of $I(\pi)$. The first arises even in the absence of technical progress, where any new investment captures only a small proportion of the total increase in profits during the year, with the old equipment capturing the rest. We write the profits accruing to new equipment as a proportion n of the change in profits ΔP, i.e. $n.\Delta P$.

The second determinant arises when technical progress is occurring. One effect of technical progress is that new machines are more productive than old ones, and thus the real costs of operating old machines rise as a result of the introduction of new machines. The profits yielded by old equipment falls, and is in effect transferred to the new machines. The profits yielded by old machines will fall in a year by a proportion x of real labour costs. The proportion x will be larger, the greater is the increase in productivity resulting from technical progress. Real labour costs will be equal to output (Q) minus profits (P), both in real terms. Thus from this source, the profits gained by new equipment will be $x.(Q-P)$.

With a rate of profit π, the sum of profits gained by new equipment is $\pi.I(\pi)$. From the two determinants discussed above, we have the sum of profits as $n\Delta P + x(Q-P)$. Putting those two together yields an equation for investment of $I(\pi) = (n\Delta P + x(Q-P))/\pi$.

Now profits and output are related via the degree of monopoly, and using equation (3.15) above (with the simplification of $B = E = 0$ as noted above), we have $Q = P/1 - a$, and hence $x(Q-P) = x.\dfrac{a}{1-a}P$, which we write as $d.P$. The use of the symbol d is not entirely coincidental for it does reflect the rate of depreciation. It is depreciation in the sense that it indicates the declines in profits yielded by old equipment each year.

The actual investment decisions are influenced by three groups of factors. The first, for the reasons explored above is gross entrepreneurial savings, denoted by E. The second related to the 'prerequisite for reinvestment of entrepreneurial savings'. Investment decisions will exceed actual savings when the rate of profit is high and *vice versa*. At a 'normal rate of profit' (labelled π^*) investment decisions $I(\pi^*)$ are taken as equal to actual savings and investment, i.e. $I(\pi^*) = I$. In other cases, investment decisions are different by a proportion r of $I(\pi^*) - I$. The third factor is the stimulus to investment which results from innovation and invention. The speed of invention and innovation is taken to change relatively slowly, and the impact on the level of investment decisions is summarised by the function $B(t)$ which is a slowly changing function of time.

Bringing these three factors together, with the additional assumptions that entrepreneurial savings are a constant and high proportion of total savings, and with $I = S$, we arrive at the investment decision equation:

$$D_t = eI_t + r\frac{(n\Delta P_t + dP_t - I_t)}{\pi} + B(t)$$

The equation for actual investment is generated by repeating the previous observation that there is a lag between decisions and implementation, so that D_t in the above can be replaced by $I_{t+\tau}$. From the equation above for profits, we can derive and then substitute an expression for ΔP_t. Simplifying down yields:

$$I_{t+\tau} = sI_t + v\Delta I_t + F(t)$$

where

$$s = e - r(1 - m\delta/\pi)$$

$$v = \frac{r}{\pi} + mn$$

$$F(t) = \frac{r}{\pi}.m.\delta A(t)\left(1 + \frac{n}{\delta}\frac{\Delta A(t)}{A(t)}\right) + B(t)$$

Kalecki then argued that the equivalent of s will be less than unity and that $F(t)$ will be a slowly changing function. This equation is not unlike equation (3.20) above, for investment derived on a somewhat different basis.

Here again, Kalecki separated out the trend and the cycle by defining the trend component (labelled I^* here) as the solution to the equation

$$I_t^*{}_{+\tau} = aI_t^* + b\Delta I_t^* + F(t)$$

leaving the cyclical component to satisfy

$$I_{t+\tau} - I_t^*{}_{+\tau} = a(I_t - I_t^*) + b\Delta(I - I_t^*)$$

and, of course, $I_t = I_t^* + (I_t - I_t^*)$ provides the division into trend and cyclical components.

Kalecki derived two important results from this analysis, though these results are also present in Kalecki (1962a). We do not reproduce the mathematics here, for which the reader is referred to Kalecki (1971a) pp. 179–82, or for the earlier version to Kalecki (1962a) especially pp. 143–53. The first conclusion is that the ceiling on the rate of growth of capital is closely linked to the ceiling on the rate of growth of $F(t)$, i.e. to changes in technology. This is perhaps not a surprising conclusion, but the model has been developed such that it is derived as a conclusion and is not imposed as an equilibrium requirement.

The second conclusion is rather more interesting. It is that the extent of utilisation of equipment (and also of labour) is considerably affected by the maximum growth rate of $F(t)$ (i.e. technical progress) and by the degree of monopoly. Kalecki argued that taking plausible values for the key parameters indicates that chronic under-utilisation would be a frequent phenomenon in developed capitalist economies. The mechanism at work here is that the lower is technical progress, the lower will be the incentive to invest, and hence the lower will be the general level of demand and output. This conclusion is usually derived for the static case for a given level of investment (see pp. 79–83 below). In the long run it is generally asserted within the neo-classical framework that there will be full employment (see, e.g., growth models of Solow, 1956 and Swann, 1956). Indeed a part of the neo-classical synthesis which dominated economics in the 1960s drew heavily on the idea that which the short run could be analysed in broadly Keynesian terms with an emphasis on the role of aggregate demand and the possibility of unemployments, the long run analysis would be neo-classical whereby price flexibility and factor substitution would maintain full employment (see, for example, the discussion of Hacche, 1979, pp. 35–6). It was however a continuing theme of Kalecki that this view was mistaken, as can be seen by papers such as Kalecki (1941a) and Kalecki (1968b).[5] It can be seen that it is a clear conclusion from Kalecki (1962a) and (1968b) that there is likely to be under-utilisation of people and equipment in capitalist economies.

Development Factors

In his discussion of investment, Kalecki made frequent reference to the obvious but often overlooked fact that investment will move towards replacement level covering only depreciation on existing capital stock unless there are inventions and innovations which stimulate the demand for investment. However, Kalecki did not provide any intensive discussion on invention and innovations and, as can be seen above, introduced the effects of technical change in a simple way.

Kalecki thought (e.g. Kalecki, 1954, p. 159) that there would be a slowing down in the growth of capitalist economies in the later stages of development. The slowdown would, he thought, arise in part from a decline in the intensity of innovations, which in turn were seen as arising from three broad reasons. First, there is the declining importance of discoveries of new sources of raw materials, of new lands to be developed etc. Second, the increasing monopolistic character of capitalism would hamper the application of new inventions. Thus, for example, firms would be under less competitive pressure to introduce new products. Third, he argued that 'assembly industries' (e.g. electrical goods) would involve a form of technical progress which is largely concentrated on improving the organisation of the assembly process, which does not involve large-scale investment. Thus technical progress would have a less stimulating effect on investment than hitherto. One could add (though Kalecki did not) that these industries have also turned out to be those in which production is relatively easily shifted from developed to developing countries in pursuit of low wage costs.

Kalecki discounted the growth in population as a stimulus to economic development. He argued that growth in population did little to ensure a growth in purchasing power, and it was the latter that was relevant for development. Further, faster growth in population might depress wages (on basis of increase in supply of labour), raise degree of monopoly, which would *ceteris paribus* reduce level of output.

We have noted above that Kalecki saw the division of the source of savings as between entrepreneurs on the one hand and rentiers and salary earners on the other as influencing entrepreneurs' investment decisions (p. 45 above; further explored pp.101–6 below). Kalecki did not speculate on how this division of savings would develop, but it is clear that if the division moves against savings by entrepreneurs that growth would be thereby retarded.

Growth

Whilst the study of algebraic formulae relevant to the growth process (such as equation (3.2) above) is necessary to be aware of the implications of the theory and the interactions between various elements, nevertheless certain key elements for growth are portrayed as exogenous. These key elements could include factors such as the rate of technical progress, response of investment to technical progress etc. Kalecki drew on this view in a number of respects.

First, he argued (Kalecki, 1971a, p. 183) that

> the rate of growth at a given time is a phenomenon rooted in the past economic, social and technological developments rather than determined fully by the coefficients of our questions as is the case with the business cycle. ... To my mind future inquiry into the problems of growth should be directed not towards doing without such semi-autonomous magnitudes as $A(t)$ and $B(t)$ but rather towards treating also the coefficients used in our equations (m, n, δ, q) as slowly changing variables rooted in past developments of the system.

The symbols in this equation have the same meaning as those used in the section above labelled Kalecki's last version.

Second, apparently similar equations for growth can be obtained for a wide range of economies (specifically capitalist and socialist). Kalecki (1970) quoted the equation for the rate of growth $\Delta Y/Y = (1/m).(I/Y) - a + u$, where m is the incremental capital output ratio, I gross investment, a depreciation, scrapping etc. and u increase of output due to better utilisation of equipment. This equation is derived below (p. 240) for a socialist economy. The major point to note here is that whilst the equation holds for both types of economies, its interpretation is quite different. Specifically, investment decisions are taken by different bodies (private firms, central planners), and that the u-factor is dominated by aggregate demand changes under capitalism and by improved resource utilisation under socialism.

In Kalecki (1970), he discussed the two major approaches to growth in capitalist economies, namely the neo-classical approach and the Harrod approach.[6] He was very critical of both approaches to growth under capitalism, and we outline these criticisms here drawing also on Kalecki (1962a).

The neo-classical approach involves perfect competition, price flexibility and thereby a tendency towards full employment, with supply-side factors dominant. Kalecki regarded this as 'some sort of idealized *laissez faire* capitalism' which was 'fairly remote from the realities of the present capitalist, socialist or "mixed" economies' (Kalecki, 1970). Full employment cannot be assured (or predicted) merely because the analysis is long-run rather than short-run, for unemployment is a persistent feature of capitalism.

Price flexibility was not a characteristic of developed capitalism recognised by Kalecki. Instead he argued that '(t)he monopolistic and semi-monopolistic factors involved in fixing prices – deeply rooted in the capitalist system of all times – cannot be characterised as temporary short period price rigidities but affect the relation of prices and wage costs both in the course of the business cycle and in the long run' (Kalecki, 1970).

Kalecki was scathing about the use of the neo-classical approach to growth under capitalism. He described it as one of those theories which 'are being created which may raise problems of great interest but are not conducive to understanding what actually happened, is happening or should be happening' (Kalecki, 1970). He also argued that the advocates of a neo-classical approach were presuming a high level of utilisation of labour and capital equipment in their analysis of a *laissez-faire* economy, but forgetting that it was government intervention in capitalist economies which brought about the high level of utilisation. Thus 'the government acts to achieve a high utilisation of resources and the economists take this state as the point of departure in their discussion without mentioning who is responsible for it' (Kalecki, 1970). The actual growth process in post-war capitalist economies would need to pay regard to the role of government.

Kalecki also argued that the neo-classical approach was more applicable in a socialist economy than in a capitalist one. The reasoning here was that under a socialist economy prices were flexible being adjusted by the planners to secure full employment and that inadequate effective demand was not a problem in the socialist system. Inflexibility of prices and inadequate effective demand were the two reasons why the neo-classical model did not apply to capitalist economies. However, even for socialist economies, the neo-classical approach was not entirely adequate. Specifically, the neo-classical model did not pay attention to some of the crucial problems of socialist planning. These included the difficulties of moving from one 'warranted' growth path to another, the removal of 'bottlenecks' and the problems of foreign trade. These are discussed at much greater length in Chapter 11.

Kalecki also argued against the Harrod approach. The relevant points of that approach here are that it concludes that there is a warranted rate of growth equal to s/v, where s is the propensity to save and v the incremental capital–output ratio, and that there is a 'knife edge' problem which means in effect that the warranted (equilibrium) growth path is unstable.

In Kalecki (1962a), he argued that the simple Harrod approach would generate two trend growth rates. In the case of no technical progress one of these growth rates would be zero and stable, whilst the second would be a rate equivalent to s/v (i.e. Harrod's warranted growth rate) but would be unstable. The latter conclusion accords with Harrod in the sense of a trend growth rate of s/v which is unstable (the 'knife edge' rate). There is the problem that with another trend growth rate possible which is stable, the economy would tend towards that growth rate. In the absence of technical progress there would be a lack of forces to maintain a positive growth rate and investment would decline to replace to replacement level only leaving zero net investment. Thus the Harrod approach would be one of stagnation not growth. The introduction of inventions and innovations which generate investment leads to a similar conclusion of two trend growth rates, with the lower being stable (but now above zero) and the higher unstable. But this requires the introduction of a stimulus to investment from technical progress which is generally absent in the Harrod approach.

In Kalecki (1970) he went some way further when he dismissed the Harrod approach along the following lines. 'It is generally known that the trend represented by the [Harrod] case is unstable: ... The belief that [a] disturbance creates merely a downswing followed by an upswing is mathematically indefensible: the underlying equations are incapable of producing a solution corresponding to a combination of an exponential curve with a sine line.' This would be needed for fluctuations around a rising growth trend. However Kalecki (1962a) did not fill out the details of this argument, but we can see that the argument is that the Harrod model would generate a zero growth rate as the stable trend rate.

The basis of Kalecki's approach to growth under capitalism can be seen as twofold. First, 'the problem of the long-run growth in a *laissez-faire* capitalist economy should be approached in precisely the same fashion as that of the business cycle' (Kalecki, 1970). We have seen above how Kalecki built up from investment decisions to reach a business-cum-growth equation (equation (3.20) above). The trend rate of growth is then solved out from that equation. The rate of technical progress to some degree made endogenous within that system though factors like the intensity of technical progress are taken as constant. It should also be noted that Kalecki stressed the role of technical progress in generating growth.

Second, 'no "general" theory of economic growth is conducive to understanding economic realities of different social systems for the institutional framework of a system exerts a profound influence upon its dynamics' (Kalecki, 1970). Thus whilst algebraic formulation is needed to understand some of the mechanics of growth and cycles, nevertheless such formulations are not enough. The development of economic models must incorporate the social and institutional realities, and the interpretation of such models must take account of such realities.

Conclusion

This chapter has focused on Kalecki's ideas in the areas of business cycles and growth. Kalecki saw that the business cycle and growth were both part of the same process, and that the analysis of them should be integrated. This also involves an integration of the short-run and the long-run, where the long-run is seen as a series of gradually evolving short-runs. Further, those problems of effective demand which are often seen as short-run problems are seen as long-run problems in the sense that they persist through time. The analysis of growth has to take proper account of social and institutional differences, and we shall return to the analysis of growth in mixed developing economies and in socialist economies in later chapters.

Notes to Chapter 3

1. For a critique of the 'surprise supply function', see Tobin (1980), Fitoussi (1983a), and Sawyer (1985).
2. If the function f is linear, then we can write $y_{t+1} = ay_t + bX'_t + c$ and the trend value of y conforms to $y'_{t+1} = ay'_t + bX'_t + c$ the detrended value of y conforms to $(y_{t+1} - y'_{t+1}) = a(y_t - y'_t)$.
3. There are particular severe problems in the aggregation of different types of capital equipment, when the demand for capital (in aggregate) is to be related to the rate of interest in order to derive a negative relationship between the demand for capital and the rate of interest. See, for example, Harcourt (1972, 1975a, b).
4. There is, however, a very important difference between Keynes and the neo-classical approach. This relates to the emphasis placed by Keynes on the difficulties of forming expectations about an unknown factor, and that such expectations are likely to be flimsily based and liable to sharp changes. These changes in expectations would lead to significant changes in the propensity to invest. In neo-classical theory, firms are usually pictured as holding firmly based expectations about the future.
5. The paper which was published as Kalecki (1941a) was initially submitted to the *Economic Journal* for consideration. Keynes in his role as editor rejected the paper for inclusion in the *Economic Journal* after some considerable correspondence. Part of that correspondence is reproduced in Keynes's *Collected Works* Volume 12 (Keynes, 1983, pp. 829–36). One interesting feature of the correspondence is Keynes's reluctance to accept a long-term analysis which included excess capacity as a feature.
6. For discussion of these approaches to growth economics see, e.g. Hacche (1979), Jones (1975).

4
Differential Savings, the Degree of Monopoly and the Level of Income

Introduction

The first part of this chapter is concerned with the savings behaviour postulated by Kalecki, namely that the savings propensity out of labour income is taken to be much smaller than the savings propensity out of profits. The reasons for this view and some of the consequences of it are then explored. When this differential savings proposition is combined with the degree of monopoly approach, a theory on the determination of the level of income and the distribution of income is obtained. We also examine the mechanism envisaged by Kalecki whereby savings adjust to the level of investment. In Kalecki's approach, investment and savings are brought into equality through changes in the level of income and its distribution, with the rate of interest not involved. In the next chapter, it will be seen that Kalecki regarded the rate of interest as a monetary phenomenon, and not related to savings and investment. The final section of this chapter considers Kalecki's links with the set of ideas which come under the heading of under-consumptionist approaches.

A central assumption of Kalecki, which featured in one of his earliest papers published in English (Kalecki, 1937a) and in his last published paper (Kalecki, 1971b) was that workers spend all their incomes and that they spend them immediately, whereas there is considerable savings out of profits. On some occasions, Kalecki began his analysis involving some savings by workers, and then simplifies by assuming those savings to be negligible or zero. It is an important part of this approach that savings out of labour income are proportionately much less than savings out of property income (loosely described as profits). We use the term differential savings propensities to summarise this view.

Kalecki would seem to have regarded this general view of differential savings propensities as self-evident and not requiring specific justification. The postulate that savings out of wages were zero and that profits are largely saved to finance investment is often termed the classical savings postulate, and is commonly assumed in the Ricardian–Marxian tradition within which we have argued Kalecki generally worked. Further in developed capitalist economies, the basic class division is seen to be between those who own and control the means of production (i.e. capitalists), receiving property income, and workers who do not own the means of production and receive labour income.

This dichotomisation can present difficulties where some groups (e.g. managers) may share some of the attributes of both these classes. But these difficulties are similar to those which arise with any use of dichotomies, groups or aggregates. Conventional macroeconomics dichotomies such as consumer expenditure/investment, money/bonds are not rejected merely because there are difficulties of classifying certain types of real world expenditure (e.g. consumer durables) or real world financial assets (e.g. three-month Treasury bills) in those dichotomies.

In the approach of Kalecki (and more generally in the Ricardian–Marxian tradition) the roles of the two classes (capitalists and workers) and the types of income (property income and labour income) are quite different from each other. Workers supply labour mainly because it is their only means to income and labour income is mainly used to finance consumption expenditure. This may arise because wages are at or close to some notion of a subsistence level (which may rise over time). Even in the neo-classical life-cycle hypothesis, the emphasis is on the redistribution of purchasing power over the life-cycle, with (for the individual) no net savings planned during the complete life-cycle.[1]

The aims of capitalists are quite different. They hire labour in order to produce output at a profit, and profits and survival are the key aims of capitalists. In a competitive struggle, future profits require the ploughing back of current profits as investment to maintain and expand market shares, reap economies of scale and incorporate technical progress. This indicates the linkages between the surplus (of output over wages) and investment (the difference between output and current consumption). Further, it is central to this approach that savings are closely linked with investment decisions (i.e. both savings and investment decisions are made by or forced upon firms) and savings arise from production and profit decisions and not from utility calculations (as in the life-cycle hypothesis referred to above).

At the level of the system, Kalecki argues that '(t)he capitalist system is not a "harmonious" regime, whose purpose is the satisfaction of the needs of its citizens but an "antagonistic" regime which is to secure profits for capitalists. ... The production of "coal and steel" is as justified as production of bread if it is profitable. Consumption is the final aim and proof of a "harmonious" but not of an antagonistic regime' (Kalecki, 1971a, pp. 147–8). Thus, in Kalecki's view, capitalism is not to be analysed in terms of consumption as the final aim (whereas neo-classical economics is founded on such an analysis), but rather that profits are the central driving force of the system.

In Kalecki's approach, ownership of firms (and hence of the means of production) is limited to the capitalist class. This can be divided into the entrepreneurs and rentiers. The latter group, whilst having an ownership interest, do not actively participate in control. The terms on which rentiers are prepared to supply finance to the entrepreneurs can limit the expansion of firms, as we shall see below (pp. 101–6). The entrepreneurs are controllers and part-owners of firms and make the effective decisions on the operation of firms.

Implications of Differential Savings Behaviour

In order to draw out the implications of the view that workers save little and capitalists save a lot, we begin with the simplest case of a closed economy in which the government sector is of negligible importance. This is to highlight certain features, although the extension to an open economy with a government sector is important.

The income of workers consists of wages and salaries, and we will often refer to these as labour income. However, it should be noted that this notion of labour income does not include any imputed income to the labour of the self-employed, whose income would be included under capitalists income. The income of capitalists (gross profits) includes undistributed profits, depreciation, dividends, withdrawals from unincorporated businesses, rent and interest payments.

The income view of gross national production (GNP) yields:

GNP = gross profits + wages and salaries

The expenditure view yields:

GNP = gross investment + capitalists consumption + workers' consumption

With an identification between capitalists' income with gross profits, and between workers' income and wages and salaries, and the assumption that workers do not save, we arrive at:

Gross profits = gross investment + capitalists' consumption

(4.1)

This equation led to the famous dictum that capitalists earn what they spend, whilst workers spend what they earn. In other words, this equation is interpreted as the expenditure on the right-hand side determining the income on the left-hand side. As part of the analysis it has been assumed that workers do not save, hence they spend all that they earn.

In the debates which followed the publication of Keynes (1936), there was considerable discussion over whether savings and investment (in a closed private economy) were always equal or whether they could be conceptually different. The debate was resolved by making the distinction between the *ex ante* or planned investment and savings which could be different out of equilibrium and the *ex post* investment and savings which would always be equal. Kalecki paid virtually no regard to planned savings. He did pay a lot of attention to planned investment (which was discussed in the previous chapter), but did assume that investment plans were made for some time ahead and were brought into effect. Thus planned investment and actual investment were taken as equal as a first approximation. Savings are then seen as forced to adjust to the level of investment. Subsequently the level of savings has some effect in the future through the pool of finance available to firms (see pp. 49–50).

Kalecki was not concerned over equilibrium between planned investment and planned savings. Instead, he saw investment as fluctuating over time (for reasons explored in the previous chapter) and savings, profits, etc. adjusted quickly to the level of investment. The picture presented by Kalecki is that investment decisions taken in the past largely determine current investment expenditures, and then savings are forced to adjust to those investment expenditures. Workers quickly spend their labour income, and some past profits are also spent on consumption goods. These combine to lead to the outcome described in (4.1) above. In the next period, investment expenditures will be different, and a different outcome will result.

Kalecki, as we saw in the previous chapter, argued that investment decisions lead to actual expenditure with a lag. This lag which firms allow for in their decision-making underpins the reasonableness of this assumption. However, there can be unintended investment in stocks of finished goods and work-in-progress arising from under- or over-estimation of demand. But Kalecki generally regarded this as of minor importance partly since unintended changes in inventories in one period could be corrected for in subsequent periods. However, to the extent to which actual investment does not correspond to intended investment it can be said that investment decisions do not entirely determine profits.

It could appear at first sight that equation (4.1) has been derived largely from national income accounts identities, except for the assumption that workers do not save. However there is more to equation (4.1) than that. Kalecki argued that investment decisions determine investment expenditures to which the other factors adjust. Thus within a single period of time, capitalists' expenditures determine capitalists' income. In equation (4.1) causation runs from right to left. 'The answer to this question [of the causal interpretation of (4.1)] depends on which of these items is directly subject to the decisions of capitalists. Now, it is clear that capitalists may decide to consume and to invest more in a given period than in the preceding one, but they cannot decide to earn more. It is, therefore, their investment and consumption decisions which determine profits, and not *vice versa*' (Kalecki, 1971a, pp. 78–9).

A first implication of that statement is the view of underlying, if not precise, profit maximisation in the sense that Kalecki argued that firms cannot decide to earn more profits. If firms were consciously foregoing profits (say, in the interests of increasing market shares) then even if the opportunities available to the firms did not change, the firms could decide to earn more profits. The second implication is the independence of spending decisions by different capitalists. For, at the economy level, collusion by capitalists over expenditure plans would determine the profit outcome, and thus capitalists could decide to earn more profits by agreeing amongst themselves to spend more.

The third implication is a rejection of the view held by some post-Keynesians (e.g. Wood, 1975; Eichner, 1973) that firms adjust their profit margins in order to be able to generate sufficient finance to cover their investment programme. The finance for investment may come from internal finance (which depends on volume of profits and retention policy of the firm) and external finance, access to which depends on profits. At the aggregate level, an equation similar to equation (4.1) holds, and with causation in a sense running from right to left. But whereas in Kalecki's approach this arises only at the aggregate level through the implementation of the expenditure plans, in the approach of Wood *et al.* this arises through the manipulation of profit margins by firms. Clearly in the approach of Kalecki, profit margins are seen as determined by the degree of monopoly. However, the approach of Wood and of Kalecki share the common feature of stressing the importance of profits for the availability of finance for a firm.

Steindl (1952) developed an approach which is similar to that of Kalecki in a number of respects, but leads to slightly different conclusions. It can be first noted that Steindl produces considerable evidence on excess capacity and price–cost margins which is supportive of Kalecki's approach. He extends Kalecki's approach by further discussion of the reasons for excess capacity. There are two important differences between Kalecki's work and Steindl (1952), which we wish to highlight. We deal with the second one below as it relates to technical change and investment. The first one is relevant to the relationship between profits and growth.

Steindl places importance on the role of cost differentials between firms (generally that large firms have lower unit costs than small firms) and on the differences between industries with easy entry and those with blockaded entry. Starting from the identity $S = u.(1/k).g.C$, where S is sales, u is capacity utilisation, k is capital intensity, g is gearing ratio (i.e ratio of total capital to funds of owners) and C own funds of owners, a corresponding identity linking the growth rates of all these items can be obtained. For relatively small rates of growth, this identity can be approximated by:

$$g_S = g_u - g_k + g_g + g_C \tag{4.2}$$

where g_x is the growth rate of item x. Steindl (p. 48) argues that '(t)he decisive contention is that *in equilibrium* the rate of internal accumulation is determined largely by the rate of expansion of the industry'. He then goes on to consider the possible effects which might intervene, and space considerations prevent a discussion of that aspect here. For our purpose we can note that this is an equilibrium condition applied to the industry level, with causation running from growth of sales to internal accumulation (i.e. savings out of profits). In that sense, it is an industry level counterpart of equation (4.1) above. Steindl interprets equation (4.2) as involving causation running from left to right. The interpretation of that equation has to bear in mind that, besides the possibility of offsetting moves in g_u, g_k and g_g, there is the effect of the use of profits to finance sales efforts to influence the growth of sales. Further, the internal accumulation of firms in one industry can be applied in other industries. But the mechanism underlying Steindl's approach is that there are changes in profit margins, dividend policy etc. as well as entry and exit from the industry until some kind of equilibrium is reached. One part of that equilibrium is that concentration will have also reached some kind of equilibrium. We conclude that Steindl's work can be seen as extending Kalecki's work. The degree of monopoly could be seen as determining the profit–sales ratio, though with the degree of monopoly perhaps being modified over time as entry, exit and growth occur, and equation (4.2) serving to determine the rate of growth of owners' capital (rate of internal accumulation).

Finally, we can note that the causal mechanism in equation (4.1) being from right to left is particularly important in a dynamic context where profits and expenditures are fluctuating. These fluctuations arise because capitalists do not spend in one period precisely what they earned in the preceding period. If profits were stationary over time, and the economy in a repetitive equilibrium then the problem of interpretation of (4.1) would lose its importance. For in equilibrium it would not be possible to say which side of equation (4.1) determined the other. Indeed in such an equilibrium, equation (4.1) is little more than a consistency requirement under the assumption that workers' savings are zero. It could be interpreted by saying that (i) the level of profits determines the level of expenditure by capitalists (via a budget constraint argument), or (ii) profits are determined in order to cover the expenditure (which is based on other considerations, such as growth rate). Kalecki's response to those interpretations might be as follows. On (i), whilst past profits influence investment, firms are not constrained by profits in their investment and consumption expenditures. Firms who want to make investment expenditure greater than can be financed by their own savings out of profits can try to borrow the extra. If firms in general wish to invest more than the currently available level of savings then banks may be able to fill temporarily the gap between planned investment expenditure and previous savings by increasing loans and thereby money supply. The creation of money in response to the demand for loans by firms to finance their investment is a major factor in the evolution of the economy through time (see pp. 91–6 below). On (ii) this has been dealt with above in that Kalecki argued that firms are not in a position to increase profits, having earned as high profits as they could in the past. It should be noted that Kalecki said little about the savings decisions of capitalists, and did not consider firms using dividend policy (i.e. varying the proportion of profits paid out as dividends and the proportion retained) to generate required finance. The implicit assumption would appear to be that, since firms find internal finance more attractive than external finance, they will push direct savings out of profits to the limit.

Extensions

In the general case of an open economy with a significant government sector, the income view of GNP at market prices becomes:

> GNP = profits (net of direct taxes) + wages and salaries (net of direct taxes) + taxes (direct and indirect).

The expenditure view of GNP becomes:

> GNP = gross investment + export surplus + government expenditure on goods, services and transfers + capitalists' consumption + workers' consumption.

Kalecki assumed that government transfers were paid to workers and can here be amalgamated with wages and salaries as they all spent and are added to wages and salaries in the income–GNP and to workers' consumption on the expenditure–GNP.

Manipulation of the equality between income–GNP and expenditure–GNP yields

Gross profits net of taxes = gross investment + export surplus + budget deficit – workers' savings + capitalists' consumption.

(4.3)

This can be slightly rearranged to give:

Gross profits = gross investment + export surplus – workers' savings + capitalists' consumption + government expenditure- – taxes on labour income.   (4.3′)

Interpreting equation (4.3) as an equation for the determination of the level of post-tax profits, it can be seen that gross investment, export surplus and budget deficit are equivalent in terms of their effects on profits (provided that a change in one of the items does not lead to offsetting change in the others). Two important conclusions which can be drawn from equation (4.3) are now considered.

First, since export surplus raises profits, fights over foreign markets to secure increases in exports can be interpreted as fights over the sharing out of profits between the capitalists of different countries (cf. Kalecki, 1971a, p. 85). Further, equation (4.3) can be interpreted to apply at the level of the capitalist system as a whole. Rosa Luxemburg had stressed the role of total exports, from the capitalist system to the non-capitalist world, in the maintenance of profits, Kalecki criticised that view since, as can be seen from equation (4.3), it is the export surplus rather than the level of exports which is important (cf. Kalecki, 1971a, pp. 152–3). But, further, Kalecki argued that export surpluses can only support profits (in the capitalist sectors) provided that the capitalist system is prepared to lend to the non-capitalist world to enable the latter to finance their import surplus (which corresponds to the export surplus of the capitalist sectors).

Second, a government budget deficit helps support profits. This would appear to lead to capitalist support for budget deficits as leading to profits, though this factor may be more than offset by others, such as the fear of a growing public sector, which is further discussed in Chapter 7. However, some forms of public expenditure may be acceptable to capitalists, and Kalecki focused on armaments expenditure in this category. In a comparison of unemployment in the American economy in 1938 and in 1955, Kalecki (1972b) argued that:

1. The increase of the relative share of big business's accumulation of the national product was absorbed by armaments (mainly through the tax on corporate profits and the export surplus, whose realisation was also closely connected to the expenditures of the armament-imperialist complex).
2. The decline in unemployment was associated to a great extent with an increase in the armed forces and in government employees: as a result, the rise in the degree of employment did not have much effect on the standard of living, which increased mainly owing to a higher productivity of labour.

Kalecki grouped budget deficits and export surpluses together as 'external' markets for an industrialised capitalist economy. Without these 'external' markets of government budget deficit and export surplus, the profits of capitalists are conditioned by their own spending on consumption and on investment. Kalecki then linked 'external' markets with imperialism.

The fight for the division of existing foreign markets and the expansion of colonial empires, which provide new opportunities for export of capital associated with the export of goods, can be viewed as a drive for export surplus, the classical source of 'external' profits. Armaments and wars, usually financed by budget deficits, are also a source of this kind of profits (Kalecki, 1971a, p. 86).

The Degree of Monopoly and the Level of Income

In Chapter 2, the idea was developed that the share of profits plus overheads in value added was related to the degree of monopoly. In particular, we can write:

$(P+F)/Y = d$ (for convenience) $= (k-1)(j+1)/(1+(k-1)(j+1))$ i.e.
$P+F = d.Y$ (4.4)

From equation (4.2) above we have:

$$P = I + C_c + BD + XS + WS \tag{4.5}$$

where C_c is capitalists' consumption, BD is budget deficit and XS export surplus, WS workers' savings. The combination of these two equations yields:

$$I + C_c + BD + XS + WS + F = d.Y \tag{4.6}$$

and hence

$$Y = (I + C_c + BD + XS + F - WS)/d. \tag{4.7}$$

This last equation is useful for organising discussion around, although as far as we know Kalecki never formally brought together the degree of monopoly and differential savings.

In this approach, we can see that the share of profits in national income (cf. equation (4.4)) is determined by the degree of monopoly (k'); and the relationship of imported input prices to domestic wages (j). The volume of profits is determined by capitalists' expenditure, budget deficit and export surplus (equation (4.5)). When the two ideas are brought together (equation (4.7)), the level of income depends on the balance between the expenditures mentioned in the previous sentence and the degree of monopoly with the relationship between imported input prices and domestic prices. A rise in investment, capitalist consumption, budget deficit, or export surplus has a one for one impact on profits (cf. equation (4.4), and leads to a rise in income which depends on the d-term. A higher degree of monopoly (k), leading to a higher value of d, would lead, *ceteris paribus*, to a lower level of income and an unchanged level of profits. Effectively, the mechanism here is that an attempt to gain higher profits via a higher degree of monopoly would be frustrated in the absence of changes in capitalists' expenditure and the adjustment would be through a change in the level of income.

Profits can only be realised if there is sufficient expenditure and we saw above that Kalecki emphasised the role of the budget deficit, export surplus and capitalists' expenditure. Here, it can be seen that a rise in the degree of monopoly would raise the profits share, but would not lead to a higher volume of profits unless expenditure was increased alongside. Indeed, the effect of a rise in the degree of monopoly could well be a fall in the levels of output and employment.

The approach of Kalecki has some similarity with that of Kaldor (1955) although it is clear that Kalecki's development predates Kaldor's, and indeed that whilst Kaldor labels his theory Keynesian there is more reason to label it Kaleckian (Pasinetti, 1974, p. 99). However, Kalecki did not use the same mode of expression, and did not assume that there were constant marginal propensities to save out of wages and profits. There is also a substantial difference between the versions of Kaldor and that of Kalecki (as well as a number of minor ones). In order to facilitate comparisons we take the Kaldor version where propensity to save out of wages is zero. Then we have, with s_p as the propensity to save out of profits

$$s_p P = I \tag{4.8}$$
$$Y = W + P \tag{4.9}$$
$$Y = Y_f \text{ (full employment output level)} \tag{4.10}$$

so that:

$$P/Y_f = (1/s_p)(I/Y_f) \tag{4.11}$$

The substantial difference is that Kaldor takes the view that, at least over the long-term, there will be generally full employment. In a technical sense, the full employment equation (equation (4.9) above) in Kaldor's presentation replaces the degree of monopoly equation (determining the share of profits) in Kalecki's approach. The rationale for the full employment assumption is given in Kaldor (1955), and further discussion in Hacche (1979), Chapters 11 and 12.

In the approach of Kalecki, full employment is not assumed and the share of profits in national income is determined by I, C_c, F, k and j and the level of national income in a sense adjusts to satisfy the requirement given by (4.4) above.

It can also be noted that whilst the degree of monopoly plays a central role in Kalecki's approach, it comes in a side-constraint in Kaldor's approach, in the form of a minimum acceptable profits to sales ratio. But if this side-condition (and others which Kaldor introduced) is binding then it determines the distribution of income rather than the differential savings propensities. But if the constraint is not binding then it is not directly relevant to the distribution of income. If the constraint is sometimes binding and sometimes is not, then the theory would require some indication of when it was binding and when not.

The ideas which are formally expressed in the system of equations given by equations (4.3), (4.4) and (4.7) above find strong echoes in the writings of a number of radical economists, notably Baran (1957), Baran and Sweezy (1967), Cowling (1982) and Steindl (1952).[2] The key equations from above for this discussion are:

$$Y = (I + C_c + BD + XS + F - WS)/d \qquad (4.7)$$
$$P + F = d.Y \qquad (4.4)$$

Two ideas arise from these equations upon which we focus. First, it can be seen that, *ceteris paribus*, the level of income depends upon d, the term related to the degree of monopoly. The view of many writers, including Kalecki was that industrial concentration, sales promotion through advertising would tend to rise over time, leading to a rise in d.[3] Thus the share of profits plus fixed costs in income would be expected to rise (as indicated by equation 4.4)). Although the correspondence is not exact, this idea is closely related to the central idea of Baran and Sweezy (1967) on the tendency of the surplus to rise. Note, however, that how profits move relative to income depends on movements in d and in F/Y. Although F is labelled fixed costs, it does include expenditures such as advertising, managerial salaries etc. Thus a rising d and, say, constant profits to income ratio could arise from a rising F/Y ratio. Cowling (1982, e.g. p. 171) suggests a tendency for the ratio F/Y to rise overtime arising from rises in managerial consumption and salaries.

Second, high level of income (relative to full capacity income) require appropriate levels of the factors in the numerator on the right-hand side of equation (4.7). Indeed if d tends to rise over time, then high levels of income (relative to capacity) and low levels of unemployment require that these terms grow (relative to income) over time. We can note that the budget deficit (BD) and export surplus (XS) require the government and 'other countries' to run deficits, which may be unsustainable over prolonged periods of time. There may be some tendency for workers' savings to grow over time. This will tend to depress income for two reasons. From equation (4.7) we can see that workers' savings (WS) have a direct depressing effect on income. Further, as the proportion of savings made outside of firms, the greater will be the resource of firms to external rather than internal finance, and as argued above (pp. 101–6) this tends to make firms more reluctant to invest.

Investment appears as a crucial factor in the achievement of high levels of income. However, Kalecki argued that the investment required from a growth perspective would be inadequate for the maintenance of full employment, and we examine that argument in detail below. Steindl (1952) (especially Chapter 13) develops the ideas hinted at by Kalecki. Specifically, Steindl argues that the growth of monopoly may have an adverse effect on the rate of growth. The main two strands of reasoning behind this are that monopolistic conditions will involve high profit margins and thereby a fall in aggregate demand and that monopolies will involve a higher planned rate of capacity utilisation reducing investment incentives. Steindl (1952) Chapter 13 sets out these arguments at length. He concludes that '(o)n the basis of the present model it is thus possible to demonstrate that the development of monopoly may bring about a decline in the rate of growth of capital'.

Baran and Sweezy (1967) particularly focus on various means by which sufficient expenditure is generated to, in their words, absorb the surplus. Baran and Sweezy, in common with Kalecki, place considerable weight on the role of armaments expenditure in this respect. But their Chapters 4 to 7 deal with the absorption of the surplus through capitalists' consumptions and investment, the sales effort, civilian government and militarism and imperialism.

Kalecki and Under-consumptionist Approaches

There has been a long history for a set of ideas which are often put under the heading of under-consumptionism, and Bleaney (1976) provides an extensive discussion of this stream of ideas. The general idea of under-consumptionism is that the level of demand is inadequate for the maintenance of full employment, and that the predominant reason for the inadequacy of demand is a shortfall of consumer demand. In turn, it has been argued that the reason for the inadequacy of consumer demand is the maldistribution of income. With lower income groups having a higher propensity to consume the policy suggestions contained in this is to shift income from high income groups to low income groups to raise the level of demand.

If one adopts the general view that it is possible for the level of demand to be inadequate to take up all of the potential supply then there is a certain arbitrariness in which component of demand is identified as the cause of the lack of demand. For simply it requires some bench-mark against which each item of demand is to be measured. Nevertheless, those authors who are firmly within the under-consumptionist tradition placed particular emphasis on the inadequacy of consumer demand. On that criteria Kalecki cannot be classified as under-consumptionist (cf. Bleaney, 1976, p. 243), for his emphasis is on the inadequacy of investment. It is still the case that within the framework provided by Kalecki the level of demand would be higher if the degree of monopoly were lower (and so wages and consumer demand higher), if investment and capitalist consumption were higher. The degree of monopoly strongly influences income distribution, and in that sense part of the inadequacy of aggregate demand results from a 'maldistribution' of income.

The discussion in Chapter 3 indicated the crucial role of investment in the determination of the level of aggregate demand and hence of output. A low level of output can then be seen as arising from a low level of investment. Kalecki (1945a) sought to indicate why investment would usually be too low for the generation of full employment. Further, Kalecki was amongst those economists who felt that the post-war period would encounter severe problems facing the inadequacy of private demand for full employment once the main thrust of post-war reconstruction was complete (see pp. 133–4 below).

The argument of Kalecki (1945a) was phrased in terms of the comparison of two levels of private investment. The main feature of private investment here is that it is undertaken for profit, and hence any public sector investment undertaken for profit-related reasons could easily be included in the argument. The first level of investment, denoted by I_f, is that level which would create sufficient demand for the maintenance of full employment. This level of investment would have to be calculated for a given degree of monopoly and propensity to save. The second level, labelled I_c, is that level which would expand the capital stock in line with increases in population and the productivity of labour. Kalecki argued that I_f was likely to be larger than I_c. The basis of the argument was by reference to interwar period data for the USA and the UK.

Before we present the relevant figures, we set out formally the argument (which Kalecki appears not to have done). We signify the relationship between full employment incomes and investment by $Y_f = m.I_f$, where the value of m depends on, *inter alia*, propensities to save and the distribution of income. The term m could be labelled the multiplier in this context, though note that it may differ from the relationship between changes in investment and changes in income. The value of I_c is the sum of net investment (equal to growth in the capital stock of $g.K$) plus depreciation (amounting to $d.K$), where K is the capital stock. Thus the ratio of I_c to I_f is equal to $(g+d)K/(Y_f/m) = m(g+d)k$, where $k = K/Y_f$ is the capital–output ratio at full employment.

From Kalecki's calculations, we can find an estimated value of m of around 4 (though he assumed in the course of calculations a lower value of 2 to 2.5 for the ratio of changes in income to changes in investment). He argued that g would be around 4 per cent per annum and d also of the order of 4 per cent. The implied value of k was 2.5. On that basis, the ratio of I_c to I_f was estimated at 0.8. Kalecki's own presentation was to express I_c and I_f to the amount of depreciation, and he calculated $I_c = 2D$ and $I_f = 2.5D$ where D is total depreciation provision.

The difficulty with this approach arises in part from the difficulty in quantifying the key variables involved. Clearly, relatively small errors on, say, g could throw out the whole conclusions. In the case of g (holding the value of other parameters constant) a rise from 4 per cent to 6 per cent would lead to a move from the position of insufficient demand to a position of balance between I_c and I_f.

A basic point raised by this approach, which would be lost by arguments over the precise values of the crucial parameters, is that there is no particular reason to think that I_c will equal I_f, and no apparent mechanism for bringing about that equality. I_c and I_f are seen as independently determined. Whilst Kalecki took the view that $I_f > I_c$ usually, there may be periods of time when actual investment I is greater than I_f. This could arise from a combination of reasons, such as I_c being temporarily high as the productivity advances are particularly high (e.g. following an important new discovery), or where there is a strong element of 'catch-up' with a technologically more advanced country.

Now if $I_f > I_c$ then attempts by government to secure full employment through the stimulation of investment would, if successful, lead to the capital stock expanding faster than output. For I_c is the level of investment which expands the capital stock in line with growth of labour force plus productivity, and the actual level of investment is raised above I_c. As capital intensity rises (capital stock rising faster than output), the rate of profit on capital will decline unless profits rise relative to output. As the rate of profit falls, firms will be more reluctant to invest and a government seeking full employment via investment would be pushed towards raising the incentives to firms to invest. Kalecki (1945a); argued that the further stimulation of investment would require ever increasing incentives as the rate of profit continued to decline. However, as his former colleague Łaski (1983) has pointed out (and indeed is implicit in Kalecki's writings on growth under socialism reviewed below), there would be a lower limit to the decline in the rate of profit. For eventually as the capital stock increased the point will be reached where even though investment is at the high level of I_f the rate of growth of the capital stock is back into line with the growth of output. At that point, capital intensity stops changing and the rate of profit ceases to decline, and the required incentives to investment no longer spiral upwards. At this general level there is little indication of the volume of investment incentives which would be required to maintain full employment, bearing in mind that whilst the rate of profit has stopped declining nevertheless it is lower than at the beginning of the process.

Notes to Chapter 4

1. See, for example, Ando and Modigliani (1963), Modigliani (1975); for critical appraisal see, e.g. Green (1981), Sawyer (1982a) (pp. 18–23).
2. Baran (1957) acknowledged the help of Kalecki (amongst others) in the discussion of topics covered in that book. Steindl was a close friend of Kalecki, and he acknowledges his intellectual debt to Kalecki in the introduction to Steindl (1952). The influence of Kalecki on Steindl is also clear from the introduction for the reissue of Steindl (1952) in 1976. Baran and Sweezy (1967) in their chapter entitled 'The Tendency of the Surplus to Rise' wrote that

   [t]he leader in reintegrating micro and macro theories was Michal Kalecki. ... A further long step in the same direction, which owed much to Kalecki's influence, was Josef Steindl's *Maturity and Stagnation in American Capitalism* (1952). And anyone familiar with the work of Kalecki and Steindl great will readily recognise that the authors of the present work owe a great deal to them. If we have not quoted them more often or made more direct use of their theoretical formulations, the reason is that for our purposes we have found a different approach and form of presentation more convenient and usable.

Cowling (1982) opens with the statement that the book 'was inspired by the work of Kalecki (1938, 1939 and 1971a) Steindl (1952) and Baran and Sweezy (1967) . . .'.

3. Kalecki often indicated (e.g. Kalecki, 1943a, pp. 20–1) that he expected the degree of monopoly gradually to rise over time as capitalist development proceeded. However this overall tendency arises from a number of counteracting tendencies. On the one hand, he expected that concentration, cartelisation and sales effort would rise over time, thereby pushing up the degree of monopoly, but on the other a fall in transport costs and increased standardisation of goods would tend to lead to a decline in the degree of monopoly.

5
Money, Finance and Interest Rates

Introduction

In this chapter, we begin with a consideration of the views of Kalecki on the nature of money, specifically that in conditions of developed capitalism money is predominantly credit money created by the banking system. This leads into consideration of the way in which the banking system and the expansion of the money supply is an important ingredient in any expansion of the economy. Specifically, there is a need to consider the financing requirements of an expansion of investment demand. The interaction of the demand for money by the public and the banks' willingness to supply money are seen as determining short-term interest rates, with long-term interest rates based on the expectations on future short-term interest rates. The final section of the chapter deals with the restrictions placed on the expansion of any single firm by the finance capital market.

The Nature of Money

It is usual to recite three functions of money – operating as a unit of account, medium of exchange and a store of value or wealth. It is of some importance whether money is regarded as a store of value or a store of wealth. If money is to be held if only temporarily between its receipt and its disbursement then it must hold its value reasonably well, and in that sense be a store of value. But to say that money is a store of wealth tends to imply that money is held (along with other assets) as part of the wealth of the individual. In which case, the demand for money is portrayed in terms of its attractiveness as an asset relative to other assets (e.g. bonds, shares, physical assets).[1] Much recent work in macroeconomics has tended to emphasise the store of wealth role of money, rather than its medium of exchange role. In contrast, Kalecki placed most emphasis on money as a medium of exchange, and virtually disregarded its role as a potential source of wealth.

Placing emphasis on money as a medium of exchange leads quickly to two important aspects of the approach to the way money is treated in economic theory. The first is that the transactions related demand for money is focused upon, rather than the portfolio related demand for money (e.g. the speculative demand for money).[2] It will be seen below that Kalecki adopted a transactions related approach to the demand for money, in which demand for money was a function of short-term interest rates as well as the volume of transactions. The second and frequently neglected aspect is that plans for expenditure cannot lead to actual expenditure unless those plans are backed by the possession of money (and a willingness to spend the money). The expansion of the economy derived from an expansion of expenditure plans will usually require an expansion of the money supply first to permit the expansion to take place and second to underpin the higher level of transactions.

Money which takes the form of bank deposits, and which can be created by the banks to some degree (which may be limited by government or Central Bank) can be usefully labelled credit or bank money. An important feature of credit money from the perspectives of macroeconomic debates of the 1940s and later is that credit money does not represent net worth for the private sector. In the terminology introduced by Gurley and Shaw (1960), credit money is 'inside money'. Whilst a bank deposit, which represents a part of the money supply, is an asset so far as the depositor is concerned, it represents a liability as far as the bank is concerned. Similarly, the expansion of the money supply by the granting of a loan, introduces a set of assets and liabilities which balance out.

Within the IS–LM framework, Pigou and others argued that the real balance (or Pigou) effect on the level of expenditure would eventually lead an economy back to full employment. The mechanism envisaged was that low levels of output and employment would lead to price falls, which would raise the real value of the money supply (and other forms of net wealth with a value fixed in nominal terms). The real wealth of the private sector would thereby be increased and consequently, it was argued, the propensity to consume would be increased. Kalecki (1944b) was one of the first to put the counter arguments to this. He argued that Pigou (1943) had assumed that the banking system would maintain the stock of money constant in the face of declining incomes, although there was no particular reason why they would. This recognises that banks, rather than government, determine the amount of money in circulation. Further, he argued, the increase in the real value of the stock of money does not mean that the real wealth of the community or the private sector has increased when the money stock consists of credit money, that is credits granted to people by other people and organisations especially banks. In those circumstances, the gain to money holders when prices fall is exactly offset by the loss to money providers. Thus, whilst the real value of a deposit in a bank account rises for the depositor when prices fall, the liability represented by that deposit for the bank also rises in size. Indeed, Kalecki argued that '[t]he total real value ... increases only to the extent to which money is backed by gold' (Kalecki, 1944a). This would imply that even government provided cash when unbacked by gold (as is now usually the case) does not generate a 'Pigou-effect', which can be more formally expressed as saying that cash does not constitute net wealth. This arises from the asset provided to the holder of cash being offset by the liability of that cash to the government (as it forms part of the National Debt).

Kalecki also argued that falling prices and wages would mean that the real value of outstanding debts would be increased, which borrowers would find it increasingly difficult to repay as their real income fails to keep pace with the rising real value of debt. Indeed, when the falling prices and wages are generated by low levels of demand, the aggregate real income will be low. Bankruptcies follow, debts cannot be repaid, and a confidence crisis was likely to follow.

The key property of money in Kalecki's work is that it is an immediately accepted medium of exchange. The only sense in which money is a store of value is that it is held between receipt and disimbursement but money is not seen as held as part of long-term assets. In the discussion of the determination of short-term rate of interest (Kalecki, 1954, Chapter 6), he defined the stock of money as current bank accounts and notes, and elsewhere (e.g. Kalecki, 1971a, Chapter 3) the implicit definition of money is similar with money being taken as an immediately accepted medium of exchange. It is also accepted that the banking system can change the supply of money (e.g. Kalecki, 1954, p. 77) though in some earlier papers the role of the Central Bank is stressed. In much discussion, it is implicitly assumed that there is little constraint on any increased demand for loans (which thereby increase the money supply) being granted by the banks. In a footnote, Kalecki (1971a, p. 149) said that he is 'assuming tacitly that the supply of money by the banks is elastic [with respect to demands for money and loans]'.

The Financing of Investment

The stress of much macroeconomics is on the equilibrium between *ex ante* savings and investment, in which the finance made available by savings is passed through the capital market to firms who wish to undertake investment. The problem which is overlooked in the discussion of movements between different equilibria is where do firms obtain the necessary finance for increased investment ahead of the rise in savings which will follow *if* the increased investment is to take place. Since Kalecki was mainly concerned with non-equilibria rather than with equilibria, particular attention has to be paid to this problem. However, we find that discussions of this problem was involved throughout the development of his ideas on effective demand and its translation into actual output. In his first paper on the business cycle (Kalecki, 1933) he considered how investment was to be financed. In Kalecki (1971a), Chapter 3 (a translation of Kalecki, 1935c, d), we find the following:

> Let us assume that as a result of some important invention there is an increase in investment associated with its spreading. ... The financing of additional investment is effected by the so-called creation of purchasing power. The demand for bank credit increases and these are granted by the banks. The means used by the entrepreneurs for construction of new establishments reach the industries of investment goods. This additional demand makes for setting to work idle equipment and unemployed labour. The increased employment is a source of additional demand for consumer goods and thus results in turn in higher employment in the respective industries. Finally, the additional investment outlay

finds its way directly and through the workers' spending into the pockets of capitalists (we assume that workers do not save). The additional profits flow back as deposits to the banks. Bank credits increase by the amount additionally invested and deposits by the amount of additional profits. The entrepreneurs who engage in additional investment are 'propelling' into the pockets of other capitalists profits which are equal to their investment, and they are becoming indebted to those capitalists to the same extent *via* banks. ... [T]he increase in output will result in an increased demand for money in circulation, and thus will call for a rise in credits of the Central Bank. Should the Bank respond to it by raising the rate of interest to a level at which total investment would decline by the amount equal to the additional investment caused by the new invention, no increase in investment would ensue and the economic situation would not improve.

Therefore the precondition for the upswing is that the rate of interest should not increase too much in response to an increased demand for cash.

This quote of Kalecki's gives much of the flavour of his views on macroeconomics. We can see the prime role attributed to investment, the generation of profits by investment expenditure and the importance of the creation of money for the evolution of the economy.

The nature of Kalecki's style of argument here is that of a thought experiment, to seek the conditions which are needed for an expansion to occur. These include increased investment opportunities, which entrepreneurs anticipate would be profitable, and for which it is worthwhile those entrepreneurs going into debt (by bank borrowing, etc.), although for entrepreneurs as a whole find the extra profits generated cover the increased investment expenditure. But there are financial transfers from those who invest to those who do not invest. The firms who invest may well finish the year with more debt and less financial assets (than at the beginning of the year), but with the hope that the investment will yield profits in the future. The firms who do not invest find themselves in a more favourable short-run position, as some of the profits generated by higher investment and other expenditures flow to them. Another condition is that there is an increase in bank borrowing, and thereby in the money supply as the bank deposits created by the borrowing are regarded as part of the money supply.

Kalecki's ideas on money and finance are not systematically developed, and we use our own formulation to express these ideas. This allows us to draw together Kalecki's ideas, and at the same time to show aspects which need further development.[3] Using a period analysis, which has its drawbacks, suppose that firms have investment plans drawn up for execution during the period t of I_t. If those investment plans actually take place (and no other unintended investment or disinvestment in inventories occurs), then during the period savings of $S_t = I_t$ will arise. But the finance from that volume of savings cannot actually be used for investment finance since the savings only arise after the investment has taken place. In this we see the crucial role of investment as a driving force in the economy to which savings adjust.

Suppose that the capital market works slowly such that savings in the current period only become available for the finance of investment at the end of the period. Then the finance from savings available in period t is savings in the previous period of S_{t-1}, which matched the level of investment in period $t-1$. A higher volume of investment in period t of I_t would require extra finance of $I_t - S_{t-1}$. This can be provided by the banking system through loans to the firms concerned which thereby create bank credits and add to the stock of money. In this simple example, the increase in the money supply, $M_t - M_{t-1} = I_t - S_{t-1}$.

There is no doubt that this expansion of the money supply is crucial to the expansion of the economy. However, the full effect on the money supply can be modified by two effects. First, the capital market may be able to 'recycle' most of the increased savings as they arise during the period. The importance of this may well depend on the length of period being considered. Second, as the money is spent it passes round the economy, and some of those who receive the money may decide to pay off existing bank loans. Decisions on paying off loans may depend on the nature of the loans (e.g. overdrafts versus fixed period loans) and the relative costs and benefits of repayment of loans. The repayment of loans will have the reverse effect of the initial increase in lending, namely the money supply will now be reduced.

These effects can be summarised to say that $M_t - M_{t-1} =$

$a(I_t - S_{t-1})$, where the coefficient a will be closer to zero as the capital market is quicker at recycling savings and more loans are paid off. One consideration which may limit the extent to which loans are repaid is that, as the nominal value of output (whether through a rise in output or prices) rises, the transactions demand for money is likely to rise. Thus some of the money created through the granting of loans is retained by people to satisfy the increased transactions demand, rather than being used to pay off loans.

The above line of argument has been cast in terms of an expansion in investment expenditure. Similar arguments would also apply for a decline in investment expenditure. The differences would arise that the role of banks would become more passive as firms would be able to pay off loans and the money supply declines. Thus to some degree, banks may be able to choke off a potential expansion by not meeting the demand for loans, but would have little influence on a potential contraction.

Kalecki put his argument in terms of an expansion of investment expenditure and the key role played by an expansion in the money supply in permitting that expansion of investment to occur. This is related to the key role ascribed by Kalecki to investment, but it is possible to extend the argument to cover other forms of expenditure. Basically, any expansion of expenditure requires additional finance. This can be seen in two particular ways. First, whilst investment can be seen as a particularly important item of expenditure, the need for finance clearly applies to all forms of expenditure. Consumer expenditure as seen by Kalecki is closely constrained by labour income. But in recent years, consumer access to credit has grown considerably so that consumers may not be so constrained by their current income. So, again, credit expansion may permit the expansion of consumer expenditure.

Second, when production takes a significant time and when firms wish to produce output to meet demand (rather than meet an expansion of demand immediately by a run down of stocks), firms must expand their use of inputs ahead of an expansion of output. The expansion in the use of inputs may need to be financed by extra borrowing to the extent to which firms cannot finance it by the proceeds of sale of previous output and own retained funds.

The general ideas that the money supply is endogenous to the private sector, and that the money supply responds through bank loans to planned increases in expenditure are widely accepted within the post-Keynesian tradition (see e.g. Moore, 1979; 1983; Kaldor, 1982). Although the epithet Keynesians (or post-Keynesians) is often applied to these ideas, it is recognised (e.g. Kaldor, 1981 especially pp. 19–22) that there is little in the *General Theory* along these lines, although there is in Keynes's *Treatise on Money* (Keynes, 1930).

The importance of these ideas can be seen by reference to the monetarist approach to macroeconomics. Monetarists (e.g. Friedman, 1969) argue that changes in the money supply determine changes in nominal income in the economy. Further, since the economy tends to operate around the 'natural' level of output, most changes in the money supply will lead to changes in the price level. Control of the money supply becomes necessary and sufficient for control of inflation, since the government is postulated to have control over the money supply, directly or indirectly, it follows that it is the fault of the government if the money supply grows quickly and the resulting inflation. Each of these ideas can be seen as being rejected by the approach of Kalecki. We examine his rejection of the notion of the economy tending to operate around some 'natural' level of employment, corresponding to full employment below (pp. 115–16). In this chapter, we have discussed how the interaction of banks and the public, rather than the government, determine the expansion of the money supply. It is planned increases in expenditure which are seen to require an increase in the money supply, at least initially, leading to actual increases in expenditure. Thus increases in the money supply are seen as the permissive factor in the expansion of expenditure, and not the initiating factor as seen by monetarists.

There are a number of ways in which the above analysis by Kalecki may need to be modified. We examine three ways. The first two are 'spill-over' effects from, first, the current period to future periods and, second, from past periods to current ones. There may be complications arising from an open economy and from government sector.

The spill over effects would arise from the following considerations. During the period, savings of $S_t = I_t$ were made. Some of these savings may have been forced savings in the sense that some individuals received income which they would have liked to have spent but did not through unavailability of supply, etc.[4] We could interpret Kalecki as assuming (as a first approximation) that wages are immediately spent and all profits (voluntarily) saved. In this case there would be no spill-over on the savings account. The other aspect is that firms may not be able to fulfil their investment plans, specifically that inventories change in an unintended manner. Further, although investment plans are drawn up with anticipations of delays, etc. these may turnout to be different from those antici-pated. When bank loans are taken out on a short term basis even though used to finance long-term projects (and whether that hap-pens will depend on policy of banks which varies from country to country), then firms with loans may seek to refinance those loans by the issue of bonds, equities, etc. The exchange of bonds equities, etc. for loans will also affect the value of *a* above.

The second modification follows directly from the first. Since the economy never starts from a position of equilibrium (which here would mean constant level of income, *ex ante* savings and invest-ment equal, portfolios 'balanced'), there are inevitably spill-overs from the past. Specifically of importance here is that the willingness of banks to extend loans in current period will depend on their liquidity position, etc. inherited from the past.

The third modification arises when we consider an open economy with a role for government, then the simple conclusion what investment generates savings has to be modified. Now the basic equation becomes: Investment equals Domestic savings plus govern-ment savings (taxation minus expenditure) plus foreign trade deficit (imports minus exports). Thus an increase in investment expenditure would now be seen to generate some combination of domestic private savings, government savings and trade deficit. Thus the savings which are generated by the increase in investment can be seen as spread over the domestic private sector (which in Kalecki's approach would mainly be made out of profits), public sector/ government savings and foreign savings (= trade deficit).

Interest Rates

Kalecki examined the determination of two sets of interest rates. The first set is summarised by the phrase short-term interest rates. The typical short-term financial asset is taken to be a 'short bill' (i.e. financial assets yielding interest and repayable within a relatively short period of time say, up to three months), which include banks time deposits (cf. Kalecki, 1954, pp. 73–4), as well as Treasury bills etc. The second set of interest rates are long-term rates, with the long-term assets labelled as bonds, and the discussion proceeds in terms of undated bonds. The third set is interest rates charged on loans by banks and other financial institutions.

The financial assets and liabilities which Kalecki focused upon are money, bills (short-term assets), bonds (long-term assets) and loans. In reality there are, of course, numerous financial assets and this generates problems of classification in that any particular financial asset will only imperfectly fit into one of these broad categories, and could have some of the features of more than one category. Further using this particular classification certain features are emphasised (e.g. money has a zero interest rate), whilst others are overlooked (e.g. the differences between cash and current account deposits).

Kalecki's use of three financial assets means that there are three interest rates on these assets to be determined. The rate of interest on money is taken as zero, leaving the interest rates on short-term and on long-term assets to be determined. In contrast, conventional macroeconomics (following to some degree Keynes (1936)) used two assets, usually labelled money and bonds. The interest rate on money is again taken as zero, leaving one interest rate to be determined. One effect of the further disaggregation used by Kalecki is that money and bills are seen as being held essentially for transactions purposes, whilst bills and bonds are held for essentially wealth-related reasons. Thus the demand for money is 'unhitched' from wealth or portfolio considerations.

Kalecki regarded interest rates as essentially financial or monetary phenomena. Like Keynes (e.g. Keynes, 1973, pp. 206, 229), Kalecki argued against the proposition that interest rates were determined by the interplay of the forces of thrift (reflected in savings) and of the productivity (reflected in investment). In his review of Keynes (1936), Kalecki stressed the point that 'saving does not determine investment, but on the contrary, it is precisely investment which creates savings. The equilibrium between demand for "capital" and the supply of "capital" always exists, whatever the rate of interest, because investment always "forces" savings of the same amount.'[5]

From this, it follows that if 'investment "finances" itself, whatever the level of the rate of interest, [then] the rate of interest ... is the result of the interplay of other factors' (Kalecki, 1954, p. 73). In Kalecki's view (and, to some extent, Keynes), these other factors are the demand and supply of money.

Keynes's attack on the notion that interest rates were real phenomena and his advocacy of the idea that they were monetary phenomena were diffused by a combination of two devices. First, it could be pointed out that Keynes had made the demand for investment a function of the rate of interest, and had allowed that savings could be a function of the rate of interest (amongst other variables). Second, within an equilibrium framework such as the IS–LM model, the rate of interest is determined by the interaction of both the real (IS) factor and the monetary sector (LM), and *inter alia*, individuals could be seen as adjusting savings to the point where the rate of interest was equal to rate of time preference and firm adjusting investment until marginal profitability was equal to rate of interest.[6]

These two lines of rebuttal cannot be used against Kalecki's arguments. The previous chapters have indicated that the propensity to save depends on the distribution of income but not on interest rates, and interest rates as seen as having a minor impact on investment decisions. There is no implicit or explicit identification of the rate of profit (or marginal rate of profit) with the rate of interest. Indeed, Kalecki (1937a) concluded that 'the rate of investment decisions is an increasing function of the difference between the prospective rate of profit and the rate of interest'. Further, he sought to show (Kalecki, 1943a, Chapter 3) that generally the rate of profit would exceed the rate of interest, with the level of profits determined by capitalists' spending decisions (cf. pp. 72–5 above), and the rate of interest determined by monetary factors.

We begin the discussion of the determination of interest rates by considering the short-term rate since, we will see, the long-term rate is built upon the short-term rate. The short-term rate is the remuneration for holding short-term assets ('bills') rather than money, which involves the inconvenience that an exchange of 'bills' for money has to be made prior to expenditure being undertaken. Thus the individual is portrayed as holding money and 'bills' as temporary stores between receipt of income and expenditure. Thus money is held for transactions purposes and some 'bills' are also held for this purpose.

Kalecki argued that the velocity of circulation of money would depend upon the short-term rate of interest. This arises from the simple argument that when short-term interest rates rise, people will seek to manage on a smaller stock of money and a larger stock of 'bills' to take advantage of the higher interest rate on 'bills'. This line of argument was later formalised as the inventory approach to the demand for money (Baumol, 1952; Tobin, 1956). Kalecki expressed his approach in terms of the velocity of circulation V being an increasing function of the short rate of interest r_s so that $T/M = V(r_s)$, where T is the nominal value of transactions and M is the supply of money which is determined by banking policy, i.e. the interaction between Central Bank's monetary policy and decisions taken by banks. He further argued that when velocity of circulation is high (and so money holding small relative to turnover), it requires relatively large increases in the short-term rate of interest to reduce money holding further. Thus the first and second derivatives of $V(r_s)$ are positive.

The equation $V(r_s) = T/M$ was interpreted by Kalecki as indicating the determination of the short-term rate of interest by the value of transactions and the supply of money. The former is determined by the investment demand etc. and the latter by banks and banking policy. If the banks decide to, say, reduce their cash ratio (ratio of notes and Central Bank deposits to deposits) and buy bills, then the purchase of bills pushes up their price and reduces the corresponding rate of interest. The fall in the rate of interest continues until the short-term rate of interest has fallen to such a level that the non-bank sector (the 'public') are prepared to increase deposits with the banks to the extent to which banks wish to buy bills.

The long-term rate of interest is the rate of interest on long-term assets and thus does not have any connotation of being an underlying, natural or equilibrium rate of interest. Kalecki considered that the long-term rate of interest was determined by decisions made concerning the holding of wealth as between short term assets (bills) and long-term assets (bonds). The short-term rate of interest is taken at this stage as determined by substitution between money and bills (as indicated above). The key feature of short-term assets in the present context is that the rate of interest on them varies over the decision period (for holding wealth). The key feature of long-term assets is that their price (capital value) varies over the decision period, whilst their interest rate is fixed at the time of purchase.

Kalecki portrayed security holders considering how to invest their reserves and wealth. Over the relevant period, the expected short-term rate of interest is denoted by r_s, and the long term rate of interest is r_l. The difference $r_l - r_s$ is then explained by the relative advantages and disadvantages of the two types of securities. The disadvantage of bonds is the risk that they may depreciate in value during the period for which they are held. This is a permanent capital loss arising from a change in the value of bonds relative to other goods and assets. Short-period fluctuations in the value of bonds are, Kalecki argued, not important for should the bond holder wish to convert the bond into money at a time when the value of the bond was low there was the alternative of using loans until the value of the bond recovered. This view would seem to be based on the implicit assumption that it is relatively prosperous households and firms who hold bonds and that these groups have an easy access to loans. The contrast can be made between the approach of Kalecki in which the disadvantage of bonds is the prospect of a long-term loss of capital value with the approach associated with Tobin (e.g. Tobin, 1958, also see Moore, 1968, especially Chapter 2) in which the disadvantage of bonds (and other assets) arises from short-period fluctuations in capital value and/or return. Kalecki argued that a provision, labelled c, for the risk of depreciation was the way to summarise the disadvantages of bonds.

The value of c is seen as related to the relationship between the current price of bonds (labelled p) and the minimum price which experience indicates is possible (labelled p_{min}). Then c is taken as $g.(p - p_{min})/p$, with g as a factor of proportionality, with $(p - p_{min})/p$ as the maximum relative fall in the price of bonds that it is thought possible. With undated bonds, the price is the inverse of the long-term rate of interst, so that we can write $c = g(1 - r/r_{max})$, where r_{max} is the long-term interest rate corresponding to price of bonds p_{min}.

The disadvantage of short-term assets is that the expected rate of interest on them is subject to some uncertainty. Further, for Treasury bills and the like, which have a life of three months, there are costs associated with purchase of bills every three months. The disadvantages of short-term assets is summarised by a coefficient e.

The advantages and disadvantages of bonds and bills balance out when:

$$r_l - c = r_s - e$$

Substituting for c and rearranging yields:

$$r_l = \frac{r_s}{1 + g/r_{max}} + \frac{g - e}{1 + g/r_{max}} \tag{5.1}$$

Thus equation (5.1) makes the long-term rate of interest (r_l) as linear function of the short-term rate (r_s), provided that g, e and r_{max} are constant. Further, the impact of a change in the short-term rate on the long-term rate in those circumstances depends on $1 + g/r_{max}$ and since that term is greater than unity the long-term rate changes less than the short-term rate.

This led Kalecki to stress (e.g. Kalecki, 1971a, p. 11; 1954, p. 87) that the long-term rate of interest changed relatively little during the course of a business cycle even when the short-term rate varied considerably. Since investment is seen as a long-term decision, Kalecki saw the long-term interest rate as the rate which would influence investment decisions if any rate of interest did. As the long term rate did not fluctuate much (in Kalecki's view) whether in comparison with the short-term rate or the rate of profit, Kalecki adopted the view that the effect of long-term interest rate changes could be amalgamated with the effect of changes in the rate of profit.

The Nature of Financial Markets

In this section we examine the nature of financial markets postulated by Kalecki, paying particular attention to the cost and provision of loans to potential borrowers. Kalecki viewed the financial markets as essentially imperfectly competitive in at least the technical sense that the cost of finance rises with the amount borrowed, and the ease of borrowing is related to profits and wealth of the borrower. This can be constrasted with the general assumption, often implicit, made in conventional macroeconomics and elsewhere that the capital market is perfectly competitive. This means that a firm is able to borrow as much as it wishes at the prevailing and constant rate of interest, which does not depend on the firm's credit rating, and the difference between borrowing and lending rates of interest is negligible. These assumptions allow theorists to talk of *the* rate of interest, though this creates measurement problems when theories involving a single rate of interest are applied or tested (see, for example,

discussion of Helliwell, 1976). Implicitly many theories of investment appeal to the Modigliani–Miller theorem (Modigliani and
Miller, 1958) to the effect that, under conditions of perfectly
competitive capital markets with an absence of uncertainty, transactions costs and taxation, the cost of finance to a firm is independent
of the source of finance and amount. In contrast, Kalecki argued
that the cost of finance will depend on source, with internal funds
usually available at a lower cost than external funds, and on amount
with the cost arising with amount borrowed. Further, the cost and
availability of external funds depend on the profits of the firm.

The key ideas in this section are that the access of a firm to the
capital market for finance depends on its own entrepreneurial
capital, and that there is definite upper limit on a firm's ability to
borrow (where the limit depends on its own capital). This means that
ratios such as the debt–equity ratio become seen as important
restraints on the ability of firms to raise new finance. 'The size of a
firm thus appears to be circumscribed by the amount of its entrepreneurial capital both through its influence on the capacity to borrow
capital and through its effect on the degree of risk' (Kalecki, 1971a,
p. 106). The limitations on the size of a firm may be short run ones
on expansions, since as time passes profits accrue which may enable
the firm to expand by the use of internal finance and external finance
secured on the basis of the internal finance.

An important implication of this line of argument is that the
actual profitability of a firm has a strong influence on investment. It
has an effect through the availability of finance for investment, both
directly as retained earnings and indirectly through enhancing the
borrowing opportunities. Past profitability will also have a marked
effect on the views of future profitability, and thereby also on the
investment decisions. The important point here is that the expansion
of a firm depends on its own savings out of current profits. Savings
out of current profits can themselves be invested in the firm, and
enable the firm to secure new loans.

In the discussion on investment in Chapter 3, investment decisions
were related to a proportion *a* of current savings. The value of *a* will
depend upon the proportion of total savings made directly by firms
out of profits and the extent to which firms can borrow further funds
relative to their own funds. Since workers are assumed not to save,
savings are made by two groups – rentiers and entrepreneurs. The
savings by rentiers are, in a sense, passed to the entrepreneurs via the

capital market. If savings by rentiers rise relative to savings by entrepreneurs, then a greater proportion of savings pass through the capital market. Thus the extent of external finance rises relative to internal finance. But external finance may be more costly than internal finance (through, for example, transactions costs) and the supply of external finance to a particular firm may be limited by the principle of increasing risk discussed below. Thus Kalecki argued (Kalecki, 1954, p. 159) an increase in rentier savings may have a depressing effect on the economy through a depressing effect on investment. Although Kalecki usually treated workers' savings as zero or of trivial importance, we could extend this argument for the case where workers' savings become of some significance. In post-war Britain savings by the personal sector (which is not exactly the same as workers' savings) have risen substantially partly through the rise of often compulsory pension arrangements. Here, as with rentiers' savings, a rise in workers' savings will swing the balance away from internal finance to external finance, and tend to have a depressing effect on investment.

The principle of increasing risk is based on the simple proposition that the greater is a firm's investment relative to its own finance the greater will be the reduction in the entrepreneur's income if the investment is unsuccessful. Thus an entrepreneur will be reluctant to increase borrowing, relative to own wealth, because of the increased risk of bankruptcy resulting from a 'bad year'. Similarly, the capital market is more reluctant to lend to an entrepreneur whose debt is large relative to own resources because of this increased risk of bankruptcy and hence an increased risk of default on the loan. This may be reflected in higher interest charges to an entrepreneur with a higher ratio of debt to own wealth, which in turn heightens the bankruptcy risk in that the interest charges payable are increased. This may form an absolute limit on a firm's ability to borrow. For as a firm wishes to borrow more, the interest rate charged rises, and higher interest rates place further doubt on the firm's ability to repay and its future solvency.

There has been a long-standing debate on the limits to the size of a firm. In neo-classical theory, the firm is portrayed as operating subject to a U-shaped long-run average cost curve. In circumstances of perfect competition, free entry into the industry pushes price down to the minimum level of average cost. For the individual firm, the increasing cost which would eventually be encounterd by expansion limits the size of the firm. In the case of a monopoly, the firm's size is limited by a combination of U-shaped cost curve and a downward sloping demand curve. Kalecki, like Kaldor (1934), dismissed the idea that plant-level diseconomies could limit the size of the firm, for simply those diseconomies can be overcome by operating the number of plants. Further, Kalecki argued that '(t)he argument with respect to difficulties of management arising out of large scale enterprise also seems doubtful since adequate measures of decentralisation can always be introduced to meet this problem' (Kalecki, 1971a, p. 105). Kaldor (1934) had similarly argued that the limits imposed on a firm by management problems were more limits on growth and change rather than on size *per se*. Kalecki can also be seen as emphasising the limits on growth of firms but not the ultimate size of firms.

Another factor which is seen as limiting the size of a firm is the size of the market in which it operates. However, that factor may be overcome by moving into other markets or by taking over rivals. But, further this limitation 'leaves unexplained the existence of large and small firms in the same industry' (Kalecki, 1954, p. 91). This coexistence is explained by Kalecki in terms of differences in entrepreneurial wealth. Firms start at different times, with different amounts of entrepreneurial wealth (supplied usually by their founders) and then grow at different rates depending on ability, motivation and luck. The profitability of firms are an important ingredient of their ability to grow.

The question now arises as to whether the above arguments apply to joint-stock companies, or whether such companies are able to overcome these limitations. Kalecki argued that similar limits applied to the joint-stock companies. Such companies are likely to be larger than other firms, and hence the absolute amount of finance which they can raise will generally be larger, but not in relative terms. The 'principle of increasing risk' arising from borrowing via issue of bonds, debentures or raising of loans remains much the same. For the raising of additional finance by the issue of ordinary shares (which do not commit the joint-stock company to interest payments) Kalecki pointed to three ways in which the company is restricted in their use. First, there is the possible dilution of the control exercised by the current controlling group of shareholders. There may be ways, such as building up holding companies, which can circumvent some of these problems. But even here the problem of the maintenance of control by the key shareholders restrains the willingness of those shareholders to issue further shares. It can be suggested that these considerations may exert considerable influence on relatively new companies where the founder and associates are still in effective control. Kalecki, however, considered the more general case. He argued that 'a joint-stock company is not a "brotherhood of shareholders" but is managed by a controlling group of big shareholders while the rest of the shareholders do not differ from holders of bonds with a flexible rate of interest' (Kalecki, 1971a, p. 107). This notion is rather similar to the distinction between 'insider' and 'outsider' shareholders with the former group exercising effective control and the latter group being rentier shareholders, drawn by Aaronovitch and Sawyer (1975). The discussion by Cowling (1982), Chapters 3 and 4 on the possible conflicts between top managers and shareholders is in a similar vein.

Second, there is the possibility that the investment which is financed by a share issue yields a lower rate of profit than existing capital assets of the firm. Kalecki regarded this as another form of the principle of increasing risk. It can also be seen as a form of dilution in which the profit per share is diluted as the number of shares rise faster than the volume of profits.

Third, there can be a limited market for the shares of any particular company, and hence there are limits to the amount of shares which can be sold at a constant price. Instead, each company is faced with a downward-sloping demand curve for its shares, so that the issue of further shares leads to a fall in the amount paid per share and hence the finance raised. The other way of looking at this is that the cost of finance (to the existing shareholders) rises with the amount required. The reason for this feature is that a major method of reducing the risk attached to share ownership is the holding of a diversified portfolio. Thus there may be an upper limit on the extent to which an individual shareholder would wish to hold shares in one particular company. Large financial institutions are likely to operate in this manner to avoid being locked into one company.

In terms of macroeconomics, the main implication of the above discussion is to indicate the relevance of profits for the finance available and thereby for the effective investment decisions of a firm. There is a broader significance in that 'the limitation of the size of the firm by the availability of entrepreneurial capital goes to the very heart of the capitalist system. Many economists assume that at least in their abstract theories, a state of business democracy where anybody endowed with entrepreneurial ability can obtain capital for starting a business venture. This picture of activities of the 'pure' entrepreneur is, to put it mildly, unrealistic. The most important prerequisite for becoming an entrepreneur is the *ownership* of capital' (p. 109). Thus there is an element of *monopoly* in the sense that only a limited section of the population has the wealth and access to wealth required to become an entrepreneur.

Kalecki's arguments point to the importance of internal finance and wealth for investment and the size of the firm. He does not indicate how the average rate of interest on loans is determined, though it is clear that an unwillingness by banks to extend loans would lead to rationing or a rise in interest on loans, both of which would have the effect of restricting investment.

Conclusions

It can be seen from this chapter that Kalecki took approaches to the nature of money and the determination of the money supply, the nature of financial markets and the forces determining interest rates, which contrast to the orthodox approach. It was seen that the creation of money through loans is an important aspect of any reflationary process, and that interest rates were seen as determined by financial factors, and not related to the 'real forces of productivity and thrift'. We have also seen that the availability of finance becomes an important restriction on the growth of firms.

Notes to Chapter 5

1. Tobin (1969), Friedman (1956), and others have treated money largely as a store of wealth, and viewed the demand for money as part of the analysis of the portfolio of assets held by individuals.
2. The nature of the speculative demand for money as developed by Keynes (1936) and the portfolio approach of Tobin (1958) and of Friedman (1956) are quite different, as argued by Chick (1983), Appendix to Chapter 10. The feature which these approaches share is to see part (or all) of the demand for money related to wealth.
3. For an extended discussion of Kalecki's views in this area and comparisons with the ideas of Keynes, see Asimakopulos (1983).

4. It may also depend on how income is calculated and paid. By income we may mean the income (of an individual) which arises within a given period (e.g. for work done during that period), but which may actually be paid later. Then during a period, the current income being earned is not available for spending, and current expenditure may be restricted by last period's income.
5. The quote in the text is taken from the translation of Kalecki's review of Targetti and Kinda-Hass (1982). In this quote, Kalecki appears to be summarising his concept of Keynes's views. But Kalecki (1954), p. 73 expresses the same views as his own.
6. Shackle (1961) summarises the approach of Patinkin, which was within the IS–LM tradition as follows:

> The threefold role of the interest rate is to equalise for every individual (in his private or his entrepreneurial capacity) the utility of consuming a marginal amount now with the utility of having the prospect of consuming the compound interest increased equivalent of this amount in the future; to equalise for him the utility which his marginal unit of money holdings affords by its liquidity with the utility which a bond, purchased with it, would afford by promising interest; and to equalise for him the interest he could obtain (or avoid paying) on the marginal bond with the rate of profit promised by the equipment purchasable with the price of this bond.

The difference between a Keynesian outcome and a neo-classical one is simply whether these marginal conditions hold at less than full employment (Keynesian) or at full employment (neo-classical).

6
Wages, Employment and Inflation

Introduction

In the first part of this chapter, we focus attention of Kalecki's views on the determination of real wages, and the relationship between real wages and employment. A crucial feature of Kalecki's views on the links between real wages and employment is an emphasis on the *positive* impact of wages on the level of demand and thereby on employment and the down grading of the conventional concern with the *negative* impact of a rise in real wages on the demand for labour and thereby on employment. In the second part of this chapter, we examine various aspects of Kalecki's writings on inflation.

Real Wages and the Degree of Monopoly

Kalecki paid relatively little attention to the workings of the labour market, but, as we will see below, viewed the product market as rather more important than the labour market for the determination of real wages. Money wages are determined in the labour market, and trade union activity can be an important feature of the determination of real wages. But real wages are effectively determined by the degree of monopoly, though the speed of increase of money wages and trade union activity are features of the labour market which may modify the degree of monopoly.

From equation (2.2′) in Chapter 2, we have the relationship between price of output p, average prime costs u:

$$p = k.u \tag{6.1}$$

where k is related to the degree of monopoly. We interpret this as an equation for the aggregate level, where p is price of final output. We can expand average direct costs u as $(w.L + f.F)/Q$, where w is money wage, L is labour input, f is the price of imported materials and F their volume, and Q is output. When suggested by equation (6.2) prices immediately adjust to costs, then manipulation of (6.2) and the expansion of the u-term yields:

$$w/p = (Q/kL) - (fF/pL) \tag{6.2}$$

Equation (6.2) provides a relationship between money wages and output-prices. In order to infer the movement of real wages from this equation, three factors need to be borne in mind. First, the term p relates to the price of final goods, including both consumption and investment goods. Kalecki thought that as a first approximation, the prices of consumption goods and of investment goods tended to move together. If that is so, then the discussion of movements in real wages does not need to distinguish between movements in prices of consumption goods and of investment goods. Clearly, in equation (6.2), for real wages it is consumption goods prices which are relevant. Second, equation (6.1) is advanced only for cost-determined prices, and some of the goods purchased by workers (and hence relevant to calculation of real wages) will have demand-determined prices. Over the trade-cycle the relationship between cost-determined prices and demand-determined prices may fluctuate. Kalecki expected that demand-determined prices would rise (relative to cost-determined prices) during a boom and would fall during the slump. Third, there are prices which are effectively determined by government and those determined by long-term contracts (e.g. often rents), and movements in these prices will also influence movements in real wages.

This equation suggests three key factors determining the relationships between money wages and output prices in those sectors with cost-determined prices, and bearing in mind the qualifications in the previous paragraph, influencing real wage. These key factors are (i) the degree of monopoly as reflected in k, (ii) the techniques of production and the intensity of labour as reflected in Q/L and F/L and (iii) the relationship between imported input costs (f) and domestic output prices. A fourth factor can also be introduced, and this is the speed with which prices adjust to costs. Thus, for example, money wages are rising rapidly such that prices take some time to catch up with wage increases, then there will be some temporary increase in real wages.

There are two important implications to be drawn from equation (6.2). The first is that real wages are not determined, and are relatively little influenced, by conditions in the labour market. Although the underlying mechanisms are different, Kalecki and Keynes shared the common view that money wages are determined in the labour market but real wages are mainly determined in the product market.[1]

The second implication is that the relationship between real wages and the level of output is not straightforward to predict. The approximately constant average direct cost assumption of Kalecki would be reflected in Q/L and F/L varying little with the level of output. There might, if anything, be some increase in Q/L as output increased (up to capacity). The degree of monopoly is seen as unlikely to change dramatically as output (following demand) varies, though Kalecki argued that if anything the degree of monopoly would tend to rise as output fell (cf. p. 40 above). The final term relates to the ratio of material prices to output prices (i.e. f/p). If we take the industrial sector as a whole, and treat the material inputs as coming from outside the industrial sector with prices that are demand-determined, then the argument advanced above applies. Thus we might then expect f/p to rise when the general level of demand is rising, and to fall also with the level of demand. Thus a number of countervailing forces are at work. These types of argument led Kalecki to conclude that the direction of the change of real wages as output changes cannot be predicted (cf. Kalecki, 1966, p. 61).

A major neo-classical explanation of unemployment, which comes to the fore in most recessions, is that real wages have been set 'too high', usually seen as pushed up by trade unions or minimum wage legislation. Kalecki's approach challenges this explanation on a number of fronts. The first challenge is on the grounds that real wages are largely determined outside of the labour market (cf. equation (6.2) above), and hence it is difficult to pin the blame on events or organisations in the labour market. Thus, for example, according to equation (6.2), trade unions can only effect the real wage (relative to average productivity) in so far as they can affect the degree of monopoly.

The second challenge could be seen to be in terms of causation. Even if the assumption of perfect competition is accepted and if there is found to be a negative relationship between real wages and output, what is the implication of that finding? If, as both Keynes and Kalecki argued the level of output is determined by the level of aggregate demand, then with a rising marginal cost curve it would be predicted that a rise in the level of aggregate demand and hence output would lead to a rise in marginal costs. Under perfect competition, prices rise with marginal costs, which in turn have risen relatively to input prices including wages. Thus prices rise relative to wages, leaving real wages declining as output increases. But, there is no implication here that low real wages causes high output, rather that both result from a high level of aggregate demand.

This line of argument led Keynes (1936, Chapter 2) to expect a negative association between real wages and output, and he was disconcerted by the evidence of Dunlop (1938) and Tarshis (1939) which did not confirm this expectation. This and Keynes's use of some of the work of Kalecki to explain the Dunlop–Tarshis findings is evident from Keynes (1939) and the correspondence between Dunlop and Keynes reproduced in Keynes's *Collected Works, Volume 29* (Keynes, 1979).

The argument is often put that a reduction in money wages (or a lower increase than otherwise) would generate an increase in employment. There are two steps in this argument – namely that a reduction in money wages leads to a reduction in real wages, and that a reduction in real wages stimulates employment. Both Kalecki and Keynes challenged these arguments in a similar manner. They argued that a reduction in money wages does not necessarily imply a reduction in real wages. Kalecki argued that prices relative to wages are determined by the degree of monopoly and the other factors indicated by equation (6.2) above, and Keynes argued that prices relative to wages depended on the marginal cost function and the user cost of capital. If the factors determining the relationship between prices and money wages do not change, then a fall in money wages is followed by a fall in prices leaving real wages unchanged. However, to the extent to which real wages decline (arising from, for example, lags in the adjustment of prices to money wages), the impact on the level of aggregate demand has to be examined. Keynes (1936) touched on this question in Chapter 19 (which deals with the effects of changes in money wages), and we examine Kalecki's views below. Here we should note that both authors noted the adverse effect on aggregate demand of a shift of income away from wages, though Kalecki placed much more emphasis than Keynes did.

Kalecki argued that the empirical evidence for the USA (Kalecki, 1939, Chapter 3) and Poland (Kalecki, 1966, Chapter 6) supported the conclusions drawn from equation (6.2) above of virtually no relationship between real wages and output. Kalecki used that evidence to argue against the acceptability of the theory of perfect competition (which would have predicted a negative relationship) and against arguments for wage-cutting to cure unemployment. Indeed, Kalecki argued for money wage militancy on the part of the workers. He wrote (Kalecki, 1939, p. 91) that

[t]here are certain 'workers' friends' who try to persuade the working class to abandon the fight for wages, of course in its own interests. The usual argument for this is that the increase of wages causes unemployment, and is thus detrimental to the working class as a whole. . . . Our investigation above has shown that a wage increase may change employment in either direction, but that this change is unlikely to be important. A wage increase, however, affects to a certain extent the distribution of income: it tends to reduce the degree of monopoly and thus to raise real wages . . . . If viewed from this standpoint, strikes must have the full sympathy of 'workers' friends'.

In the study on real wages and output in Poland (originally published in Polish in 1939), he attacked the study of Wątecki, who was a disciple of the French economist Rueff. Rueff was well known in the interwar period for his argument and evidence to the effect that high real wages were the cause of unemployment. Kalecki argued that some rise in real wages (of those remaining in work in the industrial sector) might arise in a slump from a relative fall in demand-determined prices. In terms of equation (6.2), this could be reflected in a fall in the ratio f/p and in prices of consumption goods not included in p falling relative to those included in p. Kalecki argued that Wątecki had obtained his results of rising real wages through a comparison of money wages with general wholesale prices, where the latter included the effect of imported prices. The relevant comparison for the supply decisions of domestic industrial firms was between the prices of output of that sector and the prime costs of that sector (based on costs of imported raw materials, domestic agricultural production and labour costs).[2] In Kalecki's words, 'it is clear . . . that the ratio of wages of the British worker to the prices of Brazilian coffee is rather irrelevant to the conditions of industrial production in Great Britain' (Kalecki, 1966, p. 60). When the correct comparisons were made, Kalecki found that if anything the ratio of output prices to prime costs rose in depression (i.e. in terms of equation (6.2) the ratio w/p fell), thus contradicting the view that a rise in real wages was responsible for the fall in employment.

The actual relationship between money wages and real wages is also influenced by the speed of adjustment of prices to changes in money wages (and hence in costs). Kalecki tended to argue that a reduction in money wages would lead to some initial fall in real wages as firms took the opportunity of a reduction in costs to enhance their mark-up. Conversely, a push for higher money wages may lead to some rise in real wages. As Cowling (1982) points out this line of arguments depends on 'a variant of the kinked demand curve hypothesis which is based on pessimistic expectations on the part of each firm regarding the reactions of rivals to its own price changes'. Thus, prices may not immediately rise to offset a money wage increase, particularly if the money wage increase is specific to a few firms or industries.

Kalecki considered the impact of trade unions through their effect on the degree of monopoly. Trade unions are seen as only able to raise real wages and wage share in so far as they are able to modify the degree of monopoly. Thus power in the labour market is seen as of little use without some corresponding power in the product market or some constraint on firms in that market to offset power in the labour market.

Kalecki (1971a), Chapter 14 argued that trade union activity could influence the degree of monopoly. The mechanism envisaged was that high mark-ups (resulting from a high degree of monopoly) would encourage strong trade unions to push for higher wages, in the knowledge that the high profit margins will permit the firms to pay higher wages. To the extent to which these high wage claims are granted and the degree of monopoly remains unchanged, then prices in the high mark-up sectors rise relative to prices in the low mark-up sectors. The high profit margins remain, leading to further union push for higher wages. At some stage, the high mark-up firms have either to concede a lower mark-up or resist the above average money wage claims, for otherwise their prices will have risen so substantially relative to other prices that the demand for their goods will be strongly affected. It was through this type of mechanism that Kalecki thought trade unions could influence the degree of monopoly. But it does require strong unions who push for higher wages in high mark-up industries, and with collective bargaining undertaken on an industry-by-industry basis.

This line of argument may apply in terms of the fears of firms or industry of the problems of raising their prices following a wage increase for their workers. The firms would be less worried about, say, a 10 per cent wage increase if they thought that that rate of increase was the norm than if they thought wage increases would average 5 per cent elsewhere. But in a decentralised wage determination system, with other wage increases imperfectly predicted, there will be pressure from the firms to hold down wage increases. However, on this line of argument a generalised wage push (which was widely anticipated) would raise money wages but would do little to raise real wages, since prices would be raised at the same rate as money wages. The situation might be a rather different one when an open economy is considered depending on the behaviour of the exchange rate. In a fixed exchanged rate regime, a rise in money wages would have a twofold beneficial effect on real wages. Prices in the traded goods sector would be constrained by international competition. The price of inputs would remain constant in nominal terms and fall relative to domestic prices. Both of these would enhance real wages (cf. equation (6.2) above). In a flexible exchange rate regime, account needs to be taken of the response of the exchange rate to domestic price changes. If the exchange rate changes exactly offset the rise in domestic prices then there will be no change in the level of foreign demand and real wages as the result of a rise in money wages.

In this discussion on trade unions, and the degree of monopoly, Kalecki linked union pressure for higher wages with high mark-ups, which suggsts that unions have some notion of a bench-mark against which the actual mark-ups are compared. The context of Kalecki's discussion would suggest that he had in mind a high mark-up and profit margin in an industry relative to the norm. This would generate, if the unions were successful in reducing higher than average profit margins, a mechanism by which profit margins are moved towards equality. Thus wages rise and profit margins fall in high profit industries in response to union pressure, alongside or instead of movements of capital and other resources. The other interpretation would be that workers have some notion of an acceptable profit margin in general, and press for higher wages when the actual profit margin exceeds the norm.

Kalecki's discussion at this point is mainly at the level of the industry. As he acknowledged, union pressure for higher money wages (in response to high mark-ups) would continue if the firms' reaction to the initial wage increase were to be a price increase of the same magnitude. The process would only end when the mark up has been reduced, i.e. prices having risen by less than wages. Although Kalecki did not consider this, it is clear that there is no automatic end to the process. At the industry or economy level, there is no strong reason why the mark-up which the firms are prepared to accept and that which the unions find reasonable (and so stop pushing for higher wages) are mutually acceptable.

Real Wages and Employment

There are two propositions which are close to the heart of neo-classical monetarism, and which strongly influence much current policy discussion. These are Say's Law (that supply creates its own demand) and that high wages are a major factor in the generation of unemployment. Say's Law effectively rules out the possibility of generalised unemployment, for the potential supplies of labour and capital, which are capable of certain amount of output, generate sufficient demand to absorb that output.

Kalecki worked with the general view that excess capacity and unemployment were normal features of capitalist economies, though there would be some periods of high employment and capacity utilisation. He supported the general view of unemployment and excess capacity by a number of arguments. First, since he viewed the capitalist economies as inherently cyclical and the height of a boom reaches at most full employment and capacity utilisation. Thus

[n]ot only is there mass unemployment in the slump, but average

employment throughout the cycle is considerably below the peak reached in the boom. The reserve of capital equipment and the reserve army of the unemployed are typical features of capitalist economy at least throughout a considerable part of the cycle (Kalecki, 1971a, p. 139) (cf. p. 57 above).

Second, full employment over a prolonged period would lead to social and political changes, with the power of workers considerably enhanced. We discuss this line of argument in full in the next chapter. Here we can note that the view of Kalecki is that full employment may not be politically sustainable unless there are substantial changes in the political and social character of capitalism.

Third, Kalecki dismissed the mechanism of changes in relative prices by which neo-classical economists have seen the restoration of full employment occurring following some exogenous shock to the system. Kalecki argued that the relationship between prices and costs, being determined by the degree of monopoly, would not be flexible. Indeed, as we saw in Chapter 3, Kalecki saw socialist economies as displaying more price flexibility than capitalist economies.

Fourth, Kalecki believed that there were strong tendencies for capitalist economies to generate insufficient aggregate demand to maintain full employment. These arguments were examined in some detail in Chapter 4.

Kalecki's analysis of the impact of wage changes on employment was undertaken against this background of less than full employment. His analysis often used a three-department schema, similar to that used by Marx. The departments are taken as being vertically integrated, with department I producing investment goods, department II consumption goods purchased by capitalists ('luxury goods'), and department III consumption goods purchased by workers ('wage goods'). Workers spend all their income immediately, whereas there are delays in capitalists' spending (on investment and luxury goods) after receipt of profits. The analysis is carried out for a closed economy.

Wages are derived as income in each of the three departments, and total $W_1 + W_2 + W_3$, where W_i is wage payment in department $i, i = 1,$ 2, 3. They are spent on wage goods which are produced by department III, so with income arising in that sector ($W_3 + P_3$, where

P_3 is profits in department III) equal to expenditure on the output of that sector, we have $W_1 + W_2 = P_3$. The same result can be obtained by considering capitalist income. That income is $P_1 + P_2 + P_3$ and is divided between savings and consumption. Savings out of profits (which is here the only source of saving) equals investment. Thus capitalist income equals expenditure in departments I and II. From this we have $P_1 + P_2 + P_3 = W_1 + P_1 + W_2 + P_2$, i.e. $P_3 = W_1 + W_2$, which was labelled equation (1) in Kalecki (1968a). He argued that 'the modern theory of effective demand ... may be derived in full from the Marxian equation (1) representing the exchange between Departments 1 and 2 on the one hand and Department 3 on the other, if this equation is considered in the general context rather than in that of uniformly expanding reproduction'.

Now consider a rise in wage bills of the proportion a, and look at the case where there is no corresponding rise in prices, so that real wages rise. For department III, the rise in wages leads to a rise in demand, and from the equations given above that would mean a rise in profits in department III by $a(W_1 + W_2)$. In Departments I and II, if prices remain unchanged then profits fall by an amount equivalent to the rise in wages, i.e. by $a(W_1 + W_2)$, noting here that the volume of investment and capitalist consumption is assumed predetermined, expenditure in departments I and II remains unchanged if prices are constant. Under these assumptions profits in aggregate remain unchanged although there is redistribution between departments. Employment and output remain unchanged in departments I and II, but rises in department III. Since aggregate profits remain unchanged, the unchanged nature of investment and capitalist consumption is validated.

In the case of imperfect competition and oligopoly, Kalecki considered that prices would rise in line with wage increases (with the degree of monopoly remaining unchanged). When investment and capitalist consumption remains unchanged in real terms and with real wages unchanged then there is no change in real terms to the initial position.

We have to consider now how investment and capitalists' consumption might respond to rises in wages. It can first be noted that in the two cases considered above, profits remain unchanged. If capitalists' consumption and investment are linked to profits (or the rate of profit) then there would be no reason for those expenditures to change. However, there may be some impact effects of the change in wages on capitalists' expenditure which then lead to changes in profits, and then to further changes in expenditure. The rise in wages may signal to firms that their costs are rising, appearing to threaten their profits, which lead to a cut-back in investment plans. But as the effect of higher wages feeds through the economy, demand rises helping to hold up total profits. It was seen in the first case considered above that even when prices did not rise the volume of profits remained unchanged. Kalecki argued that there were considerable lags between investment decisions and actual investment, and thus a rise in wages would have no immediate impact on actual investment which had been determined by previous decisions. But this argument relies on the wage rise being unanticipated (at the time when the investment decision is made).

The important differences here between wages and profits are that wages are immediately and completely spent whilst profits are not spent either immediately or completely. A shift from profits to wages will tend to stimulate the economy since a higher proportion of wages is spent, and also that the shift leads to a quick rise in consumption out of wages but only a delayed cut in consumption out of profits. If all income were like wages, then something like Say's Law would operate. But the existence of income like profits denies Say's Law, since those forms of income are not spent completely and immediately.

Inflation

Kalecki did not present a fully worked treatment of inflation, and his writings on inflation suggest that there could be different types and forms of inflation. Kalecki discussed the causes of and policies for inflation under wartime conditions in a series of papers, especially Kalecki (1941d, e), and hyperinflation in Kalecki (1962b). Kalecki's ideas on inflation can be conveniently divided into three groups. The first group relates to inflation in conditions where there are capacity constraints in some or all sectors of the economy. These conditions are seen as arising in periods of war, immediate post-war reconstruction and in developing economies. These capacity constraints may arise through a high level of demand in the economy ('overheating' of the economy) and through an imbalance of supply between different sectors. The feature of importance is that when there are capacity constraints, the expansion of output faces problems of rising unit costs, which leads to prices rising relative to wages and other costs. Thus real wages are likely to decline in these circumstances.

The second group relates to inflation under 'normal' peacetime conditions. In those circumstances, there is usually excess capacity and output can be expanded at constant unit costs. Then, inflation may arise from a tendency for money wages to rise. In this context, Kalecki saw full employment as likely to lead eventually to a continuous upward pressure on money wages. With unit costs constant with respect to output, when the degree of monopoly remains unchanged, prices rise in line with cost changes.

The third group relates to conditions of hyperinflation, which is characterised by high rates of price change, the widespread expectation of continuing inflation and long-term spending coming to a halt. The periods of hyperinflation were seen as relatively rare but having a continuing effect on the economy through the resulting redistribution of income and the folk memory of inflation.

In this section, we outline Kalecki's ideas under each of these three groups in turn. Developments of the ideas of Kalecki on inflation to help explain the stagflation of the 1970s and 1980s are considered in Chapter 12. One theme which will arise throughout this discussion is Kalecki's concern for the income distribution consequences of inflation, which stands in contrast to most discussion of inflation which ignores the distributive consequences.

The first group of ideas were set out in Kalecki (1941d, e) for wartime Britain, and in Kalecki (1976) for developing countries, to which we return in Chapter 10. In these circumstances, Kalecki saw 'the problem of inflation [arising] in wartime because the volume of employment is maintained or even increased, whereas the output of consumption goods falls considerably . . .' (Kalecki, 1941e). The rise in employment raises the wage bill and thereby the demand for comsumption goods, which in these circumstances cannot be fulfilled. A similar mechanism is seen at work in developing countries where, Kalecki argued, the agricultural sector is often unable to increase food production. The rise of demand pushes output into the range where unit costs are rising (with respect to output), and 'the characteristic of inflation will be the rise in price of consumers' goods in relation to the relevant costs of labour and raw materials', and thereby a fall in real wages. As an aside here we can note that in a number of articles (e.g. Kalecki, 1941d, e; 1944c), he strongly advocated rationing as the appropriate policy response. It has two particular advantages in that rationing recognised that supply could not in those circumstances respond to demand and in sharing out the available supply could do so in a fair way.

Thus both *laissez-faire* inflation and the stabilisation of money wages will have this in common: that the lower income grades are hit, and it is the reduction in their consumption which keeps in balance the demand for and the supply of consumption goods. This is not only an evil in itself but it tends also to reduce productivity of labour. (Kalecki, 1941e).

In these circumstances, a 'vicious spiral' of inflation could be set off. The rise in prices, as capacity constraints are met, lowers real wages, triggering off money wage rises in an attempt to restore the previous level of real wages. But the restoration of those real wage levels may be difficult. First, in due course prices will respond further to the money wage rises, preventing the attempted rise in real wages from taking effect. Second, the economy is unable to produce the necessary consumption goods because of the capacity constraints which would permit real wages to be spent (unless there could be imports of consumption goods).

Whilst this type of inflation could be labelled demand inflation in the sense that it results from demand being high relative to supply, there are substantial differences in Kalecki's treatment as compared with conventional wisdom. We can note that Kalecki saw this type of inflation as arising in capitalist economies in the relatively unusual circumstances of war or post-war reconstruction. There is no notion of the level of excess demand, but rather a focus on the physical difficulty of the economy producing any more output. There is also a focus on the income distribution consequences of this type of inflation, specifically a decline in real wages.

The second group of ideas could be seen as relating to the normal peacetime conditions under capitalism. Of importance here is the view that excess capacity and the linked condition of constant unit costs are normally found. This clearly means that the typical fluctuations in demand can be accommodated by existing capacity, and thus prices (relative to costs) do not change in response to a change in the level of demand. This was summarised above (pp. 20–3) as cost-determined prices.

The experience under capitalism prior to the Second World War was of unemployment (with fluctuations) and often no general upward trend in money wages and prices. In that sense both Kalecki and Keynes wrote against a background of a generally stable price level so that the impact of double digit inflation was not investigated. However, Kalecki's experience in Poland of the 1920s would include some periods of hyperinflation (and of substantial unemployment). But this was a period following the First World War and the first years of Poland as an independent country.

In his discussion of the post-war prospects, on which we draw in the next chapter, Kalecki (1944b) gave some brief consideration of inflation. He argued that inflation would result in peacetime under conditions of a general scarcity of labour and/or equipment, but that would only happen in either the immediate post-war reconstruction or if governments pushed the level of demand too high. Otherwise, increases in demand would mainly lead to rises in output as output can be expanded at approximately unit costs. However, Kalecki also argued that under prolonged conditions of full employment, the bargaining power and confidence of trade unions would be enhanced. This may lead to a 'spontaneous tendency for money wage rates to increase which leads to a rise in prices and the cost of living; this in turn leads to a secondary rise in wages and so on' (Kalecki, 1944b). The conditions for this type of inflation include union power which push up money wages (though there is little effect on real wages as firms preserve their degree of monopoly), and an accommodating money supply. Kalecki did not specifically discuss the role of money in the inflationary context, but it is not difficult to relate Kalecki's view on the endogeneity of the money supply (cf. pp. 88–91) with the accommodation of the money supply to rises in wages and prices.[3]

The concluding chapter of Oxford University Institute of Statistics (1944) (which was subscribd to by the authors of the volume) argued that at full employment it might well 'be necessary to exercise wide control over prices, either directly or indirectly by means of subsidies'. This was to prevent 'the possibility of cumulative price increases, not so much due to bottlenecks in production, but to pressure for higher money wages'. This statement is of some interest for two reasons. First, it clearly recognised that full employment could bring inflationary problems which had to be dealt with by controls and not by resorting to unemployment. Second, despite the view that the inflationary pressures came from the labour market in terms of higher wages, the controls were to be applied in the output market on prices. The contrast can be drawn between those proposals for price control (which may well have the effect of redistributing income towards wages and away from profits) and the main thrust of post-war UK incomes policies which have generally been more concerned with wage control than price control and have had the effect of reducing real wages (cf. Tarling and Wilkinson, 1977).

Kalecki's discussion of hyperinflation is contained in Kalecki (1962b).[4] This paper is of interest in part for the light it throws on Kalecki's attitude to the quantity theory of money. He indicated that the quantity theory could in normal (i.e. not hyperinflation) conditions be expressed as:

$$M.V(r_s) = P.T \tag{6.2}$$

(where we have amended the notation to conform to that used above). In normal circumstances (p. 99 above), this equation serves to determine the short term rate of interest r_s. But in conditions of hyperinflation, long term lending comes to a halt and there is a scramble to obtain real goods rather than financial assets. People also then anticipate future rises in prices. Then the free market rate of interest closely approximates the anticipated increase in prices. Thus we have:

$$r_s = \dot{p}^e - cc \tag{6.3}$$

where $\dot{p}^e$ is the anticipated rate of inflation, and cc the carrying cost of goods (which is now the alternative to holding money under the conditions of hyperinflation). Thus r_s becomes determined by the inflationary experience rather than by the interaction between the demand and supply of money. In turn the velocity of circulation is then determined. It is under conditions of hyperinflation that the quantity theory operates, with the velocity roughly constant, leaving prices rising with the money supply. In contrast '(i)n normal conditions the increase of the quantity of money in circulation results directly in a greater liquidity and lower velocity of circulation rather than in increase in prices' (Kalecki, 1962b).

Thus Kalecki makes a sharp distinction between normal conditions and hyperinflation. The question arises as whether Kalecki would have regarded the 1970s double digit inflationary period as normal or hyperinflation (or some mixture of the two), and hence whether and to what extent the quantity theory applied. One would guess that the 1970s did not display the conditions of hyperinflation with a flight from money, and that period of stagflation may have fitted in with the prognostication of Kalecki (1943b), with the prolonged full employment of the 1950s and 1960s leading to inflation. There may have been elements of hyperinflation in the sense that interest rates rose to some extent in line with inflation.

Kalecki also argued that 'the theory of hyperinflation is of interest even though the phenomenon is rather exceptional, because this phenomenon is striking because even though hyperinflation does not last too long, it leaves considerable traces in the economy in the years to come, one of the consequences being the wiping out of the wealth and income of the rentier' (Kalecki, 1962b). Hyperinflation also involves some other redistribution of income. Initially, Kalecki argued, wages lag behind prices, partly because there is a time lag in negotiation and there are difficulties in making arrangements for the continual adjustment of wages comparable to continual adjustment of prices. Since the government budget deficit is one of the contributory factors to the growth of the money supply the real budget deficit is likely to be higher than usual. Investment in capital equipment may be higher than usual, as part of the flight into goods and partly encouraged by easy bank credits, which are also fuelling the increase in the money supply. On Kalecki's usual line of argument (cf. pp. 77–9 above) higher real budget deficits and investment would swell business profit. Further, there is impoverishment of rentiers, which has the side effect of reducing the real interest charges on entrepreneurs. Each of these effects serves to shift income towards profits and away from wages and rentiers income. However, the time comes when 'their [big business] interest in [hyperinflation] it begins to vanish at the point where the techniques of fixing wages are so perfected as to enable workers to increase real wages' (Kalecki, 1962b) and when the rentiers cannot be squeezed any more.

Conclusions

The first part of this chapter has indicated that the approach of Kalecki to the determination of real wages stresses the role of the degree of monopoly, and can be constrasted with the conventional neo-classical approach. Following on from that, it was seen that Kalecki emphasised the demand-stimulating role of increased wages. The last part of the chapter considered Kalecki's views on inflation. It can be seen that he took an eclectic approach, stressing structural factors in conditions of reconstruction and in developing countries, suggesting the possibility of cost push inflation under conditions of low levels of unemployment, and also discussing the specific attributes of hyperinflation. Throughout the discussion of inflation, there is the concern with the income distribution aspects. We will return to consider Kalecki's approach to inflation in Chapter 12, when we ask how it should be amended to deal with the double digit inflation of the 1970s and the occurrence of stagflation.

Notes to Chapter 6

1. For Keynes with given money wage, the real wage would depend upon the level of output. As the level of output increased, marginal cost and hence price rose, so that real wage declined as output rose.
2. Keynes (1939) indicated that Pigou advanced a similar argument in respect of the study of Rueff.
3. I have also attempted to do so in Sawyer (1983) Chapter 1.
4. Johnson (1978) used this discussion of hyperinflation using the quantity theory and expectations to place Kalecki outside the Cambridge (England) stream of Keynesian economics. He wrote that

   > [T]here is another ironical possibility, that had Kalecki been kept in Cambridge, he would have developed an economics far more relevant to, and capable of handling Britain's post-war economic difficulties than 'Keynesian economics' as it developed at Cambridge, and more specifically at the Institute of Statistics at Oxford. My reason for thinking this is that, on the one occasion on which I met him at Cambridge (his being *en route* back to Poland) Kalecki delivered a lecture on inflation that employed a simple quantity theory of money together with expectations about the future trend of prices – and which met with a reception from his former admirers so hostile that he was discouraged from publishing it.

   Johnson was at Cambridge until March 1956, and this lecture would seem to be the one referred to by Feiwell (1975), p. 212. Feiwell links that lecture with the article published in 1962 (Kalecki, 1962b) discussed in the text; and the article itself indicated that it was based on a lecture in Cambridge in 1955.

7

The Political Economy of Full Employment

Introduction

In the previous chapter, the general view held by Kalecki that unemployment was a normal feature under *laissez-faire* capitalism was set out (pp. 115–16). However, Kalecki felt that with the understanding provided by Keynesian ideas it would be technically feasible by the manipulation of aggregate demand by governments to ensure full employment. In the first part of this chapter, we outline Kalecki's views on how full employment could be achieved and his counter-arguments to those who argued against the possibility of achieving full employment. However, Kalecki considered that there would be considerable political and social obstacles to be overcome if full employment were to be maintained. Further, certain 'crucial reforms' would be needed. These aspects are considerd in the second part of the chapter.

The Economics of Full Employment

The Oxford University Institute of Statistics, for which Kalecki worked for most of the period of the Second World War, provided a regular commentary on economic events and also participated in debates on the future post-war economy. In this section we consider his contribution (Kalecki, 1944b) on 'three ways to full employment' to a volume on 'The Economics of Full Employment' (the title of Oxford University Institute of Statistics, 1944), and in the next section on an article dealing with the political and social constraints on the achievement of full employment (Kalecki, 1943b).

Kalecki considered that in developed capitalist economies in normal peacetime conditions the main economic cause of unemployment would be the inadequacy of aggregate demand. Since that inadequacy had now been recognised as the cause, it should be possible for government intervention and management of aggregate demand to avoid (or at least reduce) unemployment. This general conclusion would have to be subject to two important caveats. First, there could be economic obstacles to the achievement of full employment. These would include inadequate capacity, insufficiently trained labour force, lack of certain skills, etc. These were some of the characteristics of underdeveloped economies, and we will consider Kalecki's discussion of methods to overcome those obstacles in Chapter 10. In the immediate post-war period, shortages of capacity and labour would be likely to be problems requiring planning and rationing. But when the post-war reconstruction was over these problems would be much reduced. Kalecki also regarded 'the problems of foreign trade . . . [as] perhaps the greatest *practical* difficulty in the achievement of full employment'. Kalecki (1944b) did not deal with problems created by foreign trade constraints since that was dealt with elsewhere in the book of which the article by Kalecki was a part, while those constraints were outlined in Kalecki (1946a).

The second *caveat* is that Kalecki considered that 'the assumption that a government will maintain full employment in a capitalist economy if it knows how to do it is fallacious' (Kalecki, 1971a, p. 138).[1] This line of argument is considered in some detail below, and here we merely note the general point that even if full employment is technically possible it does not follow that it will be achieved or even attempted.

Kalecki (1944b) considered the three ways of achieving full employment as:

(i)   Governments spending on public investment and subsidies to mass consumption, covered by borrowing, i.e. deficit spending;
(ii) Stimulating private investment;
(iii) Redistributing of income from higher to lower income classes.

The discussion by Kalecki is in the context of a closed economy, which was undertaken for analytical convenience and, as mentioned above, since problems of foreign trade were dealt with in another essay in the same book. We use the three categories listed above to organise our discussion.

Kalecki (1944b) began by setting out the conventional multiplier argument that an increase in government expenditure financed by borrowing will increase the level of employment. He then listed four points which had been made against the proposal to create employment by government deficits and these arguments have continued to be raised in part because of a failure of Keynesian economics to deal with them adequately.

The first counter-argument raised is 'where does the money come from?' Kalecki's answer is 'that the budget deficit always finances itself – that is to say, its rise always causes such an increase in incomes and changes in their distribution that there accrue just enough savings to finance it – the matter is still frequently misunderstood'. Political discussions of the 1970s and 1980s indicate that this last sentiment is still true. In a closed economy, gross savings will cover private investment plus the budget deficit. An increase in government expenditure generates a rise in incomes sufficient to create enough savings to equal the increase in the budget deficit. The problems posed by continuing budget deficit are considered below.

Kalecki then considered the second counter-argument that budget deficits force up interest rates and thereby reduce investment. Here he argued that 'the rate of interest may be maintained at a stable level however large the budget deficit, given a proper banking policy'. Following from the discussion of the determinants of the rate of interest (pp. 96–101), it can be seen that Kalecki regarded interest rates as a monetary phenomenon. It follows that interest rates can be kept stable provided that the money supply, bills and bonds can be changed in an appropriate manner to fulfil the objective of stable interest rates. The appropriate policies would be for the Central Bank to expand the cash base in line with the demand for bank deposits, and for the government to issue bonds of various maturities on tap in response to demand to maintain interest rates.

The third counter-argument related to the dangers of inflation. Kalecki argued that budget deficits would not themselves generate inflation, provided that output was not pushed past full capacity levels and provided that proper regard was paid to any shortages of plant and equipment (e.g. after a war). Conditions of prolonged full employment might well generate inflation, but that would be a consequence of full employment however achieved and not a consequence of budget deficits *per se*.

The fourth point is the perceived burden of the National Debt. Clearly, in contrast to some Keynesian discussion, Kalecki was fully aware of the monetary and financial implications of government budget deficits. A continuous deficit will mean that the national debt will expand continuously, and it is likely that interest payments will rise relative to national income. Kalecki considered how those interest payments on the national debt could be met without disturbing output and employment. If the interest payments are funded through further deficits, then this would constitute further stimulus to an economy which by assumption is fully employed.

The proposal made here and elsewhere by Kalecki (e.g. Kalecki, 1943d) to avoid the national debt growing relative to national income was for an annual capital tax levied to finance the interest payments on the national debt. This annual capital tax would have some similarities with an annual wealth tax, except that it would be levied on firms and persons (with the assets of firms directly taxed, and the equity in firms held by households being excluded). The argument was that such a tax would mean that aggregate consumption would be little affected. Capitalists income would be raised by the interest payments on the national debt, and lowered (to an equivalent amount) by the payment of the capital tax. Thus the aggregate income of capitalists would be unchanged, leaving little impact on consumption (the only change being some redistribution of income within the capitalist class). Since all forms of capital assets would be taxed, there would be no change in the relative attractiveness of different assets. Specifically there would be no change between the attractiveness of investment in physical assets and in government financial assets.

The second way to full employment considered was the stimulation of private investment through, for example, reduction in the effective rate of interest, tax concessions linked to investment expenditure. Kalecki considered two reasons for stimulating private investment. The first was to raise the level of investment to a level which expanded productive capacity proportionately to the long-run increase in full employment output (i.e. investment labelled I_c in Chapter 4). He considered it quite possible that actual investment would fall below I_c. The second reason, and of particular relevance to this discussion, was as part of raising effective demand. In

Chapter 4 we saw that Kalecki argued that the level of investment required for full employment (I_f) would usually be above I_c. Thus whilst it is possible that the investment demand would have to be restrained to prevent overstraining the economy, Kalecki regarded it as much more likely that investment would be inadequate to secure full employment. In her review of Oxford University Institute of Statistics (1944), Joan Robinson (1945) commented favourably on Kalecki's contribution but felt that he had dwelt on the lack of investment and overlooked the possibility of too much investment demand.

Kalecki adopted the view that I_f would be usually greater than I_c and used that as the basis of his argument. Suppose in those circumstances a government sought to stimulate investment as a means of reaching full employment. Then there are two possible consequences considered by Kalecki. The first is that capacity rises faster than output, there is a fall in capacity utilisation, a rise in excess capacity and a decline in the rate of profit. This fall in the rate of profit would in turn tend to depress the level of investment. If the government is seeking to maintain the level of investment, further subsidies are required. If investment rises again, capacity again increases followed by a further fall in profitability requiring further rises in subsidy.

The second possible consequence is capital deepening, that is the capital to labour ratio rises as more capital intensive techniques are introduced. Kalecki thought that interest rates had little influence on the choice of techniques so that changing interest rates would have little impact (Kalecki, 1939, pp. 102–5).

However, as we pointed out above (p. 85), the fall in the rate of profit and the capital deepening would eventually come to a halt. Hence, the government would not have to increase its incentives indefinitely if it sought to maintain investment at I_f. But if the gap between I_f and I_c were of some macroeconomic significance, then the investment incentives involved would be of considerable size.

Kalecki also argued that governments would find the accurate prediction of the reactions of private entrepreneurs to investment incentives difficult. In particular, when entrepreneurs are pessimistic about the future or dislike the political colour of the government they may not respond at all to investment incentives. Thus the stimulation of private investment is seen as having a limited role in reaching full employment.

The third way to full employment considered is the redistribution of income from rich to the poor. This would be a policy which Kalecki would welcome on moral grounds but here advanced on economic grounds. He considered the familiar argument that low income groups have a higher propensity to consume than higher income groups, and hence a redistribution of income from rich to poor would raise consumer expenditure. He broadly accepted that argument, though he suggested that a rise in income tax on high income groups, imposed to achieve this objective of redistribution could have a depressing effect on the level of investment. Thus the design of the taxes needed to take these possible side-effects into account, and Kalecki's main suggestion was that the taxable income of a firm be regarded as gross profits minus actual investment expenditure.[2] Thus income used to finance investment would be exempt from tax, but depreciation provision which was not spent on investment replacement would be taxable. In this way, Kalecki hoped to avoid the disincentive impact of income taxes on investment.

The extent of the redistribution (and hence the structure of the income tax system) was to be designed to secure full employment with investment at the level adequate for the expansion of capital equipment in line with increases in the working population and in productivity. In the notation used above, that is for investment to be equal to I_c, Kalecki's emphasis was on investment needed to support full employment growth, and at least in this discussion he took the rate of growth as largely circumscribed by the underlying rate of technical progress and of the population.

Kalecki recognised that the achievement of full employment by redistribution through the tax system was more egalitarian than achieving that objective through budget deficits. 'But precisely for this reason, "full employment through taxation" is likely to encounter a much stronger opposition that a "Budget deficit policy". One cannot, therefore, make any definite choice between the Budget deficit and the income tax method' (Kalecki, 1944b). In his discussion of the use of redistribution we can see Kalecki's egalitarian commitment, his awareness of the possible detrimental side-effects of some forms of redistribution and of the political and social restraints on economic policy.

Although investment and public expenditure on capital equipment were important components of aggregate demand, in Kalecki's view these forms of expenditure should not be made purely for their aggregate demand effects. Both investment and public expenditure have their social benefits and it is for those benefits that they should be undertaken. Thus

> the proper role of private investment is to provide tools for the production of consumption goods, and not to provide enough work to employ all available labour. ... Both public and private investment should be carried out only to the extent to which they are considered useful. If the effective demand this generated fails to provide full employment, the gap should be filled by increasing consumption and not by piling up unwanted public or private capital equipment (Kalecki, 1944b, pp. 42–3).

Similarly, in the case of public expenditure where '(t)he general principle must be that social priorities should decide the nature of the Government's spending programme ... Such decisions may be to a great extent affected by political factors' (pp. 49–50).

The ideas expressed in the previous paragraph taken together with the view that private sector aggregate demand was likely to be inadequate for full employment leads to the view that the achievement of full employment lies through the expansion of consumption. In Kalecki (1946b), he advocated a range of social benefits (e.g. old age pensions, child allowances) to stimulate consumption and to aid the lower income groups. In general he advocated the stimulation of mass consumption as a major part of a macroeconomic package to ensure full employment. He argued this on the grounds of the inadequacy of other methods, on grounds of social justice and on the grounds that consumption was the intended end product of economic activity.

Kalecki (1943c) was a strong defence of the ideas behind the Beveridge Plan on Social Security, meeting a number of the criticisms made by the political right against that plan (see Addison, 1976, Chapter 8). He argued that the 10 per cent unemployment rate on which the calculations of the Beveridge Plan were based was too pessimistic provided that governments pursued the necessary demand management policies. Indeed, the spending power provided by the social security payments envisaged would help the achievement of full employment. Kalecki argued also that 'the objections to the Beveridge Report on the ground that it will seriously impair the competitive position of British exports are, to put it mildly, not very well substantiated . . .'. The argument here was that the addition to industrial costs was not large and if necessary could be offset by an appropriate devaluation. It is also of some interest to note that Kalecki considered the disincentive to work argument against unemployment benefits, and argued that if such benefits did constitute a disincentive problem for low-paid workers, the appropriate policy response was to raise low wages rather than to lower benefits.

Kalecki foresaw that armaments expenditure might be an important component of aggregate demand in the post-war world as it did not raise the same objections from business that many forms of public expenditure did (see pp. 137–8 below). We saw above (p. 79) that he thought that post-war American experience illustrated the role of armaments expenditure as wasteful and dangerous and saw the apparent need to resort to this form of expenditure to maintain high levels of demand as a major shortcoming of capitalism.

Kalecki generally argued that both private and public investment should not be encouraged for aggregate demand purposes of seeking full employment, but only used in so far as the investment was needed to aid production (whether in the private or public sector). There was some role for shifting of investment expenditure over time to even out fluctuations of demand might be useful. However this shifting of investment over time might become of limited importance if macroeconomic policies designed to limit fluctuations were successful. For fluctuations in investment arise from fluctuations in the rate of growth of output, and if output grew smoothly then investment would be roughly constant. In turn, the lack of variation in investment expenditure would enhance stability in the level of economic activity.

Thus Kalecki stressed the role of the subsidising of consumption, through social security provision, reduction in indirect taxes, etc., in the maintenance of full employment. He did this for reasons of the effect on aggregate demand and because 'the higher standard of living of the masses . . . [is] . . . the purpose of all economic activity'.

Kalecki was writing at this time against a background of debate over whether the period after the Second World War would be, like the period after the First World War, one of recession after an initial post-war boom. He took the view along with many Keynesian economists that there would be a strong tendency towards recession (after the initial boom) unless countervailing government action was taken. This general view lay behind measures such as the UK post-war tax credits, which amounted to forced wartime savings to be released as spending power in the post-war period when demand was low, though in the event they were not used for this purpose.

The protagonists in the debate over the shape of the post-war economy can be broadly divided into optimists and pessimists. The pessimists, amongst whom we place Kalecki, based their argument on a simple Keynesian approach with forecasts for the balance between full employment savings and investment. The estimates of a simple consumption function of the form $C_t = a + c . Y_t$ (where C_t is consumer expenditure, Y_t disposable income and c the marginal propensity to consume) with $a > 0$ implies a declining average propensity to consume as income rises. Hence the full employment level of savings would tend to rise both absolutely and relatively to income, so that the achievement of full employment would require some combination of increasing investment, government deficit and export surplus.

We saw above that Kalecki based his main argument on a shortfall of investment required for growth below that needed for full employment. In Kalecki (1945b), he sought to look ahead to 1950–1 for the economic situation in the UK and the USA, to see what 'the maintenance of full employment after the transition period' (the title of Kalecki, 1945b) would involve. For both countries he argued that the maintenance of full employment would involve a budget deficit. The USA 'will require a much more unorthodox policy in public finance' than the UK, which arose from a higher savings ratio in the USA than in the UK. He also argued here that it would not be possible to stimulate investment sufficiently to absorb full employment savings.[3] For the United States the budget deficit required to generate full employment was estimated to be nearly 9 per cent of national income, whilst the corresponding figure for the United Kingdom was just over $2\frac{1}{2}$ per cent. These figures on budget deficits related to the combined current and capital account. The important aspect of this article is that Kalecki foresaw the need for a long-run budget deficit at full employment (in order to ensure full employment).

A number of governments in the mid-1940s appeared to commit themselves to full employment. In Britain, the 1944 White Paper on

Employment Policy (Ministry of Reconstruction, 1944) acknowledged the responsibility of governments to prevent fluctuations in
output and employment. Kalecki (1944c) was a critical appraisal of
this White Paper. The first part of that appraisal largely approves of
the White Paper's proposals on the transition from a war economy
to a peacetime economy, whilst the second part dealt similarly with
anti-cyclical policy. But in the third part, Kalecki was severely
critical of the main weakness of the White Paper. This was that
whilst it recognised the role of the government budget in offsetting
fluctuations in private sector demand to seek to obtain a stable level
of demand, it left untouched the question of how to ensure that the
stable level of demand was a high level of demand (i.e. one which led
to high levels of employment). Indeed, the White Paper was based
on the view that whilst the government budget need not balance in
any one particular year it must be balanced over a longer period, i.e.
budget deficits and surpluses must over a run of years balance out.
In view of our earlier discussion, it should not be surprising that
Kalecki argued that 'a programme for lasting full employment ...
must be based either on a long-run budget deficit policy or on the
redistribution of income' (Kalecki, 1944d). He also restated his
proposal for an annual capital tax (see p. 128 above) as a means of
financing the national debts in a way which would both preserve the
level of aggregate demand and which would not involve disincentive
effects of high taxation.

The experience of the 1950s and 1960s appeared to be more of
vindication of the optimists than the pessimists in the sense that, set
against previous experience, the capitalist world enjoyed prolonged
high levels of employment. Further, for much of the time, governments did not run budget deficits on current accounts.[4] Increases in
private investment expenditure were seen as a factor in the higher
levels of employment in the post-war period as compared with the
interwar period, though there has been debate over the size of this
factor (e.g. Matthews, 1968; Stafford, 1970) and debates over the
reasons (e.g. did Keynesian demand management policies contribute
to a higher level of confidence and thereby higher levels of investment or was investment higher through more opportunities?).

It is notable that like the British White Paper on Employment
Policy governments did not generally accept the possibility of
perpetual budget deficits. Bispham and Boltho (1982) in reviewing
demand management policies in post-war Europe conclude the 'UK

came closest to acceptance of the idea that budget deficit *per se* didn't matter. A number of other countries accepted deficits – but either wanted them on average to balance out or to be consistent with full employment balance.' Thus the position advocated by Kalecki of a permanent budget deficit at full employment to ensure full employment was not accepted. When in the 1970s the private sector appeared incapable of sustaining full employment, governments reluctantly accepted some deficits but appeared unwilling to accept the need for permanent ones sufficiently large to generate full employment.

Kalecki (1946a) considered the difficulties of combining multilateralism (i.e. free trade between countries) with full employment. He began from the proposition that 'world multilateralism can secure a better utilisation of world resources than bilateralism or regional blocks'. His argument can be seen easily if we consider the theoretical case of world-wide full employment but with countries having a variety of foreign trade positions, some in deficit and some in surplus. Kalecki's fear was that the adjustments to that situation would take the form of the deficit countries deflating to restore trade balance imparting a deflationary bias to the system. Thus Kalecki advocated that adjustments be undertaken by the surplus countries through the stimulation of their imports and hence the exports of the deficit countries.

Kalecki argued that devaluation by deficit countries might not work as a means of correcting the deficit. He pointed to the possibility of competitive devaluation by surplus countries and advanced the argument which later became known as 'elasticity pessimism' (that is that the elasticities of demand for imports and exports are sufficiently low that a devaluation does not improve the balance of trade). He also argued that loans from surplus to deficit countries were unlikely to provide a permanent solution.

Kalecki's basic policy recommendation in this area was 'that each country should maintain full employment based on domestic expenditure and on net foreign expenditure financed by international long-term lending'. Under these circumstances, deficit countries would be able to enjoy full employment (with the trade deficit covered by borrowing), and surplus countries would be lending the equivalent of their trade surplus.

In a number of respects, the problems which Kalecki foresaw for the 1950s did not become fully apparent until the early 1970s when unemployment became a substantial macroeconomic problem again. A number of fears about budget deficits, the national debt and the inflationary consequences of full employment which Kalecki had sought to overcome (see pp. 126–8 above) re-emerged. But, in general, people (including economists) failed to address themselves to the problems raised by Kalecki. These include the question of whether the stimulation of private investment can be adequate for long-term full employment, and if not how a policy involving a permanent deficit.[5]

The Politics of Full Employment

The discussion above was largely dealing with the economic-technical aspects of the difficulties of reaching full employment. But Kalecki was fully aware of the social and political aspects of unemployment and of full employment in capitalist economies. In a paper published in 1943, Kalecki dealt specifically with the social and political aspects. In this now much-quoted article, Kalecki examined the powerful forces operating against the achievement of full employment. This section deals mainly with that paper. It was first published as Kalecki (1943b), was revised by Kalecki in the early 1960s, and the revised version is published in English in Kalecki (1971a), Chapter 12. The main effect of the revisions was the removal of some sections. (In our discussion below, when a passage is in both versions we give the 1971a reference, but when the passage appears only in the 1943 version we refer to that.)

In Kalecki's view, the maintenance of full employment would entail substantial government intervention in capitalist economies. Long periods of full employment had not previously been experienced under capitalism, and such periods would generate substantial social and political changes. The resistance to the maintenance of full employment would arise from these political and social changes and from dislike of the government intervention. Kalecki organised his discussion around three main reasons for opposition to full employment as:

(a) the dislike of government interference in the problem of employment as such;

(b) the dislike of the direction of government spending (public investment and subsidizing consumption);

(c) dislike of the social and political changes resulting from the *maintenance* of full employment (Kalecki, 1971a, p. 139).

The dislike of government interference is seen as arising from two considerations. The first is a general suspicion of extensions to government activity, possibly as foreshadowing the replacement of private capitalism with state activity and socialism. The second is that under *laissez-faire* capitalism the level of employment strongly depends on the 'state of confidence'. If the confidence falters, then so does investment, and thereby output and employment. Confidence is a fragile flower which needs great care, i.e. policies which industrial leaders approve of. Thus the use of public expenditure to maintain the level of demand is seen to remove considerable power from capitalists, whose threats not to invest if confidence is harmed become less potent. The argument against public expenditure will often be wrapped up in semi-moralistic arguments on the need to balance the budget, not to spend more than one's means, etc. and the need for 'sound finance'. But 'the social function of the doctrine of "sound finance" is to make the level of employment dependent on the "state of confidence" (Kalecki, 1971a, p. 139). In other words when a government is prepared to use public expenditure to ensure full employment, investment and the control over investment loses its power over the level of employment.

The dislike of government spending focuses on public investment and subsidising mass consumption. In the case of public investment, this dislike arises as it involves the expansion of government activity into areas which were previously seen as the preserve of private enterprise. Thus Kalecki argued that the pressure would be for public investment to be confined to areas in which it does not compete with the private business, for example hospitals, schools and highways etc. Kalecki forecasted that the subsidising of consumption, which would include social security provision, would be strongly resisted specifically along two lines. First, there would be the argument that by subsidising consumption, the Government 'would not be embarking on any sort of "enterprise"'. In recent years, this argument has re-emerged, usually under the heading that public expenditure is not wealth-creating and the public sector lives on the back of the wealth-creating private sector. Second, there is 'a "moral" principle of the highest importance ... at stake. The fundamentals of capitalist ethics require that "You shall earn your bread in sweat" – unless you happen to have private means' (Kalecki, 1971a, p. 140). We find, again, this argument forcibly expressed in recent years, with attacks on the unemployed and their standard of living.

However, these arguments against public investment and subsidising consumption would not apply against public expenditure or armaments. In the context of a discussion on Nazi Germany, Kalecki (1971a, p. 141) argued that 'the dislike of government spending, whether on public investment or consumption, is overcome by concentrating government expenditure on armaments'. In the case of armaments expenditure, the government has been a traditional employer of the military so that it does not involve government extending its role. Further, the production of arms continues to be undertaken by private sector, with the government providing an assured market.

It is worthwhile to quote Kalecki's views on the political and social changes inherent in the maintenance of full employment at some length. The maintenance of full employment

> would cause social and political changes which would give a new impetus to the opposition of the business leaders. Indeed, under a regime of permanent full employment, 'the sack' would cease to play its role as a disciplinary measure. The social position of the boss would be undermined and the self assurance and class consciousness of the working class would grow. Strikes for wage increases and improvements in conditions of work would create political tension. ... But 'discipline in the factories' and 'political stability' are more appreciated by the business leaders than profits. Their class instinct tells them that lasting full employment is unsound from their point of view and that unemployment is an integral part of the normal capitalist system (Kalecki, 1971a, pp. 140–1).

There would then be pressures against the maintenance of full employment and against the measure designed to achieve full employment. But there would also be popular pressure for full employment. The outcome of these contrary pressures were seen as twofold. First, there will be pressure on governmemts to be seen to do something. What they actually do may be cosmetic and may (under pressure from business) be directed towards the stimulus of private investment which, as seen above, Kalecki regarded as inadequate for prolonged full employment. But he also felt that even as a short term measure the stimulation of private investment faced the difficulty that when, during a slump business was pessimistic about the future, the response of investment to incentives might be small and would be rather uncertain.

Nevertheless, there could well be an emphasis on various means of encouraging private investment through, for example, lowering the rate of interest, providing subsidies on investment. The attraction of such an approach to business would simply be that the intervention is conducted through private enterprise. The relationship between these remarks and much recent policy discussion during the present recession is fairly clear. There has been the adoption of many cosmetic measures, including those specifically designed to reduce measured unemployment even though actual unemployment is not affected, and the emphasis on stimulating private investment through lowering interest rates and the encouragement of small businesses spring to mind.

Second, a political business cycle would develop. The economic political system has been seen as incapable of securing the maintenance of full employment. Popular pressure for full employment would reach its height at or near election time, leading to government-induced pre-election booms. But, between elections, unemployment would be allowed to rise to prevent the political and social changes which would result from continuous full employment.

This state of affairs is perhaps symptomatic of the future economic regime of capitalist democracies. In the slump, either under the pressure of the masses, or even without it, public investment financed by borrowing will be undertaken to prevent large scale unemployment. But if attempts are made to apply this method in order to maintain the high level of employment reached in the subsequent boom a strong opposition of 'business leaders' is likely to be encountered. As has already been argued, lasting full employment is not at all to their liking. The workers would 'get out of hand' and the 'captains of industry' would be anxious 'to teach them a lesson'. Moreover, the price increase in the upswing is to the disadvantage of small and big *rentiers* and makes them 'boom tired'.

In this situation a powerful bloc is likely to be formed between big business and the rentier interests, and they would probably find more than one economist to declare that the situation was manifestly unsound. The pressure of all these forces, and in particular of big business would most probably induce the Government to return to the orthodox policy of cutting down the budget deficit (Kalecki, 1971a, p. 144).

The group of 'more than one economist' have generally become known as monetarists!

There are two important ideas in Chapter 12 of Kalecki (1971a) which are worth separating out since they are rather conflated in Kalecki's presentation. The first is that there would continue to be a business cycle with fluctuations in the level of output, etc. This would arise partly because it would not be possible for a government to iron out all fluctuations of investment even if it wanted to. But the new (as compared with the pre-war situation) element would be the deliberate stimulation of the economy in the period preceding an election and the tolerance of recessions in other periods. Discussion of 'election booms' indicates that this idea has entered into wide circulation. Clearly the key question which arises here is whether the post-war experience of the reasons for recessions is in line with Kalecki's view that the downswing occurs as a result of the desire of business to prevent workers 'getting out of hand' and 'to teach them a lesson'. It is not to be expected that such reasons would be directly expressed, but may well be disguised in terms of the need to restrain wage increases, to reduce inflation or to maintain international competitiveness, etc.[6]

The second element is that a prolonged period of low levels of unemployment generates social and political changes and eventually strong resistance to its continuation. The length of this prolonged period is much more than the two or three years of the boom part of the business cycle. Given the experience in the interwar period of recession and the smashing of trade union organisation in a number of countries, it could be expected that a very substantial period of low levels of unemployment would have to occur before workers 'getting out of hand' became a problem for business. Further, the post-war experience of rising real wages at an unprecedented rate, may have helped to prolong the long boom. Thus the resistance by business and the political right which Kalecki foresaw may have taken much longer to develop than would seem to be implied by Kalecki (1943b).

The most significant of the deletions from Kalecki (1943b) when it was revised is the final section which dealt with the question of 'should a progressive be satisfied with a regime of the "political business cycle"?' (Kalecki, 1943b).[7] He answered the question in the negative on the two grounds '(a) that it does not assure lasting full employment; (b) that government intervention is tied down to public investment and does not embrace subsidizing consumption'.

It is clear that with any kind of business cycle, whether engendered for political reasons or not, there can only be full employment at most at the top of the boom, and hence there will be unemployment for much of the time. Thus Kalecki's argument implies an objective of full employment with as far as possible the removal of business cycles.

The concluding essay of Oxford University Institute of Statistics (1944), to which the authors of articles in the book including Kalecki subscribed, argued that 'unemployment is the most powerful of all economic controls. . . . The ideal is to replace the arbitrary undemocratic "control" of unemployment by conscious controls, operated democratically in the public interest.'[8] As the nature of controls changes and becomes visible, who controls whom and in whose interests change.

In a brief paragraph, which was not developed, Kalecki argued

> that full employment capitalism will have, of course, to develop new social and political institutions which will reflect the increased power of the working class. If capitalism can adjust itself to full employment a fundamental reform will have been incorporated in it. If not, it will show itself an outmoded system which must be scrapped (Kalecki, 1943b).

With the advantage of hindsight it can be seen that the development of acceptable conscious controls was not undertaken (and may in any event be an impossible aim) and that there was a failure to develop the new social and political institutions to which Kalecki refers.

The experience of reading Kalecki (1943b) some forty years after it was written makes one realise how ideas once thought dead come back to life. Allowing for some changes in the use of language, one finds Kalecki seeking to deal with a range of arguments used to justify unemployment and deflationary government policies which have again been at the forefront in the past decade.

Notes to Chapter 7

1. This particular passage was introduced in the revised version of the paper under discussion in place of a number of sections in the original version.
2. This proposal appears similar to that later made by the Meade Committee (Meade, 1978) for company taxation to be based on a flow of funds basis.
3. This paper was followed by an interchange between an 'optimist' Woytinsky (1946) and Kalecki (1947) in the *American Economic Review*.
4. Pedone (1982) in a review of public expenditure in post-war Europe presents statistics for six countries pertaining to each of the three decades of the 1950s, 1960s and 1970s. The ratio of general government current receipts to current expenditure is generally above 1 (implying current budget surplus), and is above 1 in 15 cases of the 17 for which data are available (there being no data for one country in the 1950s).
5. Matthews (1982a) summarises two papers in Matthews (1982b) as follows.

   The 1950s and 1960s were characterised, like earlier booms, by an unusually rapid rise in investment, more rapid than the rise in GDP. This was artificially prolonged by the tendency of governments to grant increasingly large subsidies to investment. The result was exhaustion of the best investment opportunities, a decline in the marginal efficiency of investment and a fall off in the rate at which the capital stock was increased.

   This fits in well with Kalecki's arguments against the stimulation of investment as a means of achieving full employment.
6. Tarling and Wilkinson (1977) argue for the UK that

   (i)ncomes policies as part of an economic strategy, are used to lower real wages relative to productivity, as part of a total package aimed at attacking inflation, switching resources from consumption into exports and investment and switching incomes from workers towards the State (higher taxes), capitalists (higher profits) and foreign suppliers (more expensive imports).

   Thus it could be argued that 'teaching the workers a lesson' took the form of income policies as well as deflation.

7. The other substantial change was the replacement of the opening eight paragraphs of Kalecki (1943b) by one introductory paragraph in Kalecki (1971a). But the deleted paragraph mainly dealt with the 'economics of full employment' along the lines discussed in the text above.

8. Klein (1952) notes Kalecki as having made a similar point in a lecture.

8
Kalecki and Marx

Introduction

There can be little doubt that the writings of Marx and some of his followers (particularly Rosa Luxemburg) were important influences on Kalecki's thinking (cf. pp. 3–4 above, Kowalik, 1964, p. 1, p. 3). In his first book (Kalecki, 1939, pp. 45–6) and in one of his last articles (Kalecki, 1968a), Kalecki linked his own ideas on effective demand with Marx's scheme of extended reproduction.[1] In Chapter 1 we sought to place Kalecki firmly within the Ricardian–Marxian tradition of economic analysis. These strands raise two interesting issues which we follow through this chapter. The first issue is that of the extent to which the writings of Marx permeated the thinking and writing of Kalecki, particularly in terms of conditioning the basic assumptions (often implicit) and the general intellectual framework used by Kalecki. For example, the idea of the two basic social classes of capitalism (capitalists and workers) used by Marx was also generally used by Kalecki in a way which suggested that this idea was part of his 'vision' of the capitalist economy.[2]

The second issue is how and where the ideas of Kalecki diverge from the ideas of Marx, and to see how their ideas relate to one another. A third issue, which we do not deal with, is the relationship between Kalecki and those who regard themselves as Marxists.[3]

Kalecki's major writings on capitalism were published between the early 1930s and the late 1940s, with some further writings (often developing the earlier writings) published in the later 1950s and 1960s. Marx was writing on capitalism between the 1840s and his death in 1883. Kalecki and particularly Marx adopted the general view that economies (and societies) evolve over time, and as their structure changes the laws of operation of the economies may change.[4] We would therefore expect that Kalecki and Marx may have adopted different assumptions and theories relating to capitalist economies as a result of the combination of different individuals, thinking and writing about capitalist economies, separated in time by nearly a century. It could be that whilst at one level there are differences between Kalecki and Marx, these could be the result of the application of a similar approach to different situations and times. Differences such as the competitive (Marx) or oligopolistic (Kalecki) nature of major parts of capitalist economies, the nature of money in use (i.e. gold/paper money versus credit money) *could* be seen as arising more from changes in the capitalist economies rather than from fundamental differences between the approaches of Kalecki and Marx.[5]

A further source of difference arises from differences of focus. Kalecki was mainly concerned with the analysis of the types of economies which predominate in the second half of the twentieth century, namely developed capitalist economies, centrally planned socialist economies and developing economies. Further, Kalecki diagnosed capitalist economies as having reached the oligopoly/ monopoly stage. Marx was concerned with the analysis of competitive capitalism as it existed in the nineteenth century (particularly in the most developed form in Britain), and with an understanding of other previous and current forms of society (e.g. feudalism) and of likely future developments. But his analysis of future developments was largely restricted to the analysis of future capitalist developments, with little on the organisation and operation of socialist economies.

We have seen above (and it also arises in the subsequent chapters) that Kalecki was fully aware of the impact of socio-political factors on the functioning of the economy, and the constraints which were imposed on the economy and on government economic policy by the specific social and institutional arrangements in a country. Nevertheless, Kalecki took a rather narrower view of what constituted economics (or perhaps more accurately political economy), with some consideration paid to the other socio-political factors. Marx operated in that sense on a much broader canvas, with consideration of not only political economy but also politics, history, philosophy, etc. In a sense, it could be said that Marx strove for a much greater integration between these various disciplines whereas Kalecki saw the constraints which these other forces placed on the operation of economies. It is also the case that Kalecki spent most of his working life employed working on rather immediate problems (e.g. the development of a perspective fifteen-year plan in Poland, the derivation of national income statistics in Poland in the early 1930s), whereas Marx was able through the financial support of Engels to pursue his own thoughts much more. Further, Marx sought to develop a theory of history and historical change, to set out the laws of motion of capitalist society and to develop a strategy for the proletariat in the overthrow of capitalism. Kalecki's aims were rather different, perhaps in part because he was able to build on the work of Marx (and others). Kalecki's aims could be seen to be the understanding of existing economic systems and the development of improvements in those systems, particularly within socialist economies.

Whereas Marx worked at, in his own terminology, various levels of abstraction, Kalecki generally operated at the more concrete, less abstract level of analysis. It is clear from the preceding chapters that Kalecki did extensive theorising, which inevitably involves some abstraction. But his theorising was usually directed towards some fairly immediate purpose, such as the explanation of economic fluctuations, the level of unemployment etc. His theorising was usually directed towards the explanation of real world phenomena which he regarded as important, and his abstractions and assumptions were related to the concrete conditions of the world he sought to explain. This approach to theorising has three interesting implications here. First, it means that Kalecki was concerned with the explanation of the behaviour of actual variables (e.g. investment, unemployment). This led him to reject the use of equilibrium analysis (cf. pp. 9–10 above) on the grounds that equilibrium would be rarely reached and observed. Thus, Kalecki did not adopt the view that an equilibrium position should be studied as a position towards which the economy would tend. This latter view, which occurs in both neo-classical and classical economics (albeit with different ideas of what constitutes an equilibrium position), carries the overtone of an underlying reality (equilibrium) towards which the actual economy would tend. In the case of Marx, for example, the competitive equilibrium of equalised rates of profit, would constitute a 'centre of gravity' towards which the actual market prices would tend. But this use of equilibrium analysis was in the context of one particular concern, namely the relationship between values and prices. However, the focus of Marx on the dynamics of capitalism, tendency towards crisis, etc. strongly indicate that equilibrium analysis could not be used everywhere. Kalecki had similar concerns, although his analysis of dynamics and crisis was more formal than Marx. But in the area of prices, Kalecki always undertook his analysis in terms of market (observed) prices, whereas Marx rarely used market prices but focused on long-run equilibrium prices (prices of production).

Second, Kalecki appeared generally to pitch his analysis at a fairly 'superficial' level (in the sense of being concerned with surface relationships), whereas Marx was concerned with both the 'superficial' level (e.g. discussion of the course of wages) as well as seeking to discover the nature of the underlying reality (e.g. the value of labour power). Further,

> Marx . . . believed that the appearances of commodity production, both capitalist and pre-capitalist, were illusory. Reality as it appears to social actors is deceptive; and Marx often writes of the true reality as hidden by appearances. . . . He sees it as the role of scientific economics to penetrate through the fetishism to the reality of social relations, which are expressed in terms of value, surplus value and capital (Howard and King, 1976).

Further, Marx sought to show that the relationship between commodities was a relationship between people. In terms of the terminology used in this paragraph, it could be said that Kalecki did not seek to penetrate as far as Marx through to the reality of social relations. But, here as elsewhere, it has to be recognised that Kalecki was writing after and in knowledge of Marx, and accepted and thought that he could not improve upon parts of Marx's writings.

Third, Kalecki's approach and assumptions in the analysis of a particular problem were heavily conditioned by the nature of the problem at hand and the economic factors which he saw as relevant and important for that problem. His assumptions were strongly coloured by his general background (e.g. the use of social classes, the tendency to focus on oligopolistic rather than competitive features) but as well the particular assumptions would be specific problem-orientated.

Much of this is reflected in Kalecki's attitude to the labour theory of value, which is often regarded as a central part of Marx's analysis.

'He felt . . . a strong distaste for the Marxian theory of value, which he considered metaphysical and (if I am not mistaken) never wanted to discuss' (Brus, 1977a, words in parentheses in original) and Kalecki 'made no use of the Classical labour theory of value and of Marx's concept of exploitation based on it' (Eshag, 1977). However, Kalecki did retain a rather general notion of capitalism as involving exploitation, without precision on the nature of that exploitation. But it can be said that he did not see profits as accruing to capitalists as a reward for waiting or for abstinence nor to link the rate of profit with any notion of the marginal productivity of capital. Thus profits accrued to capitalists on the basis of ownership of wealth (to which there was limited access) but not as a return for any services rendered.

It could be said, more generally, that '(w)hilst recognizing the enormous significance of the Marxist approach and of many Marxian tools of economic analysis, Kalecki never felt that he had to accept every component of Marxian economics or to retain those parts of it which have become obsolete' (Brus, 1977a). Kalecki's self-education in economics was also heavily influenced by Rosa Luxemburg, who had developed within the Marxist tradition an emphasis on the importance of effective demand and investment in the realisation of the surplus (see also Kalecki, 1971a, Chapter 13).[6, 7]

We view Kalecki as someone seeking to develop his own ideas against a background of Marxian influence, rather than someone who closely and deliberately based his own on that of Marx, or someone who was concerned with questions such as what Marx really meant? or what Marx would or should have said? It was seen in Chapter 1 that Kalecki was not the type of person who accepted a line of thought because of who advocated that line of thought, because someone in authority wished him to do so or because it was fashionable to do so. Some of the difficulties which this created for Kalecki's career have been summarised in Chapter 1 and occur again in Chapter 11. Thus it would be rather out of character for Kalecki to have adopted a particular view simply because Marx (or anyone else) had advocated it.

Making comparisons between the work of Kalecki and of Marx faces the difficulty of having to determine what Marx said in a number of areas where there is ambiguity or contradiction in his writings. This is added to here in that many of those areas of Marx's writing which we discuss are precisely the ones in which there has been considerable controversy. Our reaction to that problem is to indicate something of the range of interpretations which have been advanced. A similar problem arises in the next chapter when Kalecki and Keynes are compared, and the problem is dealt with in the same manner.

There is a difficulty in interpreting Kalecki in these comparisons. As we have pointed out before, Kalecki's style of writing was laconic, and specifically would not repeat ideas which he felt to be well known or unoriginal. Thus those parts of Marx's writings which Kalecki accepted would not be repeated in his own work, and so the absence of some of the key ideas of Marx from Kalecki's writings cannot be taken as evidence of his rejection of those ideas.[8]

Similarities Between Kalecki and Marx

There are numerous similarities between Kalecki and Marx in the sense that many of the implicit assumptions and much of the general intellectual background of Kalecki were derived from the works of Marx. In this section, we focus on those similarities which are either explicit, or, whilst implicit are of particular significance for the interpretation and understanding of the work of Kalecki.

The first general similarity considered is the class nature of capitalist societies with the two major social classes based on capital and on labour. Howard and King (1975) summarise Marx's views as follows:

> Although Marx uses the concept of class in various ways, in this context he defines classes as social strata that are 'grouped' as a result of the relationship they have to the possession of the means of production as private property. Possession or non-possession of the means of production, however, is not merely a legal relation, but also an economic relationship between men. Class relationships allow the *surplus product* to be appropriated by the possessing class, which thus stands in an exploitive relationship to the producers. In terms of their class structure societies differ primarily in the economic method that extracts the surplus social product from the labour of producers (italics in original).

A number of aspects of the class nature of capitalist societies which are evident in Marx's approach have an important role to play in the work of Kalecki. The first aspect of the two class nature of capitalism can be seen in Kalecki's work discussed above. Throughout there is a distinction drawn between capitalists who control production, make price and investment decisions and are the major savers and workers who supply labour, consume but generally do not save, with little influence over prices, real wages of investment.

The second aspect is the antagonistic relationship between the classes. Kalecki argued that 'the capitalist system is not a "harmonious" regime, whose purpose is the satisfaction of the needs of its citizens but an "antagonistic" regime which is to secure profits for capitalists' (Kalecki, 1971a, p. 147). Thus Kalecki, with Marx, would reject those attempts by some neo-classical economists to portray capitalist societies as 'harmonious'. However, the conflict between capital and labour was seen by Marx to be particularly sharp over the control of the productive process (and this is a point we return to below). In contrast, Kalecki made little reference to that conflict (though he may have taken it for granted), and focused instead on 'the class struggle and the distribution of income' (title of Kalecki, 1971b). We saw in Chapter 2 that the degree of monopoly approach indicates a conflict between wages and profits.

The third aspect is that for both Kalecki and Marx the capitalist class has control over the means of production, and there is restricted access to ownership of the means of production. But in the case of Marx, the monopoly position of the capitalist class was largely exercised through the control of the means of production. The product market situation in which firms operated was seen as competitive in the sense of involving rivalry and a tendency towards an equalisation of the rate of profit. Note, though, that there was a tendency towards concentration and centralisation within the competitive system. For Kalecki, the product market situation was one of oligopoly and monopoly, and although he stressed the role of the degree of monopoly in pricing decisions (and thereby on the distribution of income) this was in the context of a capitalist economy. In such an economy, Kalecki argued, there was a limited access to the ownership of the means of production. Thus, there is a common element in Kalecki and Marx over the class monopoly over the means of production. But there is the difference over the typical product market situation and the extent of competition, with

Kalecki generally assuming oligopoly (at least in industrial products) and Marx assuming rivalrous competition. There is also a
difference of emphasis in that Kalecki did not explicitly discuss the
control over the means of production.

The fourth aspect is that Kalecki and Marx shared similar ideas
over the income of the two classes, i.e. profits and wages. It was seen
above that Kalecki adopted the view of Marx and other classical
economists that wages are spent quickly and completely (at least as a
first approximation). In the case of Marx and other classical
economists (notably Ricardo), real wages were generally seen as
close to some notion of subsistence, though there were fluctuations
of real wages around such a level as the demand for labour varied.
The nature of that subsistence wage as seen by Marx (e.g. whether a
physical subsistence wage or a socially acceptable minimum which
evolves over time) has been the subject of much debate, and as it
appears to be one of the differences between Kalecki and Marx we
return to the point on subsistence wages below. Kalecki did not
directly adhere to any subsistence notion of wages, and implicitly
saw real wages as determined by the degree of monopoly (including
trade union strength) and productivity. But in a limited sense,
Kalecki maintained an indirect allegiance to the subsistence notion
in that he maintained the implication of the subsistence notion,
namely that wages are quickly and entirely spent.

Kalecki and Marx saw capitalists in pursuit of profits, and saving
substantial proportions of profits in order to finance investment and
accumulation. Savings are largely made by capitalists, for reasons
connected with production and profits, and not as part of utility
calculations over the optimal split between consumption and saving.
Further savings are ploughed back usually (but not always) by the
firm making the saving (i.e. internal finance) into investment. Whilst
Kalecki and Marx saw the important decisions on savings as being
made by capitalists, neither said much about the factors which
would influence those decisions. 'One part of the surplus-value is
consumed by capitalists as revenue, the other part is employed as
capital, i.e. it is accumulated. . . . [It] is the owner of the surplus-
value, the capitalist, who makes this division. It is an act of his will'
(Marx, 1976, p. 738).

There is an important difference between Kalecki and Marx in the
realm of investment, which relates to the degree of competitive
pressures on firms to undertake investment. This difference is

discussed below under the general heading of differences between Kalecki and Marx over competition and monopoly.

There is also a common view on what is meant by profits. Kalecki included in gross profits, depreciation and maintenance, net undistributed profits, dividends, interest, rent and managerial salaries. Marx took a similar view, and a large part of Marx (1981) is a discussion of the ways in which profits are divided up into interest, rent and industrial profits. Further, neither author saw an equality or tendency towards equality between the rate of interest and the rate of profit (which is generally taken to be the case in neo-classical economics), and indeed the rate of interest has to be generally below the rate of profit. Kalecki saw the excess of the rate of profit of enterprises over the rate of interest as one of the factors influencing investment, though he argued that as an empirical matter the two rates tended to fluctuate together. Kalecki (1943a), Chapter 3 sought to show that generally the rate of profit would exceed the rate of interest. The rates of interest (short-term and long-term) as seen by Kalecki were discussed in Chapter 5 above, and from there it can be seen that Kalecki regarded the long-term rate as based on the short-term rate, and the latter rate arising from the interaction of the demand for and supply of money.

Marx saw 'interest (as) simply a part of profit' and 'the average rate of profit should be considered as ultimately determining the maximum limit of interest' (Marx, 1981, pp. 480–2). Further '(i)t is in fact only the division of capitalists into money capitalists and industrial capitalists that transforms a part of the profit into interest and creates the category of interest at all; and it is only the competition between these two kinds of capitalist that creates the rate of interest'. In Marx's view there are no 'natural' laws governing the determination of the rate of interest ('there is no natural rate of interest' (Marx, 1981, p. 484)), though there are for wages and profits. But 'the relationship between the supply of loan capital on the one hand, and the demand for it on the other, is what determines the market level of interest at any given time' (Marx, 1981, p. 488).[9]

In broad terms, it could be said that both Kalecki and Marx saw profits as including industrial profits, interest, rent, etc., and that profits accrue through the possession of power by capitalists (though the precise nature of that power was seen differently as discussed below).

The fifth and final aspect of the common view on the importance of social class is that Kalecki and Marx saw capital (or the interests of capital) in control of production and distribution in a capitalist economy. In particular, although Marx discussed (e.g. Marx, 1981, Chapter 23) what has become known as the separation of ownership and management, neither author appears to have substantially diverged from the idea that firms are operated in the interests of their owners with the subsequent pursuit of profits.

There is one way in which Kalecki developed ideas on the role of social class which appears to be in conflict with the general Marxian tradition. This is in respect of the idea of intermediate regimes (which Kalecki applied to developing countries and is discussed in full in Chapter 10). This idea was summarised as follows. For intermediate regimes

the governments ... represented the interests of lower-middle class and rich or medium-rich peasants amalgamated with state capitalism (the managers' class). The antagonists of these governments from above are the remnants of feudalism left over after the agrarian reform and the native big business (often reduced in scope by nationalisation). The antagonists from below are poor peasants and agricultural workers, who in general profit little from the land reform, and the urban paupers: people without stable employment, home workers and workers in small establishments (Kalecki, 1976, p. 198).

This represented 'a clear departure from the traditional Marxist standpoint that would reject the possibility of a durable class coalition based on the hegemony of the lower middle-classes' (Sachs, 1977). The lower middle class was seen to have largely displaced property owners (with local big business 'tamed', and foreign big business held at bay by nationalist sentiments) from power, and without leading to a socialist takeover by the working class.

The second area of similarity relates to the level and role of unemployment. It is clear that both Kalecki and Marx would have had little truck with the idea often advanced by neo-classical economists that unemployment is a chosen occupation. Both saw unemployment as the result of the overall operation of the economic and social system, and not merely the sum of individual decisions. As an aside here we can note that both authors could be said to be developing a genuine macroeconomics in the sense that both macroeconomic aggregates such as investment, unemployment are explained in terms of the overall operation of the system and not solely as the adding together of individual behaviour (which underlies much conventional macroeconomics).

The views of Kalecki on unemployment have been set out above (e.g. pp. 125–43). It can be seen there that Kalecki took the view that significant amounts of unemployment were a general feature of capitalist economies. The similarity of the views of Kalecki with those of Marx is partly reflected in Kalecki's use of Marx's term of the industrial reserve army (Kalecki, 1935b, fn. 8). Further, unemployment is not seen as a temporary aberration resulting from an infrequent malfunctioning of the economic system.

For both Kalecki and Marx, the role of unemployment is to discipline workers and restrain wage increases. The view of Marx is summarised in references such as 'that the industrial reserve army, during the periods of stagnation and average prosperity weighs down the active army of workers; during the periods of overproduction and feverish activity, it puts a curb on their pretensions' (Marx, 1976, p. 792).

The third general similarity is the view that capitalism is subject to fluctuations in economic activity and to periodic crises. Kalecki took economic fluctuations as a stylised fact of capitalism which requires some explanation. Kalecki's explanation of the cycle rests largely on fluctuations in investment, which drive fluctuations in aggregate demand, with fluctuations in investment based on changes in profitability and economic activity (cf. pp. 48–58 above). The turning point at the top of the cycle arises as profitability hesitates, leading to a decline in investment demand, with the decline in profitability, arising predominantly from the capital stock rising faster than profits. Thus in Kalecki's business cycle theory, the decline in profitability around the top of the cycle does not arise from money wages rising (faster than prices).

The analysis of crises provided by Marx has some points of overlap with that of Kalecki but is rather more broadly based. Junankar (1982), Chapter 9 provides a synthesis of Marx's writings on the trade cycle and crises on which we draw here. Junankar (1982) distinguishes between the factors which provide the possibility of crises and the factors which cause a crises. The factors providing the possibility of crises are '(a) the contradiction between the use value and exchange value in a commodity; (b) the existence of money which is a medium of exchange and a store of value; (c) capitalist production for exchange; and (d) the numerous (unplanned) circuits of capital' (pp. 136–7). Kalecki did not explicitly discuss the factors underlying the possibility of crises, but the previous discussion would suggest that (c) and (d) would be the more important ones for him together with the possible incomplete reinvestment of profits. It should be noted that Kalecki's approch relates to an oligopolised economy whereas Marx's approach relates to a competitive one, but Kalecki still regarded an oligopolised capitalist economy as lacking the co-ordination necessary to maintain full employment. In other words, he did not regard the cartelisation and concentration as having reached the stage of involving co-ordination of investment plans, etc. to ensure full employment or maximum profits.

The causes of crises identified in Marx's writings are divided by Junankar into abstract and concrete causes. The former are the continual expansion of accumulation and the falling rate of profit. Both of these are long-term trends. Concrete causes include accumulation problems and effective demand problems. The accumulation problems include the impact of a falling rate of profit, and the discontinuous nature of technical change and innovations. However, the cause of the falling rate of profit is not itself fully explained. The problems of effective demand are the now well known ones, although Marx appears to have wavered on the importance of these problems and did not develop their effects within a cyclical framework. It can also be noted that for Marx the down-swing of a cycle involved restructuring of industry and bankruptcy of financially weaker firms, which formed the basis for the subsequent recovery. Kalecki's discussion did not incorporate this restructuring.

There are also some strong similarities in the ways in which Kalecki and Marx approach the subject of technical change. Kalecki (1941a) listed five important effects of technical progress on economic development. These features were:

(i) technical progress increases the productivity of labour;
(ii) technical progress changes the ratio of the maximum capacity of a plant to the amount of capital it contains. ... It seems likely that on the whole technical progress has been capital using;
(iii) technical progress increases the degree of oligopoly ...

    (iv) technical progress tends to lower the general level of prices;
    (v) technical progress keeps the inducement to invest higher
           than it would be otherwise.

He summarised his discussion by saying that 'we may say that the effect of technical progress is not to increase output but to save labour', although that conclusion is subject to a number of caveats made by Kalecki. The relevance here of this list is to see how closely they correspond to the views of Marx. The ideas under (i) and (ii) that technical change tends to be labour saving is closely in line with Marx's position (cf. e.g. Howard and King, 1975, Chapter 6; Junankar, 1982, pp. 72–4). Under (iii), the degree of oligopoly rises through a rise in concentration. In one sense this corresponds to Marx's view that technical change favours capital-intensity, large-scale production, etc. which adds to the process of concentration. There are senses in which Kalecki and Marx differ on this point. Kalecki saw the rise in the degree of oligopoly as enabling prices to rise relative to wages (i.e. the price–cost margin to rise), whereas Marx saw the effect of technical change here as raising the rate of exploitation. Kalecki saw a gradual rise in the degree of oligopoly resulting from technical change as economies of scale became more important, whereas Marx saw technical change resulting from competition and leading to competition between individual capitalists. Kalecki tended to see the 'intensity of technical change' as an exogenous factor, although the actual rate of change in the economy depends on the 'conversion' of potential change into actual change through investment. Marx placed more emphasis on his writings on technical change, on the relationship between competition, investment and technical change. Further there is the very important impact of technical change on the mode of production, etc.

    Both Kalecki and Marx attributed a contradictory nature to investment.

> We see that the question, 'What causes periodical crises?' could be answered shortly: the fact that investment is not only produced but also producing. . . . The tragedy of investment is that it causes crisis because it is useful. Doubtless many people will consider this theory paradoxical. But it is not the theory which is paradoxical, but its subject – the capitalist economy (Kalecki, 1939, pp. 148–9).

The paradoxical nature of investment would appear to arise from a combination of capital equipment being long-lived and being labour-saving. This could be said to have echoes of Marx's view that '(i)t is one of the contradictions of capitalism that capital both attracts labour (to create surplus value), but also discards labour in the pursuit of profits' (Junankar, 1982).

Some Important Differences Between Kalecki and Marx

In this section we explore the differences between Kalecki and Marx in their economic analysis, focusing on those areas of analysis which are important in the work of Kalecki. We divide these differences into five broad groupings though there are overlaps between the first four groupings and sub-themes within each of the groupings. The first broad grouping relates to the source and nature of profits, and the second to the type of exchange rates used (market prices, prices of production or values). The third grouping covers wage determination, and the fourth competition and monopoly, whilst the fifth deals with the nature of money.

The discussion of differences begins with the complex of interrelated ideas on the source and nature of profits in a capitalist economy. In the background, there are differences over the role and relevance of the labour theory of value, of which as was seen above Kalecki was rather dismissive.

It will be apparent from Chapter 2 above that Kalecki focused on the product market, and specifically on the degree of monopoly in such markets, to explain the ratio of profits to sales and focuses on the level of aggregate demand to determine the level of sales and profits. For our present discussion, there are two features of Kalecki's approach to highlight. First, it is the characteristics (sphere) of exchange (i.e. market power, investment expenditure plans) which are seen as relevant to the determination of profits. In turn, this means that production and the conditions of production are kept very much in the background, and only surface in terms of constant (or near constant) average costs facing firms. Thus, the conditions of production, the intensity of labour, conflict at the place of work which are important ingredients in the work of Marx, do not appear to have a substantial role in the analysis of Kalecki (as noted by Rowthorn, 1981, p. 4). At one or two places, Kalecki recognised that the intensity of labour affects productivity and cost conditions, but for the purpose of his analysis the intensity of labour is held constant. This is one point where Kalecki's laconic style led him to omit ideas which he took to be obvious and well-established. In other words, his general Marxian background indicated to him the relevance of conflict at the work-place, disputes over the intensity of labour, etc. so that he did not feel it necessary to repeat the points. Thus omission of discussion of the conditions of production does not necessarily mean that Kalecki felt them to be unimportant.[10]

Second, in Kalecki's approach calculations of profits, sales, etc., are all carried out within the theory in terms of actual market prices. Thus Kalecki did not deal with long-run equilibrium prices (specifically relevant here would be prices of production) nor did he deal with the values of goods based on the socially necessary time of their production, both of which were used by Marx. The differences between market prices, prices of production and values are more fully discussed below. Here we note that whilst Marx had 'little interest in explaining market prices' (Junankar, 1982), Kalecki was only interested in market prices; conversely whilst Marx was interested in the prices of production and values, Kalecki was not concerned with such concepts at all.

Marx saw the source of surplus value as derived from the monopoly of ownership of the means of production by the capitalist class, and the control which that class held over the productive process. This control permits the creation and extraction of surplus by capitalists from workers. Labour is purchased at a wage equal to the value of labour power (more on this below). The excess of the price obtained for a unit of (net) output and the labour costs (calculated at those wages) is the (unit) surplus arising from control over the means of production.

There is some overlap between the general ideas of Kalecki and Marx in this area, but with some important differences. There is the common theme that capitalists have control over the means of production (although that is generally implicit rather than explicit in Kalecki's writings). However, Kalecki and Marx can be seen to differ in three important respects.

The first respect in which Kalecki and Marx differ here arises from Kalecki's emphasis on the role of the degree of monopoly and

Marx's emphasis on the role of the intensity of labour and the competitive nature of capitalism. From equation (6.2) in Chapter 6 above, we have the equation for the real wage in Kalecki's approach as:

$$w/p = (Q/kL) - (fF/pL) \tag{8.1}$$

where it can be seen that the real wage is seen as determined by labour productivity (Q/L), the mark-up (k) which in turn is determined by the degree of monopoly and the ratio of foreign input prices to domestic output prices (f/p). In equation (8.1), the direction of causation is seen from right to left.

Using the same variables, Marx's approach could be portrayed as:

$$k = (wL/pQ + fF/pQ)^{-1} \tag{8.2}$$

where again the causation is seen to run from right to left. The mark-up is a relatively unimportant variable which results from the interaction of the real wage and the productivity of labour (which is closely related to the rate of exploitation) and in turn the underlying real wage is set by the reproduction costs of labour and productivity by the intensity of labour.

We should note (and these are points to which we return) that equation (8.1) summarising the Kalecki approach would be in terms of market prices, and would be seen as achieved in the short-run. On the other hand, equation (8.2) would often be seen in terms of values and would express long-term relationship.

This leads into the second aspect that in the approach of Marx, the sphere of production, which involves conflict between labour and capital within the productive process over the intensity of labour is given particular importance. The sphere of production is the sphere of production of surplus value. Thus surplus and profits are seen as captured by capitalists because of their ownership of the means of production. In the case of Kalecki, in Marxian terminology, the sphere of exchange is elevated relative to the sphere of production. The conflict is over income shares. In a number of papers, some of which are discussed in Chapters 2 and 6 above, Kalecki focused on the role of trade unions is raising money wages in periods of low unemployment and then discussed how far a rise in money wages would lead to a rise in real wages. Discussion of the conflict over the intensity of labour is noticeable by its absence, although as we noted above this may be because Kalecki felt he had little to add to Marx's discussion. Kalecki's approach with its focus on the degree of monopoly in the sphere of exchange also means that in so far as any source of profits is implied, that source would appear to be the extent of control by capitalists over their markets, i.e. market power.

The differences between Kalecki and Marx may not be as great over these two aspects which we have just discussed as might appear at first sight. On an initial reading, it would appear that Kalecki saw profits as arising from monopoly positions within exchange relationships. In contrast, Marx viewed the source of surplus (and thereby profits) as the control by capitalists over the means of production, and the ability of capitalists thereby to extract a surplus from a labour force which is compelled to work for a living. However, Kalecki did not cast his discussion in terms of the underlying reasons for the existence of profits. But the proximate cause of profits is market power and market demand in the sense that the absence of market power and market demand for product leads to an absence of profits. In his discussion of financial markets (cf. pp. 101–6 above) Kalecki saw that there was a limited access to finance capital and thereby limited possibilities for people to become capitalists. He wrote that 'there is . . . [a] factor which is of decisive importance in limiting the size of a firm; the amount of entrepreneurial capital, i.e. the amount of capital owned by the firm', and that 'the most important prerequisite for becoming an entrepreneur is the *ownership* of capital' (Kalecki, 1954, pp. 91 and 95, italics in original). There are clear overtones here of the Marxian idea of a class monopoly over the means of production, and specifically in Kalecki's analysis there is limited access to finance capital and thereby to the ownership of productive capital.

The second broad area relates to the type of 'prices' used in the economic analysis. The type of exchange rates between goods which economic analysis has regarded as relevant can be divided into three groups. The first kind of prices is those which are often labelled market prices, and are seen as actual prices (within the context of the analysis) which influence the behaviour of economic agents. The agents themselves may set the prices (e.g. firms), influence their determination (e.g. collective bargaining) or may find the prices as effectively fixed as far as individual agents are concerned.[11] The second kind is long-run equilibrium prices. These are the prices which are predicted to arise when some specified process has been completed. Thus, in neo-classical economics, the process is the movement of factors of production until the point where conditions such as the equality of the marginal product of each factor in line of production is achieved. The nature of the equilibrium and the route by which it is reached is different, but nevertheless Marx often used long-run equilibrium prices, labelling them prices of production. These prices are those which arise when the rates of profit across industries have been equalised. These equilibrium prices (and particularly the prices of production) are often seen as 'centres of gravity' towards which market prices tend. The long run equilibrium prices (and the associated long run equilibrium position is often analysed on the basis that it represents the underlying position (or trend) in an economy.

The third type of exchange rate is that of values. For Marx, the value of a commodity is determined by the socially necessary labour embodied in it.

> Marx analyses economic relationships mainly in the value domain. . . . The value domain is purely an *analytic* construct and is unobservable. All commodities can be reduced to 'abstract labour' and economic relationships can be analysed in terms of values to go beyond the 'appearances' to the 'essence' or 'reality' of things (Junankar, 1982, p. 16).

There has, of course, been a very long and often bitter debate over the relationship between prices of production and values (the transformation problem), particularly the relationship between surplus value (measured in value terms) and profits (measured in terms of prices of production). There has been a further debate on whether analysis in terms of values is more fundamental than analysis in terms of prices of production, or whether analysis in terms of values is largely superfluous.[12] Kalecki's view could probably be summarised by saying that he regarded both analyses (in terms of values and prices of production) as superfluous, though for different reasons.

Much of the analysis of Marx (especially in *Capital*, Volume 1 and parts of Volume 3) was undertaken on the basis of commodities exchanging at their values. It is now generally agreed that the purpose of this approach was *not* the view that commodities *do* exchange at their values, but to highlight certain features of capitalism, particularly the source of profits. It is not necessary here to become involved in these debates. Instead, we need to note that

Kalecki and Marx diverged over which exchange rates were relevant. Kalecki used market prices, whereas Marx used prices of production and values. Kalecki's rejection of prices of production could be seen as arising from his general dislike of equilibrium analysis, especially of a long-run nature. The prices of production clearly relate to a long-run equilibrium where rates of profit have become equalised. Kalecki's rejection of values (as noted above) was based on his view of their metaphysical nature.

These two broad areas of difference are reflected in the discussion of possible evolution of the rate of profit in a capitalist economy. For the purpose of this discussion, we write the rate of profit as

$$(\pi/K) = (\pi/Y).(Y/Y^*).(Y^*/K)$$

where π is profits, Y output Y^* capacity output, K the capital stock. We do not for the present say how these variables are measured.

For Kalecki, the first of these ratios would be determined by the degree of monopoly. The degree of monopoly was generally expected by Kalecki to rise over time as market power rose (cf. p. 87). The second ratio would probably have no particular trend although variations in this ratio over the course of the trade cycle would be an important element in cyclical variations in the rate of profit. The third ratio could be expected to fall, when technical progress is capital encouraging/labour saving. Throughout, these variables would be measured in money terms using market prices. Kalecki said little about the measurement of the capital stock and that measurement is notorious for the difficulties which it raises. It would be reasonable to say that Kalecki would regard K as a measure of the productive potential of an economy and would probably seek to measure the capital stock in terms of its costs of production (with allowance for subsequent inflation) with depreciation mainly accounted for by scrapping (cf. discussion on socialist economies below). It was seen above that Kalecki separated price and investment decisions. In this context that means that movements in (π/Y) and in (Y^*/K) are also separated out. But we could anticipate that technical progress would tend to push down the ratio Y^*/K, and any rise in the degree of monopoly (rise in profitability) might further encourage investment. Thus from Kalecki's approach there is no clear prediction on the course of the rate of profit but we can see that a rising degree of monopoly is required to offset any tendency towards falling capacity utilisation and rising capital intensity of production if the rate of profit is not to decline.

Marx's discussion in this area, under the heading of the law of the tendential fall in the rate of profit (title of Part III of Marx, 1981), has been the subject of much discussion.[13]

In terms of the formula given above, Marx did not discuss the second (so implicitly assuming no specific trend in capacity utilisation) and focused on the first and the third ratios. There are three aspects of Marx's discussion to which we draw attention in order to make contrasts with Kalecki's approach.

The first is that Marx's definition of the rate of profit is $s/c+v = e/q+1$, where s is total surplus value, c constant capital, v variable capital, e the rate of exploitation ($=s/v$), and q the organic composition of capital ($=c/v$), with all variables measured in value terms.[14] The capital term is thus measured as advances for a production period, consisting of materials, depreciation of fixed capital etc. (constant capital) and payments for labour time (variable capital).

The second aspect of Marx's discussion of the evolution of the rate of profit calculated the relevant variables in terms of values rather than prices of production or market prices (Marx, 1981, Part III). Marx saw the rate of profit calculated using values as the more fundamental rate of profit, even though it would be the rate of profit in terms of prices of production which by definition was the rate equalised through the process of competition. Kalecki might well (as others have) raised the point that both the rate of profit in value terms and the rate in prices of production terms are not observed in the market by capitalists, and it will be the market rate of profit which governs capitalists' decisions and actions. It can also be noted here that the transformation problem raises its head again here on the relationship between the value rate of profit and the prices of production rate.

The third aspect is that Marx expected the first term to rise over time as a result of increasing rate of exploitation but for the third term to decline over time as a consequence of labour saving technological progress. But Marx postulated that the overall effect would be for a decline in the rate of profit. In essence Marx saw labour saving technical change as leading to a rise in the rate of exploitation, but that whilst labour saving technical change was not subject to any upper limit the rate of exploitation was. Thus eventually the rate of profit would decline. However, there were a number of counteracting factors to the tendency of the rate of profit to decline. Marx (1981, Chapter 14) discussed these under the headings of more intense exploitation of labour, reduction of wages below their value, cheapening of the elements of constant capital, the relative surplus population, foreign trade and the increase in share capital.

We do not have space (nor is it central to our purpose) to discuss the status which Marx attached to the law of tendency of profit rate to decline. We can point to two similarities in the treatments of Kalecki and Marx. Both saw, albeit for different reasons, the ratio of profits to national income tending to rise over time and the capital intensity of production tending to rise. However, Marx placed more emphasis on the importance of the joint outcome of these two forces as the decline in the rate of profit, than Kalecki did. Indeed, Kalecki did not seek to forecast the overall effect. Second, both saw that during a trade cycle, it would be a decline in the rate of profit which would be an important trigger in the downswing. Here again the mechanism was somewhat different. Kalecki saw the decline in the rate of profit during the trade cycle as arising from interaction of (in the short term) constant degree of monopoly and rising capital stock. In contrast Marx saw the decline in the rate of profit as arising from the general downward tendency.

The third area of difference to which we now turn relates to wage determination and the influence of trade unions on wages. For Marx, 'the value of labour power is determined by the value of the means of subsistence habitually required by the average worker. The quantity of the means of subsistence required is given at any particular epoch in any particular society, and can therefore be treated as a constant magnitude' (Marx, 1976). 'Wages are the prices of the commodity labour-power ... the long term fluctuations of wages is function of the changes in the value of labour-power' (Mandel, 1976). Wages are discussed in value-term, and there is again the question of the relationship between wages in those terms and wages expressed in terms of prices of production (even when the bundle of goods used to define the subsistence wage is the same in the two cases). The movements of actual wages around the value of labour-power depends on the general state of demand for labour. 'Taking them as a whole, the general movement of wages are exclusively regulated by the expansion and contraction of the industrial reserve army, and this in turn corresponds to the periodic alternations of the industrial cycle' (Marx, 1976, p. 790).

Rowthorn (1980), Chapter 7 discusses Marx's changing views on wages, and we draw on that discussion here. Rowthorn distinguishes between the cost of production (of labour) and traditional life-style as determinants of wages, and argues that Marx confused the two concepts. He further argues that whilst Marx adopted a 'subsistence' approach, there is the question of whether subsistence is to be interpreted as absolute impoverishment or as traditional life-style. Rowthorn argues that in his early writings (in the 1840s) Marx adopted the absolute impoverishment view, but in later writings moved to adopt a traditional life-style view where that view could change over time in response to experience of workers.

Kalecki viewed it as likely that the degree of monopoly would tend to rise over time as concentration and centralisation proceeded. A rise in the degree of monopoly leads, *ceteris paribus*, to a fall in the real wage. But this is only a *ceteris paribus* prediction, and the general tenor of Kalecki's approach would suggest that real wages would rise alongside productivity, though perhaps not as fast as productivity, and the trend in real wages would be modified by what was happening to imported prices relative to domestic prices (cf. equation (8.1) above). However, as seen above (pp. 113–15) in a number of papers (and particularly in Kalecki, 1971a, Chapter 14), Kalecki emphasised the role of trade unions in modifying the degree of monopoly. In particular, he argued that an aggressive money wage policy by unions could have the effect of raising real wages by forcing a reduction in the degree of monopoly on firms. Thus the power of trade unions is seen as one of the factors influencing the mark-up of price over costs, and thereby the real wage.

There is the closely related question of whether trade unions are able to influence the course of real wages. Trade unions were better organised and more extensive when Kalecki was writing as compared with Marx's times, and their views may differ for that reason. Kalecki thought (cf. Chapter 7 above) that trade unions would tend to raise money wages after periods of sustained high levels of employment, with some possible impact on real wages. But any impact would depend on the lags of prices behind wages (so that the impact would be temporary) and/or on persistent pressure by trade unions on money wages which eventually modifies the degree of monopoly. An important ingredient in Kalecki's approach is the notion that the real wage is effectively determined in the product market (rather than the labour market). In this case, trade unions' ability to raise real wages depends on persistent upward pressure on money wages such that firms become unable to pass on these wages increases as prices increases, thereby reducing the degree of monopoly.

In the case of Marx, Rowthorn concluded that 'in the main argument of *Capital*, unions have no direct effect on wages, whose movement is for the most part determined automatically and competitively by supply and demand. This does not mean that workers are helpless and can do nothing to improve their situation – Marx himself points out they can affect the hours, intensity and conditions of work'. However, in *Wages, Price and Profit* Marx focused on the

> Question of how trade unions influence wages. By confining the analysis contained in these two works, one can arrive at a fairly comprehensive picture of how the activities of trade unions are conditioned and constrained by the wider laws of capital accumulation. Trade unions can certainly influence wages, and more generally the length and intensity of the working day or conditions of work. But their ability to do so depends upon economic circumstances, and in particular upon conditions in the labour market . . . [t]he greater is the reserve army of labour the less able are trade unions to achieve their objectives although the link is not a purely mechanical one, for a militant consciousness and good organisation can do much to offset the debilitating effects of unemployment on union power (Rowthorn, 1980, p. 216).

The differences between Kalecki and Marx in this area are in part differences of emphasis. The previous discussion has indicated Kalecki's emphasis on the product markets and Marx's emphasis on the production process, and those differences of emphasis are reflected here. However, for both authors gains for the workers by trade unions would not be easily achieved and would require good organisation and militancy.

The fourth area of difference relates to the concepts of competition and monopoly and their relative importance. We can begin with the remark that whilst Marx was analysing competitive capitalism (competitive in the sense of rivalry between a relative large number of firms), he foresaw that competition (in a structural sense) carried the seeds of its own destruction, through a process of concentration and centralisation. This leads to a decline in the number of firms. The question remains, though, whether that structural change in the number of firms leads to changes in the behaviour and performance of firms. The answer which would seem to be implicit in Kalecki (and made explicit in the Kaleckian approach of Cowling (1982)) is that structural change does lead to changes, such as increased market power, higher profits, etc. The alternative view expressed by, for example, Clifton (1977) is that the evolution of technologically advanced firms has increased the extent of rivalry and competition. The reasons for this include a better awareness by such firms of profit opportunities, ability to move into high profit areas through being geographically and otherwise mobile. The analysis of the monopoly stage of capitalism was not developed by Marx and thus some of the differences between Marx and Kalecki; in this area, it may simply result from Marx analysing the competitive stage and Kalecki the monopoly stage of capitalism.

However, Marx thought that the trend towards concentration and centralisation would have only a limited impact on the rate of exploitation and the rate of profit. The increased centralisation and concentration would themselves arise from the nature of technical progress favouring labour saving process and economies of scale. But the effect of concentration and centralisation *per se* would involve the redistribution of the surplus between sectors rather than raising the level of surplus, redistribution profits/surplus towards those sectors where concentration has increased and away from those sectors where concentration is unchanged.

A monopoly price for certain commodities simply transfers a portion of the profit made by the other commodity producers to the commodities with the monopoly price. Indirectly, there is a local disturbance in the distribution of surplus-value among the various spheres of production, but this leaves unaffected the limit of the surplus-value itself. ... The limits within which monopoly price affects the normal regulations of commodity prices are firmly determined and can be precisely calculated.

However, this is subject to the large *caveat* that '[i]t could press wages down below the value of labour power, but only if they previously stood above the physical minimum. In this case, the monopoly price is paid by deduction from real wages ... and from the profits of other capitalists' (Marx, 1981, p. 1001).

Kalecki argued that

> changes in the degree of monopoly are not only of decisive importance for the distribution of income between workers and capitalists, but in some instances for the distribution of income within the capitalist class as well. Thus, the rise in the degree of monopoly caused by the growth of big corporations results in a relative shift of income to industries dominated by such corporations from other industries (Kalecki, 1971a, pp. 51–2).

The implication of this statement is that a rise in industrial concentration would lead to a rise in profits share as well as a shift in profits towards those sectors where industrial concentration had risen most.

Thus the differences between Kalecki and Marx in this respect are not only that the former was analysing the monopoly stage and the latter the competitive stage of capitalism but that Kalecki placed greater weight on the impact of monopolisation on profitability and on market power reducing real wages.

Kalecki's degree of monopoly approach focused on the impact of a particular industrial structure at a specific time on the price–cost margin in that industry. Industrial structure involves elements of competition and monopoly, of rivalry and collusion, and Kalecki used the term 'degree of monopoly' to summarise these (and other) factors. In a sense a term such as the degree of rivalry or competition could have been used to represent the same phenomenon, although such terms carry different connotations. The stress in Kalecki's writings is on the monopoly–collusive elements rather than the competition-rivalry elements. Lipinski (1977), for example, noted that Kalecki in his studies on Polish industries 'always tried to detect monopolistic tendencies and linkages and the international contradictions they were breeding'. More generally, Kalecki can be seen as within the broad tradition of continental writers who have stressed oligopolistic and monopolistic elements, in contrast to the more Anglo-Saxon tradition of stressing the importance (and often the benefits) of competition.

Competition and rivalry between firms is largely seen in Kalecki's approach as restricting the degree of monopoly, and thereby the mark-up. What is largely omitted in Kalecki, but which plays an important part in Marx, is the competitive struggle between firms, and the effect which that has on attempts to reduce costs, on innovation and investment. In Kalecki's writings, there is a separation between price–cost decisions, and investment decisions. For price–cost decisions, the focus is at the firm level, building up to the industry and then economy level. Investment is analysed at the aggregate level (thereby bringing in aggregate features such as availability of finance). In a sense, the price–cost decisions (with the level of output) influence the volume of profits and thereby investment, whereas investment is not analysed in terms of any feedback effect on price–cost decisions. Thus the competitive pressures on firms which Marx stressed, where as firms struggle with one another over markets and profits, they make investments as a means of reducing costs, are largely overlooked by Kalecki. Thus Kalecki saw investment decisions as responsive to the availability of internal finance, changes in the rate of profit, and as such undertaken for profit enhancing reasons. But the pressures on firms to undertake investment are not featured in Kalecki's analysis.

> Moreover, the development of capitalist production makes it necessary to increase the amount of capital laid out in a given industrial undertaking, and competition subordinates every individual capitalist to the immanent laws of capitalist production, as external and coercive laws. It compels him to keep extending his capital, so as to preserve it, and he can only extend it by means of progressive accumulation (Marx, 1976, p. 739).

Here again we could regard Kalecki analysing investment demand in the monopoly stage of capitalism in which whilst firms still pursue profits there are not the same competitive pressures on them to invest as there would be in the competitive stage, though there is some element of new investment capturing profits from previous investments in Kalecki's last discussion on investment (Kalecki, 1968b, pp. 60–3 above). The extensions and modifications to Kalecki's approach found in Steindl (1952), Chapter 13 serve to formalise the idea that investment incentives are predicted to be less under monopoly than under competition.

Classical economists, including Marx, saw the movement of

capital in pursuit of profits as the major force in the equalisation of the rates of profits and the emergence of a competitive equilibrium (which means only that the rate of profit has been equalised across industries). In so far as Kalecki discussed the movement of capital between high profit rate industries into low profit rate industries he focused on the effects which the inward movement of capital would have on capacity utilisation in the high profit rate industries (cf. Kalecki, 1942a). There could be a further tendency towards an equalisation of profitability through the operation of trade unions in pushing harder for higher wages in high profit industries which unions saw as being able to afford wage increases (e.g. Kalecki, 1971a, Chapter 14).

The final area of difference which we briefly examine (and which is not closely related to previous areas of difference) relates to the nature and significance of money.[15] It is clear that the differences here between Kalecki and Marx arise from the different times in which they wrote, with the assumptions about the nature of money reflecting its predominant form in their respective eras.

Marx (1976) wrote that 'throughout this work I assume that gold is the money commodity, for the sake of simplicity' (p. 188). Paper money is seen simply as replacing gold; 'paper money is a symbol of gold, a symbol of money' (Marx, 1976, p. 255). An important attribute of gold is that it is a producible commodity, and as such like other producible commodities has a value in terms of the socially necessary labour to produce a unit of it. The relationship between the value of gold and the value of other commodities is then determined, so that if we treat gold as money (and hence as the unit of account of numeraire) then the price level of other commodities is determined.[16] Thus, with the price level thereby determined, the velocity of circulation seen as historically determined, and the level of transactions set by aggregate demand the equation $MV = PT$ can be used to determine the volume of money in active circulation. There is the law

that the quantity of the circulating medium is determined by the sum of the prices of the commodities in circulation, and the average velocity of the circulation of money. . . . The illusion that it is, on the contrary, prices which are determined by the quantity of the circulating medium, and that the latter for its part depends on the amount of monetary material which happens to be present in a country, had its roots in the absurd hypothesis adopted by the original representatives of this view that commodities enter into the process of circulation without a price, and money enters without a value (Marx, 1976, pp. 119–220).

Kalecki's interpretation of the quantity theory of money was discussed above (pp. 98–9). It can be seen there that Kalecki regarded the money supply as consisting of paper money and bank deposits and determined by banking policy and the action of banks. The equation $MV = PT$ was interpreted by Kalecki as determining the velocity of circulation (under normal circumstances outside of hyperinflation), and since that velocity depended on short term nominal rate of interest, thereby the rate of interest was determined.

Thus it can be seen that neither Kalecki nor Marx accepted the standard interpretation of the quantity theory whereby the volume of money determines price level. Kalecki saw the velocity of circulation and Marx saw the quantity of money in active circulation as the variable which adjusted to ensure equality between MV and PT.

Conclusion

A major purpose of this chapter has been to indicate the extent to which the general approach of Marx (particularly on the importance of class) permeated the thinking of Kalecki. It can be further seen that even when Kalecki and Marx took divergent views (e.g. to some extent over technical change) this arose from common concerns, and those common concerns often in a sense unite them (and others) in contrast to the concerns of neo-classical economics. However, there are a number of areas (especially over value theory, role of competition) where there are substantial divergences between Kalecki and Marx.

Appendix: Values, Prices of Production and Degree of Monopoly Prices

In this appendix we indicate some of the differences between Marx, neo-Ricardians and Kalecki over price, wage and profit determination using a Sraffa-type framework. It must be stressed that in doing so we are allowing the neo-Ricardians to set the terms of discussion, whereas there are many aspects of the work of Marx and Kalecki which are overlooked in this treatment. The purpose is the narrow one of highlighting differences in the area of price formation, etc. We draw heavily on the presentation of Pasinetti (1977), Appendix to Chapter 5. This appendix is highly condensed, with the purpose of highlighting differences in one specific area. For further discussion on the Sraffa-framework, see, for example, Pasinetti (1977), Howard (1983).

The production technique of an economic system is represented by the matrix of inter-industry coefficients **A** (i.e. entry a_{ij} indicates the amount of commodity i used in the production of one unit of commodity j), and **a** is a vector of labour inputs (i.e. a_j is amount of labour used to produce one unit of commodity j). Labour is assumed to be homogeneous, and receive a money wage w. Pasinetti defines an ideal wage rate w^* as the wage which would result when workers receive the whole net product. This is given by the solution to the equation:

$$\mathbf{v}.\mathbf{A} + w^*.\mathbf{a} = \mathbf{v} \tag{A8.1}$$

which has a solution for **v** in terms of w^*

$$\mathbf{v} = \mathbf{a}.(\mathbf{I} - \mathbf{A})^{-1}w^* \tag{A8.2}$$

The vector **v** is embodied labour, i.e. value of a commodity in Marx's terms. Suppose we can define a subsistence real wage in terms of a vector of commodities, denoted by **d**, and then the subsistence real wage in value terms in **v**.**d** which is only a proportion δ of w^*. Pasinetti shows that when there is exploitation (i.e δ less than 1) then the equations above can be written to give:

$$\mathbf{v}\mathbf{A} + \mathbf{v}\mathbf{d}\mathbf{a}(1 + s) = \mathbf{v} \tag{A8.3}$$

where $s = (1 - \delta)/\delta$ is the rate of exploitation.

The set of equations in (A8.3) involve $n + 1$ unknowns (n entries in the vector **v** plus s) and n equations. This allows the solution of the equations for $n - 1$ relative values and s, treating commodity i, say, as the numeraire so that $v_i = 1$. The wage = **v**.**d** is then given in terms of v_i.

For the prices-of-production system, with an equalised rate of profit we have:

$$(\mathbf{p}.\mathbf{A}. + w.\mathbf{a}) \, (1 + \pi) = \mathbf{p} \tag{A8.4}$$

where π is the rate of profit, and p the vector of prices of production. If, again, there is a subsistence wage then that wage is given (in terms of prices of production) as **p**.**d**. After substitution, we have:

$$(\mathbf{p}.\mathbf{A} + \mathbf{p}.\mathbf{d}.\mathbf{a}.) \, (1 + \pi) = \mathbf{p} \tag{A8.5}$$

Here again there are n equations involving $n + 1$ unknowns which permit the solution for $n - 1$ prices plus the rate of profit in terms of the numeraire price (say $p_i = 1$).

The transformation problem relates to the relationship between prices of production (p) and values (v), and specifically to whether the valuation of output and the rate of profit will be the same under the two sets of prices and whether total surplus value and total profits are equal. The now widely accepted conclusion is that in general these equalities will not hold (Pasinetti, 1977, Appendix to Chapter Five; Steedman, 1977).

We can now derive a degree of monopoly set of prices for this production system. However, for these prices it is necessary to work with an amended matrix of inter-industry coefficients. The inputs for any particular line of production can be divided into material inputs (fully used up within the period of production) and capital inputs (partially used up within the period of production). In Kalecki's approach, it is only the former which are relevant to pricing decisions. Thus we introduce a modified matrix $\mathbf{A}^*$, in which coefficients in $\mathbf{A}$ which relate to capital inputs have been replaced by a zero. Further, denote by $\mathbf{E}$ a matrix with column i having entries $1 + e_i$ where e_i is the mark-up over direct costs in sector i. Then the degree of monopoly price vector, $\mathbf{r}$, is given by:

$$(\mathbf{r}.\mathbf{A}^* + w.\mathbf{a}).\ \mathbf{E} = \mathbf{r} \tag{A8.6}$$

and hence:

$$\mathbf{r} = (\mathbf{I} - \mathbf{A}^*.\mathbf{E})^{-1}.w.\mathbf{a}.\mathbf{E} \tag{A8.7}$$

This is a system of n equations with $n + 1$ unknowns (n entries in $\mathbf{r}$ plus w). If commodity i is again treated as the numeraire (hence $r_i = 1$), then the equations can be solved for $n - 1$ prices and wages. Further calculations would enable real wages, profit shares and profit rates (if capital stock and volume of output are known) to be found.

There are two differences between (A8.5) and (A8.7) which need to be highlighted. The first is that at the level of price determination (at least as represented here) the prices of production approach takes the real wage as given and then solves for the prices and the rate of profit. In the Kalecki degree of monopoly approach, the mark-up is taken as given (at this juncture in the analysis) and solves for prices and wages. More generally, within the neo-Ricardian approach it is often argued that either the (equalised) rate of profit or the real wage can be treated as predetermined, at this stage of the analysis, with the rate of profit or real wage set in some general sense by the balance of power between workers and capitalists.

The second difference is that between $\mathbf{A}$ and $\mathbf{A}^*$, which partly relates to which costs are relevant. In the prices of production approach, the view is adopted that inputs (including materials, capital equipment and labour) are paid for at the beginning of a production period, and the rate of profit is applied to all those costs. In the Kalecki approach, it is only variable (direct) costs which are seen as relevant. Whereas in the prices of production approach, the rate of profit and the implied capital stock can be calculated, in the Kalecki approach the profits in each line of production would have to be compared with the capital stock used in that line of production to generate the rate of profit in that line. Further, there is in a sense a full capacity view in the prices of production approach in that the capital stock is indicated in terms of inputs actually used whereas in the Kalecki approach the capital stock is taken as outside the price framework.

In discussion of the transformation problem, Pasinetti (1977) wrote that

> (t)he fundamental diversity lies in the different ways in which that part of the net product which is not paid as wages is distributed among the various industries. In the 'value system' it is distributed (as 'surplus value') in proportion to the wages advanced to the workers (or 'variable capital'); in the 'price of production system' it is distributed (as profits) in proportion to the sum of 'variable capital' and 'constant capital'.

The Kalecki approach could be seen as allocating the 'surplus' on the basis of the degrees of monopoly in each industry and the sum of labour and material costs (direct costs). There is no particular reason to think that the resulting ratios of profits to capital will be equalised across industries. Even if the degrees of monopoly were equal across industries, then in general apart from a constant ratio of direct costs to capital stock the rates of profit will differ. In a sense this was one of the points raised by Whitman (1942) in his attack on the degree of monopoly approach, and it is an argument which has continued to be raised.

It should be stressed that the above is an exercise only in deriving a consistent set of prices under specified assumptions. There are numerous items (system of production, subsistence real wage, degrees of monopoly) which are taken as given here, but which are the subject of analysis elsewhere.

Notes to Chapter 8

1. Patinkin (1982) observes that Lange in his lectures at the University of Chicago in 1945 (which Patinkin attended) 'seems to have given at least as much emphasis to the Marxian connection of Kalecki's writings as to the Keynesian . . .'.
2. The term 'vision' is used here in the sense used in Schumpeter (1954) of a general framework of thought which forms the background of an economist's analysis.
3. One reason for leaving aside that issue is that the range of views encompassed by the term Marxist can be rather wide. It is clear, however, that whilst many Marxists (and more so many who consider the analysis of Marx to have many insights but would not regard themselves as Marxists) have a high regard for Kalecki's work, others have strongly attacked it for departing significantly from Marx's own work. 'Alexander Erlich has, however, informed me that Kalecki's 1933 booklet was severely criticised by two members of the Polish communist party, Alexander Rajchman . . . and Samuel Fogelson, who charged Kalecki both with technical errors and with expressing non-Marxian

views. Kalecki wrote a reply (1933c) to Rajchman's criticism which led to further sharp exchanges between them' (Patinkin, 1982). The 1933 booklet referred to was eventually translated as Kalecki (1966). The emphasis on the failure of effective demand sufficient to secure full employment, which also arose in the work of Rosa Luxemburg, led to suspicion amongst some Marxists. Kalecki was also attacked as a non-Marxist in the mid to late 1960s as part of the political repression in Poland. For further discussion on this see Feiwel (1975), pp. 451–2.

In the light of the differences discussed in the text between the work of Kalecki and Marx, it is not surprising that those who adhere to a strict interpretation of Marx should find themselves in intellectual disagreement with Kalecki.

4. For some discussion by Kalecki on this point see Kalecki (1965) in which he discussed the relationship between econometrics and historical materialism.

5. We emphasise the word 'could' in that sentence since we have no way of really knowing how Marx would have analysed twentieth century capitalism.

6. In a chapter headed Investment and Income (in Kalecki, 1939) he briefly discussed the relationship between his ideas, those of Marx and of Rosa Luxemburg in this respect. After a discussion on the derivation of the equality between investment and savings, Kalecki argued that

the above equations are contained in the famous Marxian scheme of 'extended reproduction'. Marx even considers the questions of how to provide 'means' for increased expenditure on investment. It must be added, however, that the problems discussed here are treated by Marx from a rather special point of view. He is interested in finding out, with the help of exchange equations, the pace of investment in investment and consumption goods industries respectively, which is necessary in order secure a steady expansion of output. (The rates of profit in both divisions of industry are assumed to be equal through-out and on this basis the process of expansion is constructed so as to make investment in each, at the end of every 'production-exchange cycle', equal to its saving so that there is no 'shift of capital' from consumption to investment goods or conversely.) He does not pay attention to the problem of what happens if investment is inadequate to secure the moving equilibrium, and therefore does not approach the idea of the key position of investment in the determination of the level of total output and employment.

Exactly the reverse attitude is represented by one of his eminent pupils, Rosa Luxemburg. In her *Akkumulation des Kapitals* she stressed the point that, if capitalists are saving, their profits can be 'realized' if a corresponding amount is spent by them on investment. She, however, considered impossible the persistence of net investment (at least in the long run) in a closed capitalist economy; thus, according to her, it is only the existence of exports to the non-capitalist countries which allows for the expansion of a capitalist system. The theory cannot be accepted as a whole, but the necessity of covering the 'gap of saving' by home investment or exports was outlined by her perhaps more clearly than anywhere else before the publication of Mr Keynes's *General Theory* (Kalecki, 1939, pp. 45–6).

7. Kowalik (1964) notes that 'though Kalecki was, in the 'thirties closely connected with the leftist socialist movement . . . he was criticized from the political standpoint by some Marxists. The tendency of suppressing anything that had a touch of "Luxemburgism" prevailing then among Marxists might have been the reason for these criticisms.'

8. Steedman (1977) writing on the debates arising out of the work of Sraffa and its relationship to Marx argues that there are those who

> allege (incorrectly) that those engaged in the derivation of such propositions either ignore or even deny many of Marx's essential insights. The usual basis for such allegations is the mere absence from the arguments involved of lengthy rehearsals of Marx's basic ideas, as if one necessarily denied the truth of all those propositions whose truth one does not explicitly affirm!

Kalecki was not usually in the business of affirming propositions for the sake of it.

9. For further discussion, see Harris (1976).

10. In conversation, Jerzy Osiatyński has told me that Kalecki did regard them as important but that Kalecki felt that Marx had adequately dealt with that topic.

11. These market prices may themselves be in some sense equilibrium prices. For example, in the traditional monopoly analysis, the firm set a price above marginal cost based on the perceived elasticity of demand. That price is both an actual price (in the context of the analysis) in that it is attained and seen as an equilibrium price (in the sense that the firm has achieved its optimal outcome) with its given perceptions. However, this notion of equilibrium applies only at the individual firm level and not at the economy level. Further, the equilibrium has only arisen in the sense that one set of agents (monopolists) has achieved its objectives, but says nothing about any other agents, in particular consumers and workers.

12. Some references which cover the debates indicated in these two sentences include: Steedman (1977), Fine and Harris (1979), Steedman *et al.* (1981), Rowthorn (1974). For summaries see Desai (1979), Chapters 2 and 3, and Part II, Howard and King (1976), Chapter 5, Junankar (1982), Chapters 2 and 3.

13. On the law of the tendency of the rate of profit to fall see Marx (1981), Part 3, and for summaries of the debates see Steedman (1977), Chapter 9, Desai (1979), Chapter 19, Howard and King (1975), Chapter 6, Junankar (1982), Chapter 6.

14. Fine and Harris (1979) distinguish three versions of the composition of capital, namely:

   (i) the technical composition of capital, as the ratio of commodities used as constant capital to labour power, where both are measured in physical terms. Whilst this ratio may have some intuitive appeal, it can only be measured unambiguously when there is only one kind of constant capital;

   (ii) organic composition of capital, where the ratio indicated in (i) is measured in terms of historical (constant) values;

   (iii) value composition of capital where the ratio is measured in terms of current values.

15. Our main aim in this section is a comparison between Kalecki and Marx on the nature of money and the interpretation of the quantity theory relationship. For a discussion of the relationship between the more general ideas of Marx on money and its circulation, etc. and those of Keynes, see Junankar (1982), Chapter 7.

16. Marx's discussion in this area (especially in Volume 1 of *Capital*) is against the background of the assumption that commodities are exchanging at their values.

9
Kalecki and Keynes: Comparisons and Contrasts

Introduction

The names of Kalecki and Keynes are often linked together as the discoverers (or re-discoverers) around about the same time of some important ideas such as the principle of effective demand, the importance of investment as a component of aggregate demand. In Kalecki's case in a number of articles over the period 1933–6, and in Keynes's case expressed mainly in Keynes (1936).[1] It is clear that there was no personal contact between the two men prior to late 1936 nor 'did either of them exert any intellectual influence over the other during that period [prior to 1936]' (Patinkin, 1982, words in parenthesis added).[2] To the extent to which the ideas of Kalecki overlapped with those of Keynes (on which more below) it is probable that Kalecki could claim priority of publication by up to three years. However, Keynes is usually given pride of place over Kalecki as reflected in, for example, the description of Kalecki as a left-Keynesian and the use of the term post-Keynesian to describe the broad alterntive to the neo-classical orthodoxy. The earlier chapters of this book have set out the ideas of Kalecki on capitalist economies, and in this chapter we seek to highlight the differences between those ideas and those of Keynes both in the area of macroeconomics and in approaches to economics (theory and policy) generally. A major purpose of this chapter is to argue that the differences between Kalecki and Keynes are substantial, such that their approaches should be separately developed and not conflated together, although there may be some places where there could be a useful cross-fertilisation of ideas.

The general idea that Kalecki could claim priority of publication over Keynes and that his approach was in some ways superior to that of Keynes has gradually developed and spread in the years since 1936. In his review of Keynes (1936) (published in Polish, and now translated in Targetti and Kinda-Hass (1982)), Kalecki indicated in two footnotes that 'an analogous idea about the demand for and supply of capital has been given by myself' (which refers to the idea that investment 'forces' an equal amount of savings, leaving the rate of interest as a monetary phenomenon, see pp. 97–8 above), and 'I have also shown the independence of production from the movement of nominal wages'. This appears to be the only extent to which Kalecki at that stage made public claims for his own priority of publication.[3] There are a number of places (e.g. Kalecki, 1943a, p. 50, fn. 1) where Kalecki makes reference to his own independent discovery of some of the ideas of Keynes. The best known is his brief statement in the introduction to Kalecki (1971a) where he said that '(t)he first part includes three papers published in 1933, 1934, and 1935 in Polish before Keynes's *General Theory* appeared, and containing, I believe, its essentials . . .'.

The review of Keynes (1936) which Kalecki wrote clearly shows that Kalecki had developed his own framework of macroeconomics within which he could interpret the *General Theory*. It is interesting to note that Kalecki highlighted the role of investment in forcing savings, the rate of interest as a monetary phenomenon and money wages (rather than real wages) determined in the labour market. This can be compared with Robinson's view of the Keynesian revolution quoted below. It can also be contrasted with the parts of Keynes (1936) highlighted by Hicks (1936) in his review paralleled in Hicks (1937) and the development of the IS–LM approach). Hicks focused on the marginal efficiency of capital and investment (in a much less critical manner than Kalecki), the liquidity preference approach to the demand for money and the role of expectations about the future.

Lange (1939) (cited in Patinkin, 1982, p. 60) and Zweig (1944), p. 167 in discussions on Polish economists in the interwar period indicate a close affinity between Kalecki's discoveries and Keynes's.[4] Austin Robinson in his memoir of Keynes makes similar suggestions when he wrote that 'Kalecki was independently approaching the same goal' (Robinson, 1947).

Klein (1951), Robinson (1964, 1976a, b, 1977a) and Johansen

(1978) and others have made stronger claims on Kalecki's behalf. These are that Kalecki had not only priority of publication but also developed a superior macroeconomics. For example, Klein (1951) wrote that 'after having re-examined Kalecki's theory of the business cycle, I have decided that he actually created a system that contains everything of importance in the Keynesian system, in addition to other contributions'. In a footnote to this sentence, Klein refers to Kalecki (1935b) thereby implying priority of publication for Kalecki. After noting that Kalecki lacked 'Keynes's reputation or ability to draw world-wide attention', he indicates that Kalecki's model is superior in being explicitly dynamic, taking income distribution into account and making the distinction between investment orders and investment outlays. Johansen (1978) wrote that '[t]he basic fact is that Kalecki developed in some respects in a more advanced form, some of the basic elements of "Keynesian" macroeconomics before Keynes . . .'.

The question of priority of publication involves questions of what were the key ideas and were they original? Joan Robinson in her introduction to Kalecki (1966) (American edition) argued that the Keynesian revolution 'may be summarized in the propositions that the rate of saving is governed by the rate of investment, that the level of prices is governed by the level of money wage rates, and that the level of interest rates is governed by the supply and demand for money'. This is significant because it corresponds closely to the features of Keynes (1936) which Kalecki stressed in his review of that book, and which Kalecki indicated he had put forward earlier. In a chapter headed Anticipations of the General Theory, Klein (1952) argued that Keynes

> certainly said something quite different as compared with what most other economists were saying at the time, but it is not difficult to find in the literature of economics many of the same ideas earlier expressed. In fact, somewhere in literature every element of the Keynesian system was at some time discussed. But no single theorist ever worked out a complete and determinate model based on (1) the propensity to consume (save), (2) the marginal efficiency of capital, and (3) liquidity preference.

In a footnote to this section which is included in the second edition Klein says that 'this should be amended to take account of Kalecki's prior, complete model'.

Patinkin (1982) in considering the claims made for Kalecki and for the Stockholm School to have anticipated Keynes adopts a somewhat different approach. He first seeks to establish what the original contribution of Keynes was, and then to investigate whether Kalecki and the Stockholm School could be said to have anticipated Keynes. Patinkin also argues that for an idea advanced by an author to be regarded as a major original advance, it must not only be original in the sense of having no predecessors (if even the idea had been largely forgotten) but also must be realised as an important idea by the author at the time. On these criteria, Patinkin argued that the original feature of Keynes (1936) was a theory of effective demand which 'in more formal terms is concerned not only with the mathematical solution of the equilibrium equation $F(Y) = Y$, but with demonstrating the stability of this equilibrium as determined by the dynamic adjustment equation $dY/dt = \Phi[F(Y) - Y]$ where $\Phi' > 0$'. In this quote Y stands for the output and $F(Y)$ is the aggregate demand function.[5]

On the question of whether Kalecki anticipated Keynes, Patinkin argues that on the basis of the original feature of Keynes (1936) which he identified, Kalecki cannot be considered as having antici- pated Keynes.[6] Since Kalecki's main concern in the 1930s was with business cycles and fluctuations, and since he did not generally deal with equilibrium outcomes (and hence not with disequilibrium adjustment mechanisms), this is not a surprising conclusion. This is recognised by Patinkin when he writes that

> my main reason for not considering Kalecki's theory to be an independent development of the General Theory is the one I have already emphasized: namely, that Kalecki's central message has to do not with the forces that generate equilibrium at low levels of output, but with forces that generate cycles of investment; more specifically, not with the feedback mechanism that equilibrates planned saving and investment via declines in output, but with cyclical behaviour of investment on the implicit assumption that there always exists equality between planned savings and invest- ment.[7]

There are many who would disagree with Patinkin's view on the nature of Keynes's original contribution and whether that contribu- tion was the important aspect of Keynes (1936). Indeed, discussion on those points have spawned an enormous literature. Our major purpose in this chapter is rather different from that of Patinkin; it is to compare the frameworks within which Kalecki and Keynes operated.

The themes which underlie this chapter are:

(i)   The work of Kalecki and Keynes should be treated on a par rather than placing Keynes in the leading role and Kalecki in the subordinate role. In the words of Johansen (1978) '[i]t is now usually considered as one of Kalecki's greatest achievements to have developed some of Keynes's most important ideas before Keynes. It is equally true if we turn this around and say that it was one of Keynes's greatest achievements to rediscover, independently, some of Kalecki's main macroeconomic ideas so shortly after Kalecki himself'.[8]

(ii) That although there are certain similarities in their work, notably the key role ascribed to investment nevertheless, there are major differences over the nature of the economy (e.g. competitive or oligopolistic) and over the construction of macroeconomic relations (e.g. investment function);

(iii) If (ii) is accepted, then the notion of linking together the ideas of Kalecki and Keynes loses some of its appeal, although it may be possible to graft the ideas of one on to the ideas of the other;

(iv) That questions of who anticipated whom on specific original ideas are not as important as consideration and evaluation of the alternative macroeconomic frameworks presented by the two authors.

In our discussion of Keynes's macroeconomics, we are concentrating on his views as expressed in the *General Theory* and the development thereof. Thus when the ideas expressed in Keynes (1936) appear to overturn previously expressed ideas (e.g. views on the nature of money as between Keynes (1930) and Keynes (1936)), we deal only with the ideas of Keynes (1936).

It could be argued that I am over-emphasising the differences between Kalecki and Keynes in that Kalecki himself did not see the differences as large. Joan Robinson described Kalecki's reaction to news of the publication of Keynes (1936) in the following way. Kalecki

began to read it (Keynes, 1936) – it was the book that he intended

to write. He thought, perhaps further on there would be something different. No, it was his book all the way. He said: 'I confess,
I became ill. Three days I lay in bed. Then I thought – Keynes is
better known than I am. These ideas will get across much quicker
with him and then we can get on to the interesting question, which
is of course the application of these theoretical ideas to policy-
making. Then I got up' (Robinson, 1976b).

There are reasons for doubting this report. Mrs Kalecki, who was
with Kalecki in Stockholm, wrote to Joan Robinson following this
article to say that she (Joan Robinson) had exaggerated the effect of
the receipt of Keynes's book on Kalecki. Mrs Kalecki indicates that
Kalecki was dismayed to find the similarities between Keynes's book
and his own proposed book, and may have felt ill but certainly did
not take to his bed for three days.[9] It is also clear from Kalecki's
review of Keynes (1936) that he felt that Keynes's treatment of the
key question of investment was unsatisfactory. Kowalik (1964),
which is based on Kalecki's dictated reminiscences, records that
'(w)hen he had already begun to dictate the book to his wife, he
received news of the appearance of a book by Keynes, solving
certain questions in a similar way' (italics added). These certain
questions would seem to be the active and changing nature of
investment and the adjustment of savings to the level of investment.
These are indeed areas of overlap between the ideas of Kalecki and
those of Keynes, but there are many other areas where they diverge.
　There is also some reason to doubt Joan Robinson's account of
Kalecki's reasons for not making bold claims for his own priority of
publication.

I do not confirm what Mrs Robinson ascribed to Michał namely:
that still in Stockholm he has made up his mind not to divulge his
pre-Keynesianism for some lofty reasons. Only later when in
London we considered the matter. Then we have come to the
conclusion that should he claim his priority he will rather
encounter disbelief. A stranger coming from Poland ... [could
not] stand up to Keynes, a personality with a well established
position and reputation. At the same time as is known his theory
was not presented in its entirety in one publication.
　I have to add that his priority after all was not a complete
secret. He had some reason to expect that on the occasion of

publishing his book *Essays in the Theory of Economic Fluctuations*
Keynes was to be persuaded to write an introduction to it. He was
supposed to mention then the author's priority to himself. This
has not materialised as Keynes became seriously ill.[10, 11]

General Differences Between Kalecki and Keynes

The social and particularly the intellectual backgrounds of Kalecki
and Keynes were quite different, and these differences flow over into
differences in their approaches to macroeconomics. Kalecki's background was described in Chapter 1. In contrast to Kalecki's social
background of something of an 'outsider', Keynes was born into a
family well-positioned on the British social ladder at a time when the
British empire was close to the height of its power.[12] He received
what was regarded as one of the best educations that money and
social position could obtain. After a degree in mathematics, Keynes
moved to economics and received his training at Cambridge, where
the dominant influence was the work of Marshall. Starting with
work on reform of the Indian currency and continuing through to
the *Treatise on Money* (Keynes, 1930) and beyond, most of Keynes's
academic work involved money and finance, as did some of his other
activities (e.g. Bursar of King's College, Cambridge).

The differences in background can be seen as related to three
major differences in their approaches to macroeconomics (theory
and policy). The first one is that Kalecki should (in our view) be seen
as operating within the classical or Ricardian–Marxian approach to
economics, whereas Keynes can be seen as firmly within the Marshallian tradition and more generally within the neo-classical tradition even though he became critical of aspects of that approach
and described the *General Theory*'s 'composition . . . [as] a long
struggle of escape . . . a struggle of escape from habitual modes of
thought and expression' (Keynes, 1936, p. viii). Skidelsky (1983,
Chapter 9) indicates the strong attachment of Keynes, at least in the
period up to 1920, to the current economic orthodoxies.

> Keynes' commitment to free trade was no less firm than his
> commitment to the quantity theory. He regarded the case for free
> trade as scientifically established; denial of it was evidence of
> incompetence in economic training. (To Keynes unsound views

on the quantity theory, free trade and marginalist analysis were expressive of some 'natural malformation of the mind' to which 'practical men' were particularly prone.)[13]

Leijonhufvud (1968) argues that 'Keynes dealt with dynamic processes by means of a 'comparative statics' period-analysis ... Marshall had made much use of it (period analysis), and in this respect of his method, as in many others, Keynes was very Marshallian'. Keynes's difference with Marshall is seen as arising from the inversion of 'the ranking of price- and quantity-adjustment velocities characteristic of Marshall's period-analysis'. The adoption by Keynes of the Marshallian short-period approach meant that the capital stock was held constant for the short-period analysis even though investment was proceeding, and we saw above that Kalecki integrated changes in the capital stock into the investment decision (cf. pp. 49–51). Keynes's use of the Marshallian general framework is further reflected in the use of equilibrium analysis in which short-run and long-run positions are analysed, and this is discussed further below.

In Chapter 1, we argued that Kalecki should be seen as within the broad classical Ricardian–Marxian approach to economics. We would argue that Kalecki should be seen as analysing the principle of effective demand within a broadly classical approach, whilst Keynes should be seen as analysing that principle within a broadly neo-classical approach. If that line of argument is accepted and the idea that classical and neo-classical traditions reflect the two basic and opposed schools of thought within economics (e.g. Dobb, 1973; Meek, 1977), then placing Kalecki and Keynes together is likely to lead to confusion.

The second area of difference relates to the particular sectors of the economy which are focused upon in the macroeconomic analysis and which are viewed as of major importance in the malfunctioning of the economy as exhibited by unemployment and excess capacity (cf. Johansen, 1978). In Keynes's work, product markets receive relatively little attention and prices are generally viewed as moving in line with marginal costs. The analytic device of a discussion in terms of wage units (which is often interpreted in terms of constant money wages), followed by a discussion (Keynes, 1936, Chapter 19) of the effects of downward wage adjustment has the effect of focusing on the labour market and wages rather than on product markets and prices. Indeed, price is largely seen as following wages, with the relationship between prices and wages (i.e. real wages) depending on the level of aggregate demand. The financial sectors are, in this context, given most attention, with the role of money seen as particularly important.

For Kalecki, the focus of attention in terms of sectors of the economy was the product markets, reflected in the attention paid to prices as a mark-up over costs. Financial factors are seen as important in terms of constraining investment. The creation of money is viewed as a crucial component in the movement of effective aggregate demand. But disturbances arising from the financial sector are not discussed by Kalecki. The labour market is usually seen as passive in the sense that whilst unions and employers may set money wages, real wages are determined elsewhere in the product market. The power of unions becomes important when they are able to modify the degree of monopoly (and thereby increase real wages) and when in conditions of continuous full employment upward pressure on money wages generates wage and thereby price inflation. A major cause of unemployment in the Kaleckian framework could be seen to be a mismatch between the degree of monopoly (and the corresponding level of profits which would be generated at full capacity), and the level of investment expenditure.

The third area of difference relates to their general political philosophy and attitudes towards capitalism and socialism. It is well-known that Keynes was associated with the British Liberal Party at various times and placed great emphasis on the liberty of the individual and respect for personal integrity (cf. Moggridge, 1976, Chapter One), though Skidelsky (1983) points to periods of political inactivity. 'Keynes's approach to the economic problems of this time was deeply rooted in this late Victorian ethic. He had a propensity for producing on any occasion a plan designed to kill any number of popularly wanted birds with a single stone' (Johnson, 1978). It is also well known that Keynes stressed the importance of ideas rather than political and social forces, revealed in the final sentence of the *General Theory* where it is stated that 'sooner or late, it is ideas, not vested interests, which are dangerous for good or evil' (Keynes, 1936).

In contrast, as indicated above (p. 4), Kalecki was associated with the socialist movement, and could be regarded as an idiosyncratic Marxist (cf. Chapter 8). Kalecki regarded 'vested interests' (using Keynes's terminology) of considerable importance, and the interplay between economic political and social factors is clearly evident in Kalecki (1943b) which was discussed in Chapter 7 (see also Eshag, 1977). Further, his essays on development (Kalecki, 1976), and particularly his essay on 'intermediate regimes' show the significance which he attached to the constraints on economic development posed by the reaction of dominant social classes to threats to their interests (see Chapter 10).

For Kalecki and Keynes, unemployment was a major economic problem. But for Keynes, unemployment was *the* important problem (at least of the 1930s) for capitalism and that 'it is determining the volume, not the direction of actual employment that the existing system has broken down' (Keynes, 1936). Further, whilst 'a somewhat comprehensive socialisation of investment will prove the only means of securing an approximation to full employment', Keynes argued that 'it is not the ownership of the instruments of production which it is important for the State to assume'. For Kalecki, unemployment was a major blemish which capitalism would find difficult to remove. At a minimum new political and social institutions reflecting the increased power of the working class would be needed.

Macroeconomic Assumptions

Macroeconomics involves, of course, aggregates and the relationship between aggregates. Whilst attention has been paid to the 'aggregation problem' (i.e. the conditions under which relations derived at the individual economic unit level yield comparable results at the aggregate level), relatively little attention has been paid to the aggregates chosen. Leijonhufvud (1968) argued that assumptions about particular modes of aggregation are 'often left implicit and particular aggregative structures are thus left to develop into undisputed conventions while at the same time controversies rage over the second type of assumption [on behavioural relationships between variables]'. More attention is paid to certain variables or sectors (e.g. financial variables in the case of Keynes) than to others in the presentation or development of that approach. Further, certain sectors are seen as 'active' and others as 'passive'. In the example of the active nature of investment and the passive nature of consumption expenditure, Kalecki and Keynes take a common view. Finally, certain variables may be viewed as taking a value close to zero or small enough to be ignored (e.g. for Keynes the rate of interest on money, even when broadly defined, was taken as approximately zero).

The common attribute of the assumptions discussed in the previous paragraph is that they are commonly made implicitly rather than explicitly. Thus there can be some dispute over what assumptions have been made since these are implicit, but we will attempt to indicate some of the differences in this respect between the two authors. The first over which there is likely to be little disagreement is that Keynes assumes an essentially atomistic competitive economy, whereas Kalecki assumes an oligopolistic economy, where trade unions may play an important role. Below, we discuss how the difference over industrial structure (i.e. whether atomistic competitive or oligopolistic) is reflected in the approaches of Kalecki and Keynes to financial, labour and product markets.

In terms of key aggregates used, Keynes's aggregation can be summarised as income, consumption, savings, investment, money and 'bonds'. For Kalecki, the key aggregates can be summarised as income, savings, investment, wages, profits, money (and of less importance), 'bills' and 'bonds'. As compared with Keynes's aggregates, that of Kalecki involves two disaggregations. The first is that of income into wages plus profits, and the second is the division of the asset which Keynes labelled money (but which included on occasions some short-dated assets such as Treasury Bills) into an asset labelled money (i.e. money narrowly defined) and short-term financial assets labelled bills. The significance of these further disaggregations are discussed below.

Whilst Keynes used households and firms as the aggregates for economic agents, Kalecki used the groupings of workers and capitalists. This difference in aggregation is partly a reflection of the difference over an individualistic (Keynes) or class-based (Kalecki) approach to economic theorising, a difference which is discussed further below. Further, there is not a one-to-one relationship between the two sets of aggregates, e.g. households and workers are not synonymous. In the case of Keynes's approach, households make consumption, savings and supply of labour decisions whereas firms make investment and employment decisions. In many presentations (e.g. conventional IS–LM) which stress the role of aggregate demand and neglect aggregate supply, the major roles assigned to households within the model is to make consumption and savings decisions. In a sense households and firms contribute on roughly equal terms to the determination of aggregate demand, though investment is often seen as a more active ingredient than consumption. In Kalecki's approach workers are seen as having little discretion over consumption decisions, and spend all their income and make virtually no savings. The role of households (at least those of the working class) is as workers, that is their role in production rather than consumption. Within Kalecki's macroeconomics, the role of workers is usually seen as a rather passive one, though he did place importance on the role of trade unions in making the role of workers a more active one. Capitalists make decisions in investment, savings prices and employment and hence have a much greater significance in the operation of the economy than workers do.

Both Kalecki and Keynes were developing their macroeconomics against a background of substantial unemployment. In the UK, prior to 1936, unemployment had only once fallen below 10 per cent (to 9.7 per cent in 1927) amongst the insured employees since 1921, and once to just below $7\frac{1}{2}$ per cent amongst total employees.[14] Chick (1983) has argued that the view that unemployment was the norm (of unregulated capitalism) was one (of six) assumptions decisive in shaping the *General Theory*.[15] In Poland unemployment had been high since independence in 1919, with a level of 7.9 per cent in the 'boom' year of 1928, and employment in industry fell by 37 per cent between 1929 and 1932.[16]

We have already (pp. 115–16) summarised Kalecki's view that unemployment was the norm. This opens the way for both authors to be accused of dealing only with unemployment periods, though the strength of that accusation clearly depends on the ease with which their analyses can be modified for situations of full employment, and how relatively important periods of full employment are.

Methodological Differences

In this section we focus on methodological differences between Kalecki and Keynes. But since the methodology of Keynes was rather similar in many of the respects discussed below with neo-classical economics, implicitly we are discussing differences between

Kalecki and the prevailing orthodoxy. There are four areas of difference which we concentrate upon. The first is the use and meaning of equilibrium analysis, whilst the second is the relative importance given to 'subjective' and to 'objective' factors. The third is the level of analysis used, specifically individual or social class, and the fourth is the usefulness of econometrics and mathematics. As far as we are aware, neither Kalecki nor Keynes discussed their own methodological approach, which therefore leaves some room for doubt on the approach used, apart from changes through time or between different areas of enquiry which they may have followed.

Equations which are or which look like equilibrium conditions are used in at least three different ways in economic theory. The first and perhaps most usual way is to view the equilibrium equations as relating to a position at which an actual economy operates or towards which it tends. This could be labelled a descriptive use of equilibrium analysis. This also means that 'it is generally taken for granted by the great majority of academic economists that the economy always approaches, or is near to a state of equilibrium' (Kaldor, 1972).

The second use is for equations to be used to illustrate or investigate certain facets under the simplified conditions of equilibrium but without any intended implication that the equilibrium position is one to which an economy is likely to move. Hahn (1973) appears to interpret general equilibrium theory in this light, and the post-Keynesian and neo-Ricardian approaches have often taken this view (e.g. Kregel, 1973, pp. 38–40; Robinson, 1978, pp. 137–45).

The third way is the use of accounting identities, which are sometimes mistakenly interpreted as equilibrium conditions. There are well known examples (e.g. savings equal investment) where one equation can be given an equilibrium or an accounting identity interpretation, depending on the precise notions of savings and investment used.

Kregel (1976) argues that Keynes 'may have had in mind three distinct classes of models of the economy', which he identifies as models of static equilibrium (where state of expectations taken as given but expectations are realised), stationary equilibrium (where expectations may be disappointed) and of shifting equilibrium. For our line of argument, the important point is that each of these three classes of model is one of equilibrium.

In terms of the three-way distinction made above, we argue that

Keynes's work fits into the first category, whereas while parts of Kalecki's work fits into the second and third categories, in general his approach can best be described as a non-equilibrium one.

There has been much discussion over whether Keynes's *General Theory* dealt with equilibrium positions or with disequilibrium ones. Davidson (1981) has argued that 'when Keynes and post-Keynesians use the term equilibrium (for example, when they speak of less-than-full-employment equilibrium) they are using the concept in its generic sense', by which he means a position in which no one would wish to act differently. Shackle (1961) argued that Keynes's *General Theory* 'so strongly repudiating some of the conclusions of equilibrium theory, was itself an equilibrium theory in method'. In Patinkin's view referred to above, Keynes's novel contribution was to see changes in the level of income as the equilibrating variable. Further, statements by Keynes to the effect that he was 'not concerned with instantaneous snapshots, but with short-period equilibrium assuming a sufficient interval for monetary decisions to take effect' (in Moggridge, 1979, p. 280) indicate Keynes's use of equilibrium analysis. The equilibrium positions, whatever their status, were intended to be positions which an actual economy would attain as indicated in the one-page first chapter and in Chapter 22 of the *General Theory*.

It is reasonable to describe the general approach of Kalecki as a non-equilibrium one. This is partly reflected in the use of words such as essentially dynamic to describe his macroeconomics (e.g. Johansen, 1978; Feiwell, 1972), and in the use of words such as dynamics, fluctuations in the titles of Kalecki's books. His distaste for the use of equilibrium in the analysis of growth will be evident from Chapter 4 above. The term equilibrium is rarely used in Kalecki's writings, although as we noted in Chapter 1, there is some use of that term in some papers published in the late 1930s.

Kalecki attacked one author (Tugan-Baranovski) for adopting the view that 'what *may* happen is actually happening' where the 'what *may* happen' is based on 'the proportions between consumption and investment, which must be established in order that the total production should be purchased'. This effectively means the assumption that the equilibrium requirements for full employment are actually fulfilled in an economy.

In a number of places, Kalecki makes use of accounting identities, combined with the view that certain factors are determining the outcome; the clearest example of this is the equality between savings and investment (e.g. Kalecki, 1971a, pp. 28–30). In conventional terminology, Kalecki focused on *ex post* rather than *ex ante* quality. The active force is investment decisions, which are made at time t to be implemented, on average, in time $t + \tau$. In discussion of investment behaviour through time, Kalecki substitutes actual investment expenditure at time t (which implement investment decisions made at time $t - \tau$) for actual savings (at time t), with actual savings having adjusted to the level of investment.

The second and third points are to some extent linked. On the second point, Johansen wrote that '(i)n the balance of "objective" and "subjective" elements, objective elements count more in Kalecki's theories and subjective more in Keynes'. Keynes (1936) p. 248 argued that 'we can sometimes regard our ultimate independent variables as consisting of (1) the three fundamental psychological factors, namely, the psychological propensity to consume, the psychological attitude to liquidity and the psychological expectations of future yield from capital-assets, (2) the wage unit . . . (3) the quantity of money'.

Keynes placed emphasis on the fragile nature of expectations about the future, and the impact of uncertainty on economic decisions. Coddington (1983), Chapter 4 drew out two particular aspects of Keynes's approach of relevance here. First, the impact of uncertainty impinges on decisions relating to investment and liquidity preference, but not to other decisions and specifically not to consumption decisions. Second, 'these ideas have the effect of driving a wedge between behaviour and circumstances; they can be used, as it were, to detach behaviour from the circumstances in which it takes place' (Coddington, 1983). If uncertainty of the form which cannot be linked to economic events is taken seriously then, as Coddington argues, the effect is devastating for economic analysis.

In contrast, Kalecki generally says little about expectations, with the (implicit) notion that views taken about the future are heavily conditioned by the present and recent past. This leads to relating decisions on variables such as investment expenditure to actual current and past values of other variables.

The third difference relates to the level of analysis – individual or class. Whilst both authors finish with macroeconomics which necessarily involves the use of aggregates, the preceding steps are different. For Keynes, individual economic agents (whether households or firms) make decisions on consumption expenditure, investment, etc. which is then aggregated across all agents to yield the aggregate equivalents. For Kalecki, the starting point is the association of specific classes (workers or capitalists) with particular activities. Capitalists undertake investment and savings, whereas workers spend all of their wages. One consequence of this is that the division between profits (= income of capitalists) and wages and salaries (= income of workers) is built in, with profits influencing consumption expenditure. Whilst Keynes mentions the distribution of income as a factor influencing the level of consumption expenditure, it is one of a list of factors with the level of income having the central role to play. In the approach of Keynes (and many others), profits are, on average, received by individuals in a higher income bracket, as compared with the income bracket of the typical recipient of labour income. But there is no basic distinction drawn between profits and labour income, and nothing rests on the presumed higher propensity to save out of profits than out of labour income. Here again it can be seen that Kalecki's class level analysis and emphasis on the distribution of income places him in the classical Ricardian–Marxian tradition (cf. Bradley and Howard, 1982, p. 8) whereas Keynes's individualistic approach with distribution as a subsidiary factor places him in the neo-classical tradition.

The fourth difference concerns the usefulness of mathematics and econometrics. 'Kalecki was unabashingly mathematical and used some rudiments of econometrics, while Keynes hesitated in using simple formulas and was very sceptical to econometrics' (Johansen, 1978). Keynes's views on the use of econometrics are made clear on pp. 285–331 of Keynes (1973). Kalecki (1964) discussed the relationship between econometrics and historical materialism. The relationship between the work of Kalecki and Keynes to macroeconometric model-building are discussed below.

One can end this methodological discussion, by noting that both Kalecki and Keynes were striving to develop a genuine macroeconomics. By this we mean a theory of 'output-as-a-whole' (in the words of Keynes) in which there are important aggregate effects which cannot be captured by merely adding up individual behaviour. Thus, for both Kalecki and Keynes, at the aggregate level savings equal investment, with the former adjusting to the latter (in a closed economy), and this is an important economy-level relationship which has no counterpart at the individual level.

Investment

The modelling of investment decisions by Keynes was one of the main aspects of Keynes (1936) which Kalecki criticised in his review. We have outlined those criticisms above in our discussion of investment (pp. 47–8). In this section we highlight the differences between Kalecki and Keynes on investment. First, Kalecki's approach is more explicitly macroeconomic in seeking directly to explain the movements in aggregate investment incorporating the accounting identity between previous investment and savings, whilst Keynes is microeconomic in the sense of beginning from investment decisions at the individual firm level and then seeking to aggregate across firms. Second, the financial sector impinges on investment decisions in Kalecki's approach through a limitation on the availability of funds (rather than the cost of such funds), whereas Keynes pays much more attention to the cost of finance (related to the rate of interest). Third, the role of uncertainty and filmsy expectations about the future are stressed in Keynes, whereas actual events (such as profits) are stressed in Kalecki. This also relates to the previous discussion on the relative roles of subjective and objective factors. Fourth, Keynes's main concern in the *General Theory* was over current investment in a static analysis, whereas Kalecki's analysis of investment was within a dynamic context (with fluctuations and growth). Keynes's discussion on investment (Keynes, 1936, Chapter 12) makes only a passing reference to technical change, although by suitable amendments the prospect of technical change could be incorporated into discussion of the marginal efficiency of capital. Kalecki's discussion on investment often stressed the role of technical progress in maintaining positive net investment, which was required for anything approaching full employment. Keynes predicted that 'a properly run community . . . ought to be able to bring down the marginal efficiency of capital in equilibrium approximately to zero within a single generation' (Keynes, 1936, p. 220), with the prospect of net investment declining to zero. Although in a sentence which follows closely on the one quoted Keynes mentioned changes in techniques among other factors leading to 'changes and progress', this is given a relatively minor role.

Views on the Financial Sectors

We have already remarked above that Keynes placed much more emphasis on the financial sectors than did Kalecki, which can be illustrated by a glance at the list of contents of Keynes's *General Theory* and Kalecki's *Selected Essays*. With that difference in emphasis in mind, in this section we look at the financial aggregates used, the nature of money, the determination of interest rate(s) and the links between the financial and real sides of the economy as discussed by the two men.

Both authors acknowledged that there are a wide range of financial assets in existence in developed capitalist economies, though Keynes (especially in the *Treatise on Money* (Keynes, 1930) discussed this point at much greater length than did Kalecki. But for the purposes of macroeconomic analysis, Keynes used a two-asset representation of financial assets, whereas Kalecki used a three-asset representation. For Keynes the distinction was between short-term liquid assets, labelled 'money' and long term less liquid assets, labelled 'bonds' or non-money financial assets. The characteristics which serve to define money in the theoretical context were zero interest rate, constant nominal price and fixed supply (see below), whereas bonds possessed a positive rate of interest and a variable price. As Leijonhufvud (1968) observed 'Keynes's definition of 'money' is much broader than that used by later Keynesians'. Not only are all kinds of deposits generally included, Keynes also argued that 'we can draw the line between "money" and "debts" at whatever point is most convenient for handling particular problem' (Keynes, 1936, p. 167, fn. 1).

It is, of course, the case that theories which utilise a two financial asset approach where one of the assets yields a zero (nominal) rate of return, that there is only one rate of interest to be determined. In Keynes's approach, *the* rate of interest is effectively the long-term rate of interst (so that when undated bonds are taken as the representative long-term assets, the interest rate becomes the bond rate of interest).

Kalecki used the three-asset disaggregation of financial assets of money, 'bills' and 'bonds' as indicated in Chapter 5 above. This introduces a second interest rate – the short term as well as the long-term interest rate, with the rate of interest on money again assumed to be zero. It was seen in Chapter 5 that Kalecki's approach limited the role of money to its medium of exchange role,and focused on the transactions demand for money. In contrast, Keynes's approach also emphasised money's role as a store of wealth. Keynes (1937a) posed the question of why anyone would wish to hold the barren asset of money. Keynes's answer was that 'our desire to hold money as a store of wealth is a barometer of the degree of our distrust of our own calculations and conventions concerning the future'. In a sense, the return on money was certain (in a time of no appreciable inflation) and money was liquid, whilst the returns on bonds and on capital equipment were uncertain and involved a loss of liquidity. Kalecki's answer would effectively be that money is held only for transactions purposes (being only medium of exchange). There were financial assets which were highly liquid, with constant nominal price but yielding a rate of interest ('bills' in his terminology). Further, whilst bonds and capital equipment involve a loss of liquidity, loans could be used to tide people and firms over any period when purchasing power was required but the bonds and capital equipment could not be realised for cash (without a substantial capital loss).

Besides the differences in the breadth of definition of money there is also the important difference between Kalecki and Keynes over the determinants of the money supply. In the *General Theory*, Keynes wrote that 'the quantity of money (is) determined by the action of the central bank' and 'in the case of money – postponing for the moment, our consideration of the effect of reducing the wage-units or of a deliberate increase in its supply by the monetary authority – the supply is fixed' (Keynes, 1936, p. 247). In some respects, Kalecki stands at the other end of the spectrum over the nature of money. In doing so, Kalecki could be said to be more in tune with much post-Keynesian writing (e.g. Moore, 1979) than Keynes, and in this limited area Keynes and Friedman share similar views (e.g. Friedman, 1969).[17] Essentially, Kalecki defined money as current bank accounts and notes. The money supply was than determined by the policy of clearing banks in terms of reserve ratios, etc. (Kalecki, 1954, pp. 77–8).

The mechanism envisaged by Kalecki and Keynes for the translation of planned increased demand into effect can be compared. Kalecki clearly saw that translation as requiring the expansion of the money supply through the extension of loans and credits by the banking system (cf. pp. 91–6). Keynes acknowledged the importance and the availability of finance ahead of actual expenditure in Keynes (1937b, c) with his introduction of the 'finance' motive for holding money. Keynes argued that 'banks hold the key position in the transition from a lower to a higher scale of activity' (Keynes, 1937c) which sounds similar to the point made by Kalecki. But whereas Kalecki assumes that banks create bank credits when there is a demand for them, Keynes indicates that the liquidity position of at least one group out of household, firms and banks has to become more illiquid. Thus for Kalecki the focus was on the provision of bank credits, whereas for Keynes it was on the private sector being willing to move (if only temporarily) into a more illiquid position with a reduced holding of money for speculative purposes. Another aspect of this point is that whereas Kalecki's approach incorporates a close linkage between the decisions for additional investment and the requirements for bank loans, Keynes (e.g. Keynes, *Collected Works*, 1979, p. 171) made it clear that the demand for finance for additional investment expenditure would be a demand for cash, and not closely approximated by the demand for bank loans.

Kalecki clearly saw the finance markets as imperfectly competitive in the sense that access to finance is restricted and that the cost of finance rises with the amount borrowed through the principle of increasing risk (cf. Chapter 5 above). In contrast, Keynes adopted an atomistic competitive view that in his discussion on investment and the marginal efficiency of capital, the rate of interest was taken as constant as far as a single firm was concerned, and by implication that the cost of finance was independent of its source (e.g. as between bank loans, internal finance, issue of new shares). Keynes did allow that the risk premium charged by financial institutions would vary between firms, but the risk premium was constant for any particular firm relative to the amount borrowed. This suggests that Keynes thought mainly in terms of external finance for investment whereas Kalecki stresses internal finance. Further, as Kalecki (1937c) pointed out, Keynes neglected the extent to which the risk premium would rise with the amount borrowed.

It can be argued that Keynes was drawing on the then current British banking policy. Firms held overdraft facilities with the clearing banks on which they could draw up to (usually) predetermined levels. Indeed, Keynes (1937c) praised this as 'an ideal system for mitigating the effects on the banking system until the finance is actually used. . . .' The rate of interest which the firms were charged would reflect their credit rating. The picture presented by Keynes fits this in that firms are required to pay a risk premium (which varies between firms) above the 'pure' rate of interest. In the short-term, increased use of overdraft facilities could be seen as the major source of finance for investment, with the raising of finance through the issue of bonds or new equity being an infrequent event for firms.

There is one significant departure from the perfect capital market approach in Keynes, in that the full force of the consumption function with the dependence of consumer expenditure on current income relies on the absence of borrowing and accumulated savings with which to maintain consumer expenditure in the face of declining income. Whilst this may be explicable in terms of uncertainty about the future, it also reflects a view about the capital market – that households, particularly unemployed households, did not borrow.

Labour and Product Markets

For both labour and for product markets, Kalecki adopts a basically oligopolistic approach, whilst Keynes maintains a competitive approach. Further, in the analysis of Kalecki the product market plays a much more important role than the labour market does, whilst for Keynes the relative roles are reversed. Kalecki's views on the labour and product markets have been set out in detail above (cf. Chapters 6 and 2 respectively).

For Keynes the price level in an industry 'depends partly on the rate of remuneration of the factors of production which enter into its marginal costs, and partly on the scale of output' (Keynes, 1936, p. 249). This kind of statement, the views expressed by authors such as Ohlin (in Keynes, 1973), Lekachman (1977), Robinson (1976b) and the assumptions used in the 'reappraisal of Keynes' literature originating with Clower (1965) and Leijonhufvud (1968) all suggest that Keynes assumed atomistic competition in the product markets (as well as elsewhere).[18] Whereas Kalecki explained the difference between price and marginal production costs by degree of monopoly, Keynes appealed to the marginal user cost of capital. Thus that user cost enters the marginal costs which are equated with the price of output.

Whilst Kalecki assumed (at least as a first approximation) that marginal costs were constant with respect to output, Keynes made the more conventional assumption that marginal costs tend to rise with output. Both Kalecki and Keynes (e.g. Keynes, 1936, pp. 13–14) share the view that whilst money wages are determined in the labour market, real wages are determined in the product market. In a general sense, the counterpart of Keynes's assumptions on cost conditions is the view that 'real wages [are] inevitably rising in the same circumstances [of falling employment] on account of the increasing marginal return to a given capital equipment when output is diminished' (Keynes, 1936, p. 10). Thus real wages are anticipated to move counter-cyclically relative to output and employment. Kalecki expected that real wages were not likely to have any strong correlation with employment levels, and movements in real wages in a Kaleckian approach would depend on movements in the degree of monopoly, material prices, and productivity (cf. pp. 108–15 above).

Keynes appears to have given greater emphasis to the labour market than he did to the product market and more than Kalecki did. This partly arises from Keynes's device of measuring variables in terms of wage units. Chapters 2 and 19 of the *General Theory* deal in details with wages and wage adjustments. The theme which runs through these chapters relates to the difficulties attendant on wage adjustments. But throughout there is little hint of departures from atomistic competition, and as Tobin (1972) argued, Keynes 'did not appeal to trade union monopolies or minimum wage laws' to explain rigidity of money wages.

Causes of 'Breakdown'

Arising from the work of Keynes, emphasis has been placed on three basic 'causes' of deviations from full employment (in capitalist economies). Here we try to avoid being embroiled in debates over whether these causes of breakdown can be taken as accurate representations of the work of Keynes. Instead our purpose is to compare these interpretations of Keynes with the approach of Kalecki.

The first 'cause' of breakdown is derived from the work of Clower (1965), Leijonhufvud (1968) and others, and relates to the co-ordination problems of a decentralised economy. However, there is considerable doubt on whether this approach can be derived from

Keynes, even though its development is linked with the name of Keynes. A shift in the structure of demand, to which prices do not instantly and completely adjust to bring about the new equilibrium position, is seen as leading through some quantity adjustments, with the short-side of the market determining quantity levels, to a downward spiral in output and employment. Effectively, within the context of competitive markets, a mismatch between demand and supply in various markets arises, and this explanation of 'breakdown' could be labelled a disproportionality approach.

The second view emphasises the fragility of expectations about the future, and the dependency of crucial relationships such as investment demand and the demand for money on expectations about the future. Pessimistic expectations lead to a higher demand for money (liquidity preference) and a lower demand for investment, thereby leading to falls in output, etc.

The third view draws on the work of Minsky (Minsky, 1976, 1978).

This interpretation of Keynes made in the *General Theory*, consistent with views that were widespread in the early 1930s: that what had gone wrong had its roots in the imperfections of the monetary-financial system. The greatness of the *General Theory* was that Keynes visualized these as systemic rather than accidental or perhaps incidental attributes of capitalism (Minsky, 1976, p. 143).

However, Keynes's policy conclusions were 'moderately conservative', and involved the maintenance of capitalism albeit with increased government involvement.

We can contrast those views with the approach of Kalecki. In terms of the first one, Kalecki assumed oligopolistic rather than competitive markets. But, more importantly here, he assumed that firms typically operated under approximately constant costs and with surplus capacity. Thus changes in the structure of demand are seen as being met by appropriate changes in production. It is also the case that a change in the structure of demand within Kalecki's approach would have little impact on relative prices unless there was an impact on the degree of monopoly. Thus the problem between the composition of demand and of supply is not a cause of breakdown in the Kalecki approach.

The only kind of 'mismatch' which Kalecki indicated would sometimes be of significance was that between the existing stock of capital equipment and the labour force. A shortage of capital equipment was seen as a possible cause of post-war unemployment (cf. Kalecki, 1944b) and an important cause of unemployment in underdeveloped economies.

Another aspect of the Clower–Leijonhufvud approach is the signal sent from households to firms when savings behaviour changes 'misleads' firms. Specifically an intended rise in savings is associated with an intended fall in consumer expenditure, and this may well lead firms to reduce investment (cf. Keynes, 1936, p. 210). A major reason for this is that those undertaking savings, i.e. households are not those undertaking investment (i.e. firms). Here again this type of breakdown does not arise in the work of Kalecki for the obvious reason that firms undertake both savings and investment and workers are assumed to spend all their income.

The second approach listed above finds little echo in the work of Kalecki. As argued above, Kalecki stressed objective rather than subjective factors, and thus would have looked to factors such as a decline in technological opportunities to explain a decline in investment and thereby a decline in output.

The third approach could be said to be consistent with the approach of Kalecki but not to feature prominently in it. In a few places, he indicated the relevance of confidence and liquidity crises in the financial sector. He also used such an occurrence to argue against price deflation as a means of restoring full employment via the Pigou effect. 'The adjustment [from a fall in prices and wages] required would increase catastrophically the real value of debts, and would consequently lead to wholesale bankruptcy and a "confidence crisis"' (Kalecki, 1944).

Why a Keynesian Macroeconomics?

We now turn, albeit briefly, to the intriguing question of why Keynes was very much more influential than Kalecki (and others), reflected in the use of the term such as Keynesian revolution, Keynesian macroeconomics. Here we concentrate on the Kalecki versus Keynes aspects of the question.

Several reasons for the importance given to Keynes immediately suggest themselves. First, Keynes as much better known and connected than Kalecki (and to a lesser extent than the Swedish school). A range of people had been arguing for reflationary policies in Britain (ranging from Mosley, Lloyd George to Bevin and Bevan), and the stamp of approval by the best known British economists could be seen as a great aid to the spread to the idea of government using the budget position and reflation to try and reach full employment. It was five years later and in the context of a war economy, that a 'Keynesian' budget was adopted. Other countries, notably Sweden, Nazi Germany and to a minor degree the United States had been groping in the reflationary budget direction.

Second, the war-time application of the general set of ideas on effective demand and macroeconomics was in the context of macroeconomic planning. Schott (1982) distinguishes between Keynesian planning and Keynesian management. The former was undertaken in the war and immediate post-war period, and in that context the ideas of Kalecki and Keynes could be seen as generating similar concepts and policy conclusions. In particular differences in ideas on how a capitalist economy would operate when left to itself were not immediately relevant, but the use of macroeconomic aggregates and national income accounting were. But even here, as Tomlinson (1981) points out, national income accounting had predated Keynes, and indeed Kalecki had been involved in deriving national income estimates for Poland in the early 1930s. By the time that Keynesian planning gave way to Keynesian management, the dominance of a macroeconomics labelled Keynesian was established.

Third, the apparent political consensus which evolved in Britain (and elsewhere) in the last years of the war, placed emphasis on post-war reconstruction built around a welfare state with extended social security and education provision and some continuation of macroeconomic planning. This consensus found its British expression in events such as the Education Act 1944 and the Beveridge report of 1942. Addison (1976) provides a detailed account of the emergence of this consensus. The consensus fitted in with a Keynesian macroeconomic policy designed to ensure full employment with some socialisation of demand (cf. Keynes, 1936 Concluding Chapter).

Fourth, Kalecki took a more sceptical view of the possibility of achieving prolonged full employment under capitalism than Keynes did. The prolonged post-war boom, and the historical low levels of unemployment appeared to vindicate Keynes rather than Kalecki. It is perhaps not entirely coincidentally that a revival of interest in the work of Kalecki has occurred over the past few years when many of his prognostications in Kalecki (1943b) have come to pass. The experience of the past ten to fifteen years have again raised the questions which were there posed by Kalecki, such as whether capitalism could change its institutions sufficiently to cope with changes in the balance of power resulting from full employment.

Fifth, in many respects Keynes appeared to offer much less of a rupture with neo-classical orthodoxy than Kalecki did. It can be argued that the ideas of Keynes on expectations and the unknowability of the future were a serious challenge to neo-classical economics (and to any economics which sought to model economic behaviour), but it was relatively easy to bury this aspect out of sight. The importance of the state of expectation on the marginal efficiency of capital and investment slips into making investment depend on expected income, and then into investment depending on income (cf. Keynes *Collected Works*, vol. 14, p. 80). The retention of an atomistic competitive view of the world and the use of equilibrium analysis (even if of a modified form) provided a strong common link with orthodoxy. It also proved relatively easy with the IS–LM approach to present a version of the Keynesian approach, which many now doubt was an adequate representation of Keynes's approach.[19] Whilst microeconomics had demand and supply curves, which intersect to provide equilibrium, macroeconomics now had IS and LM curves which also intersect to provide equilibrium. In both cases, the curves can be shifted around in response to various exogenous shifts. The development of the IS–LM approach had the effect of overlooking Keynes's arguments about uncertainty and expectations (and also of elevating the importance of aggregate demand relative to aggregate supply). Kalecki's work was never treated to a simple diagrammatic presentation, and it would probably not have been susceptible to such a presentation, particularly if it were to retain cyclical aspects. Further, Kalecki's ideas were published over a decade or so and in a variety of languages (at least, Polish, French and English) and were not concentrated in a single book as Keynes's ideas were. It was indicated above that Kalecki abandoned his intention to present his ideas in a single book after discovering the publication of Keynes (1936), though many of his important ideas were collected into a single book published as Kalecki (1939).

Sixth, there were political difficulties in spreading the ideas of the *General Theory*. Galbraith (1971) discusses some of the right wing hostility to Keynesian ideas in the United States. Skidelsky (1983) suggests that Harrod (1951) in his biography of Keynes may have omitted discussion of Keynes's one-time homosexuality and his registration as a conscientious objector in the First World War in order to avoid challenges to Keynesian economics based on objections to Keynes as a person. The resistance to the ideas of Kalecki, involving a sharper challenge to capitalism and coming from somone associated with the socialist movement, would have been much stronger.

An element of contradition has run through what is usually labelled Keynesian economics. For some purposes, including textbook presentation and much academic controversy, Keynesian economics has been closely identified with the IS–LM approach. This model has two important ingredients for our purposes. First, it is an equilibrium model for the two sectors (goods and money) of the economy. Second, consumer expenditure/savings are taken as a function of income (and possibly the rate of interest), investment as a function of income and the interest rate with the supply of money exogenously determined. In other chapters of textbooks which present the IS–LM model, alternative theories of the 'building blocks' of the IS–LM model are given. These alternative theories are sometimes in obvious conflict with the corresponding theory entered into the IS–LM model (e.g. an accelerator theory of investment compared with the marginal efficiency of capital approach) whilst in other cases the alternative theories may be regarded as 'richer' than the corresponding theory in the IS–LM model (e.g. life-cycle theory of consumption compared with consumption as a function of current income). The justification for the use of the simplified IS–LM model is usually that it highlights interdependencies, and serves as a simple general equilibrium model. But it is not obvious that the conclusions derived from an IS–LM model would remain unchanged if alternative theories of investment, consumption, etc. were used, nor are checks on this usually carried out.

Many macroeconometric models have been developed which are given labels such as Keynesian, neo-Keynesian, etc. It can be argued that such macroeconometric models depart to a considerable extent from the ideas of Keynes, and in many respects could be more accurately labelled Kaleckian rather than Keynesian. It can also be noted that models for forecasting purposes are very likely to depart from equilibrium models. Since we generally observe that there are changes in economic variables from period to period, forecasting models have to incorporate change. Equilibrium models used in this context would have to rely on exogenous changes to bring about forecast changes. Thus it is likely that the models will have to incorporate features of disequilibrium or non-equilibrium.

The ideas which enter macroeconomic models have been developed by a wide range of economists, and these models are generally eclectic. Our interest here is with the simpler question of whether the ideas in some macroeconometric models are closer to the ideas of Kalecki or to those of Keynes.

Klein (1964) argued that 'whilst it should not be said that all the basic ingredients of modern econometric system stemmed from Kalecki's model, it can be said that all the components of Kalecki's model are finding their way into strategic places in modern econometric models'.

For the purposes of looking at macroeconometric models, we could summarise Keynes's approach as follows:

(i) Consumption (or consumer expenditure) as a function of disposable private sector income;
(ii) Investment as a function of the rate of interest;
(iii) Price related to marginal cost, with the mark-up being marginal user cost of capital, and with marginal cost rising with output;
(iv) Demand for money as a possibly unstable function of income and interest rates;
(v) Supply of money determined by government.

Kalecki's approach could be summarised as follows:

(i) Consumer expenditure as a function of labour income and profits, with propensity to consume out of labour income close to unity and the propensity out of profits small;
(ii) Investment as a function of profits and change in profits (or closely related output and change in output), and the capital stock;
(iii) Prices as a mark-up over average variable costs;
(iv) Demand for narrowly defined money as a function of transactions and short-term interest rate;

(v)   Supply of money determined by banks' lending policy and the demand for loans.

Space precludes a full review of macroeconometric models here. To illustrate our point we take the model of the National Institute of Economic and Social Research (London), which has often been described as a Keynesian approach. This description may be a suitable one if the intention is to distinguish their approach from a monetarist one. However, if we look at the equations of their model,[20] we can summarise these at the cost of some simplification as follows:

(i)   Consumer demand, which is disaggregated into durable and non-durable demand, is largely a function of real personal disposable income. This incorporates the view that items such as retained earnings (by corporations), employers' contributions to pension arrangements do not influence consumption. Since, by definition, retained earnings have been saved this imposes the view that savings out of profits are higher than savings out of labour income;

(ii)   Investment in manufacturing is related to firms' cash flow position and changes in capacity utilisation. Whilst this does not coincide with Kalecki's approach, it can be said that availability of finance and changes in economic activity have a role to play in both Kalecki's approach and the equation used by the National Institute;

(iii) There are a variety of price indices which are explained, but the general approach is to relate price changes to cost changes and output changes;

(iv)   There is a demand for narrow money which is effectively a transactions demand for money (as a function of income and short-term interest rates). Further, there are equations to explain bank lending, and changes in bank lending, taken with some exogenously determined items and changes in bank lending to the public sector and in the demand for currency, determine changes in sterling M3;

(v)   The determination of wage changes is based on the notion of workers having a target real wage.

There is another and more fundamental reason for thinking that macroeconometric models are more in tune with the views of Kalecki than the views of Keynes. Following some post-Keynesians, a major contribution of Keynes is seen as his ideas of the importance of expectations about the future for current economic behaviour, taken with the essential unknowability of the future and the consequent flimsy basis of those expectations. Then the idea of developing stable economic relationships between observed variables becomes difficult to adhere to. Simply, expectations play a crucial role but are likely to be incompletely formed and liable to change, making them extremely difficult to measure. In a preliminary review of Tinbergen's application of multiple correlation analysis to investment, Keynes criticised Tinbergen's approach on the basis that 'there is no reason at all why they [the estimated coefficients] should not be different every year'. Further '(w)hat place is left for expectations and the state of confidence in relation to the future? What place is allowed for non-numerical factors . . . ?' in econometric analysis. He also said that 'the question of what determines the volume of investment itself I should regard as *prima facie* extremely unpromising material for the method of multiple correlation'. (Quotes in this section taken from Keynes (1973), text in parentheses added.)

In contrast, with the importance of 'objective' rather than 'subjective' factors, Kalecki's approach leads on to stable relationships which can be estimated. There is, however, a *caveat* to that which is elaborated in Kalecki (1964) in his essay on econometric models and historical materialism. Essentially, he argued that an econometric model was based on unchanging relationships between the variables involved in their previous values. 'Historical materialism considers the process of the development of a society as that of productive forces and productive relations [the base] which shape all the other social phenomena . . . [the superstructure]' (Kalecki, 1964). The econometric model can be used 'where no changes in natural resources, productive relations and the superstructure affect the development of productive forces'. The thrust of that paper appears to be that econometric models are useful provided that the assumptions of what is taken as unchanging are clearly borne in mind, and that at times 'the path of economic development will alter abruptly'.

Conclusion

The purpose of this chapter was a comparison between the approach to macroeconomics of Keynes and that of Kalecki. We have sought to argue that, both in terms of general background and of specific assumptions, the two approaches are rather different.

Notes to Chapter 9

1. See Patinkin (1982), Chapter 1 for a full discussion of when Keynes first expressed (in a lecture) the ideas which Patinkin regards as the original contribution of Keynes (1936).
2. The only contact between Kalecki and Keynes prior to 1936 appears to be confined to two incidents. The only reference to Keynes in Kalecki's work (with no reference by Keynes to Kalecki) 'occurred in 1932 article in a Polish socialist review in which he summarized and criticized a public lecture that Keynes gave in February 1932 on "The World's Economic Crisis and the Way of Escape". Interestingly enough, in this article Kalecki . . . referred to Keynes as "the most serious contemporary bourgeois economist."' (Patinkin, 1982). The second incident is that Kalecki sent Keynes a German translation of Kalecki (1933). It is reported (cf. Patinkin, 1982, p. 62, fn. 9, drawing on the editorial notes of Osiatyński in the *Collected Works* of Kalecki) that Keynes returned the manuscript with a note saying that he did not read German. Skidelsky (1983, pp. 55, 179, 346) indicates that Keynes was fluent in German, so that his stated inability in German may have been a polite excuse to return the manuscript.
3. It would seem an exaggeration to say that 'Kalecki advanced his claim to independent discovery of the General Theory shortly after the appearance of Keynes's book. This he did in a long review article . . .' (Patinkin, 1982: the 'long review article' is the one discussed in the text).
4. Lange (1939) (as cited in Patinkin, 1982) briefly remarked that 'a theory of employment similar to that developed in Cambridge, was independently worked out by M. Kalecki, who on its basis developed his theory of the business cycle'. Zweig (1944) indicated that Kalecki's 'theory came very near to the Keynesian *General Theory of Employment*'.
5. The work of Davis (1980) casts some doubt on even that aspect of originality when he wrote that 'it was Hawtry, not Keynes, who first introduced output changes in an equilibrating role and the concomitant identification of quasi-equilibrium positions to economic theory'.
6. Patinkin (1982, especially pp. 72, 85) argues that ideas expressed only in non-professional journals are not to be counted as part of an author's central message. This would seem reasonable for someone who regarded themselves as primarily a professional economist with easy access to professional journals. In conversation, Jerzy Osiatyński (editor of Kalecki's *Collected Works*) has suggested that Kalecki considered himself as primarily a socialist economist rather than an academic economist, and could well have published his important ideas in socialist journals rather than academic ones. Further, within Poland

there was at that time only one academic journal on economics, which was generally rather orthodox (though it did publish Kalecki's review of Keynes (1936)).

7. In my view the last phrase should read 'between actual savings and intended investment'; cf. pp. 73–4 above on Kalecki's neglect of planned savings.

8. Patinkin (1982) would appear to be amongst the group who place Keynes ideas as foremost, and evaluate how close Kalecki (and others) came. He wrote 'that Kalecki also paid a price for his intellectual isolation – and perhaps part of this price was to come so close to the *General Theory* and yet not achieve it'.

9. The information in these two sentences was supplied to me by Mrs Kalecki in a letter dated 9 February 1984, and I am grateful to her for permission to refer to that letter. She is emphatic that the story of Kalecki being ill in bed for three days is not correct. Mrs Kalecki also indicates that a former colleague of Kalecki who was in London had sent word to him in Stockholm of the publication of Keynes's *General Theory* which contained similar ideas to those which Kalecki had been developing. This confirms the lack of contact between Kalecki and Keynes prior to 1936. The reaction of Kalecki appears to be the type of reaction one would expect from a relatively unknown person to the publication of a book along similar lines by a famous person, who was likely to receive the acclaim.

10. From the letter from Mrs Kalecki to the author, quoted with permission.

11. Patinkin (1982), p. 101 reproduces the letter sent by Keynes to Kalecki to acknowledge receipt of the proofs of Kalecki (1939). In this letter, Keynes described the book as 'exceedingly clear and intelligible and most agreeable (and *almost* easy) reading. It will be a most valuable work'. There is no indication in the letter that Keynes had ever intended to write a preface for the book, but no indication why the proofs (rather than the printed book later) were sent to Keynes. Patinkin (1982), p. 101, fn. 23 argues that '[t]he misprints [which] Keynes lists here remain in the published version of the book, which suggests that Kalecki sent the proofs at too late a stage for any changes to be made in them'. Accordingly, I find it difficult to accept Osiatynski's statement '. . . that the proofs were sent to Keynes because he was supposed to write a foreword to the book, and that illness prevented his doing so'. The preface to Kalecki (1939) is dated June 1938. Keynes 'over the last years before the war . . . was very much of an invalid' (Robinson, 1947) following his heart attack in the summer of 1937.

12. For biography of Keynes see, *inter alia*, Harrod (1951), Moggridge (1976), Skidelsky (1983). The biography of Hessian (1984) was not available in time to be incorporated into the text, but deals with some of the connections between Kalecki and Keynes.

13. Skidelsky (1983) also argues that '[t]he history of the Keynesian revolution is largely a story of Keynes's escape from the quantity theory

of money. What is interesting to the student of Keynes's thought is how little hint of escape there was before the First World War. At Cambridge Keynes expounded the quantity theory with all the fervour of a true believer'.

14. For a series from which these figures is taken, see Feinstein (1972).
15. The other assumptions are:

    (a) there is broad price stability;
    (b) the money supply is quite inelastic;
    (c) the capital stock and techniques are given;
    (d) the population is not growing substantially;
    (e) the capital stock is 'inadequate'.

    We discuss (b) further in the text later, and (c), (e) briefly. Kalecki and Keynes would appear to take similar attitudes over (a) in the sense of not paying particular attention to inflationary situations (e.g. impact inflation would have an accounting profit) though this does not imply they assumed prices constant.

    For Kalecki's views on the impact of population on economic activity, see Kalecki (1954), pp. 159–61, for Keynes's views see Keynes (1973), pp. 124–33.

16. Figures derived from Zweig (1944).
17. Kaldor (1981) writes that

    [t]hough he [Keynes] sometimes recognized (as in the *Treatise on Money*) that the quantity of money can vary automatically in response to the demand for bank loans (if only because of the prevailing system of overdraft facilities which can be activated at the initiative of the borrower) most of the time he followed the Marshallian tradition of regarding the amount of money in existence as being determined by the monetary authorities who regulate the volume of credit extended by the clearing banks. . . .

    See also Chick (1983), Chapter 12.

18. Ohlin wrote that 'in this respect (the assumption of perfect competition) as in other respects Keynes does not seem to me to have been sufficiently radical enough in freeing himself from the conventional assumptions. When reading his book one sometimes wonders whether he never discussed imperfect competition with Mrs Robinson' (in Keynes, 1973, p. 196). The last sentence hints at Robinson (1933) on *The Economics of Imperfect Competition*. Lekachman (1977) wrote that

    the context made it plain that 'the degree of competition' which Keynes took for granted approximated Marshallian assumptions of sufficient competition in most markets to guarantee quick responses by sellers to shifts in the demand for their products. Certainly there were few suggestions at any point in the *General Theory* that private monopoly was a force to be reckoned with.

Robinson (1976b) argued that 'Keynes did not accept the "perfect competition" of the textbooks, but some vague old-fashioned notion of competition that he never formulated explicitly'.

19. The title of Leijonhufvud (1968), *Keynesian Economics and the Economics of Keynes*, brought the question of the relationship between the work of Keynes and Keynesian economics to the fore. On this question see, for example, Coddington (1983), Chick (1983). For Hicks's view on his creation of IS–LM see Hicks (1983).

20. Our discussion relates specifically to National Institute Model 6 (revised August 1983).

10
Development in Mixed Economies

Introduction

This chapter is intended to review the central themes of Kalecki's writings on developing economies, with the main focus on 'mixed' economies (combining some elements of capitalism with some forms of planning). Socialist economies are considered in the next chapter. We aim here only to indicate the central themes of Kalecki's writings on development and how those themes link with some of the central themes of Kalecki's writings on developed capitalist economies. But we do not intend to provide the same type of extensive treatment of Kalecki's writings on development as we did for his writings on capitalist economies. Many of Kalecki's major essays on development were written or translated into English and have been published as Kalecki (1976), and the quotes from Kalecki in this chapter relate to that volume unless there is indication to the contrary. Kalecki's work on development has been reviewed by one of his colleagues in Sachs (1977).

Kalecki was heavily involved with teaching and research in the area of development planning particularly from the late 1950s to the late 1960s. In Warsaw, he started an advanced seminar on underdeveloped economies with Oscar Lange and Czeslaw Bobrowski in 1958 which 'became a focal point for all researchers and practitioners with the less developed economies. It was addressed by a large number of distinguished foreign speakers many of whom came from the Third World' (Sachs, 1977). Kalecki was also involved as Chairman of the Scientific Board with a Research Centre on underdeveloped economies, and with running a Higher Course in

National Economic Planning for economists from less developed countries.

Underlying Themes

A first and basic theme expressed by Kalecki (e.g. Kalecki, 1976, Chapter 1) is that the cause of unemployment in underdeveloped countries is fundamentally different from that in developed capitalist countries. In the latter, unemployment arises on account of inadequacy of effective demand. But in underdeveloped countries, unemployment is seen to result from the shortage of capital equipment rather than from a deficiency of effective demand. Thus, in general, the constraints on the level of employment and the pace of development are seen as more supply-side than demand-side constraints in the specific context of developing countries. This view then leads to the identification of the particularly binding constraints in any concrete situation, followed by proposals for the alleviation of those constraints. In the next section we discuss the four major *economic* constraints on development which Kalecki identified, which will be seen as essentially arising on the supply-side. Kalecki was very conscious of the political and social constraints on development in mixed economies, and we discuss some of those constraints below. But we shall follow Kalecki in making the analytical distinction between the two types of constraints, whilst recognising that a full analysis must bring in both elements.

A second theme is the need for the expansion of agricultural production as part of the process of development, since development itself leads to an increased demand for food. If that increased demand is not satisfied, then the price of food is likely to rise, thereby depressing real wages and helping to generate inflation. The agricultural sector is seen as likely to involve low productivity, and backward techniques. In one way this offers the opportunity that 'it will be possible to produce a higher output per acre with fewer people on the farm, without using labour saving techniques' (p. 18). Thus the agricultural sector may often involve zero or negative marginal productivity of labour and productivity in that sector may increase merely through the drift of labour away from the land into the urban areas. But for substantial improvements in productivity, more than a decline in the agricultural work-force is required. These 'powerful obstacles to the development of agriculture are the feudal or semi-feudal relations in land tenure as well as the domination of the poor peasants by merchants and money lenders.' Thus a radical acceleration of the development of agriculture is impossible if substantial institutional changes are not introduced'. (p. 26).

The third theme, reflected to some degree in the first two themes, is that market mechanisms left to themselves are unlikely to produce outcomes which Kalecki would consider in any sense socially acceptable or desirable. This is reflected in a number of ways – for example, a failure to provide sufficient capital equipment to enable the full employment of available labour (theme one above), an inadequate production of food (theme two above) and the wrong mix of goods (as between consumption goods and investment goods and the type of consumption goods). Thus Kalecki saw a strong need for planning and direct government intervention particularly in the areas of investment and foreign trade. However, Kalecki (e.g. p. 17) was well aware of the resistance to planning and government intervention for development. Simply, the purpose of planning and intervention in development would be to overcome the inadequacies of the market and of existing social institutions and arrangements. Those social classes and institutions which have power to limit (or prevent) general development will challenge the use of planning and intervention to overcome their power in the pursuit of development.

The fourth theme is the distributional aspects of growth and development. Throughout his writing, Kalecki stressed income distribution aspects of his analysis, and the distributional consequences of particular policies. This is evident from his writings in wartime Britain, in post-war Poland (see next chapter) and also arises in the area of development. In his writings on development, there is (a generally implicit) concern that development should benefit the poor. This is expressed in an essay on the financing of economic development (Chapter 7) where he stated that his assumptions included no inflationary price increases of necessities and no taxes levied on lower income groups or on necessities. Further, there is an awareness of the distributional factors influencing the course and pace of development as well as the distributional consequences of different forms of development.

Economic Constraints on Development

Kalecki was quite clear that a shortage of capital equipment was a major cause of unemployment and under-employment in underdeveloped countries. Although a deficiency of effective demand could at times be a contributory factor, it was not seen as a major one. Hence 'the crucial problem facing the underdeveloped countries is thus to increase investment considerably, not for the sake of generating effective demand, as was the case in an under-employed developed economy, but for the sake of accelerating the expansion of productive capacity indispensable for the rapid growth of national income' (pp. 23–4). It is implicit in this view that the usual neo-classical notion that there are continuous substitution possibilities between inputs into the productive process (specifically labour and capital equipment here) is ruled out. It is clear that Kalecki's analysis assumed that there is a strong element of 'fixed factor' proportions (and this assumption arises also in Kalecki's work on socialist economies, see pp. 245–6 below).

The idea of 'fixed factor' proportions has two aspects of relevance here. The first one is that once a particular form of capital equipment has been installed the possibility of varying the amount of labour used with that equipment is limited, i.e. *ex post* fixed factor proportions at the limit when no substitution between labour and capital equipment is possible. But, second, Kalecki had in mind that there were considerable limitations on the *ex ante* possibilities of substituting labour for capital. He discussed the possibility of generating employment by the use of what he termed 'pick and shovel' techniques, i.e. those using very little capital equipment. He thought that such techniques could be applicable in construction and might be possible in industrial production or services (e.g. pp. 17–18). The possible generation of employment by the use of labour-intensive techniques would lead to an increased demand for agricultural products. Then, the 'bottleneck of supply of necessities which depends on the inelasticity of agricultural production' would be encountered (p. 17). Thus even when there are technical possibilities of substitution in one sector of the economy, the achievement of such substitution may be held back by lack of substitution possibilities elsewhere.

The expansion of productive capacity faces three obstacles. First, private investment may not be forthcoming at a desirable rate, which means that the government needs to step in to ensure that total investment reaches the required level. Second, the investment goods industries may be fully utilised, though since much investment goods are imported this obstacle could be overcome through an increase in exports to pay for the increased imports of investment goods or a reduction in imports of luxury goods. Third, an inflationary pressure on necessities, particularly food, arises from the increased demand which cannot be met by agricultural production.

The second important constraints involve the problems of raising agricultural production. We find it convenient to discuss these problems in stages. In the first stage, the implications of the view taken by Kalecki that agricultural production was difficult to expand and that formed a severe constraint on development. In the second stage we will look at the reasons which Kalecki gave for the difficulties for the expansion of agricultural production.

In the capitalist sectors of the economy, Kalecki adopted the view that there was generally excess capacity so that increased demand could be relatively easily accommodated by expansion of output. Over a longer time horizon, investment could ensure that capacity expanded roughly in line with demand. But in the agricultural sector this did not apply. In the short period, the nature of agricultural production is such that it is difficult to expand output in the short-term in response to a rise in demand. It can be recalled from Chapter 2 that in the markets for primary products, Kalecki saw prices as being demand determined, and this was essentially that supply in output terms could not respond to demand changes leading to price responses. But, further, Kalecki argued that even in the longer term there were severe difficulties in the expansion of agricultural supply. The semi-feudal organisation of agriculture, as will be seen below, prevented expansion.

The process of development involves the growth of real incomes, and thereby a rise in the demand for food and other outputs from the agricultural sector. Further, any growth of population will similarly generate increased demands on the agricultural sector. But, the agricultural sector may not be able (in its form) to meet those increased demands, and thereby restrict the pace of development.

Kalecki (1976), Chapter 7 presented a formal model of the way in which 'the rate of increase of supply of necessities, as fixed by institutional barriers to the development of agriculture, determines the growth of national income. But the rate of growth was subject to certain constraints'. The basic postulates for this analysis are that there must be no inflationary price increases of necessities (particularly staple food) and no taxes levied on lower income groups. The combined effect of these two requirements is that the economy is constrained to grow such that the growth of demand from lower income groups (which is largely on necessities) is in line with the growth of agricultural production. An economy which tries to grow faster than this growth rate of necessities (with or without government intervention) would run into inflationary difficulties. An increase of demand over supply would lead to price rises of necessities, especially as the supply cannot be expanded to meet the demand. A rise in price of necessities involves a fall in real wages, which may then lead to money wage rises and wage–price spiral. But, the money wage response will not restore real wages for the simple reason that the higher real wages which would result involve a demand for necessities which outstrips supply. Thus 'the inelastic supply of food lead(s) to a fall in real wages', but also 'the benefit of food price increases accru[es] not to small proprietors, but to capitalists' (p. 47). Thus there is a shift of spending power from wage-earners to capitalists, which leads to a reduction in the general level of demand. 'It is clear ... that the expansion of food production paralleling the industrial development, is of paramount importance for avoiding inflationary pressures' (p. 48). In the context of development, Kalecki adopted a basically structuralist view of inflation in that it is structural imbalance between sectors which cannot be easily overcome which are seen to lie at the root of inflation. Further, this type of inflation involves a reduction in real wages. 'The primary inflationary pressure experienced in the course of rapid economic development is ... the result of basic disproportions in productive relations'. In those circumstances, Kalecki argued, monetary and credit restrictions will have little impact on this type of inflation. It could be added that even if the actual rate of price increase were reduced by such means, the basic problems (particularly the reduction of real wages and imbalance between sectors) would remain. Indeed, 'the solution of the problem (of inflation) must be based on economic policies embracing the whole process of development' (p. 62).

Clearly when inflation arises from basic disproportions between sectors in terms of their supply potential relative to demand then the removal of inflationary pressures requires the removal of these

disproportions. In Kalecki's view the removal of those disproportions is not something which the unfettered market mechanism
would easily bring about (particularly in the context of underdeveloped countries) and the implementation of a conscious plan
would be required.

The development of agricultural production can be seen as
particularly important. A development programme will involve the
development of many sectors, but the development of agriculture is
seen as particularly important for the restraints which its lack of
development would pose for the rest of the development programme.

The agricultural sector is seen as largely characterised by surplus
labour (so that further employment in agriculture would not increase production) and by feudal and semi-feudal social organisation. It is the existing institutional (broadly conceived) arrangements
which are seen to limit the expansion of agricultural production.
Kalecki argued that in India, for example, the development of
agriculture was hampered by the poverty of the peasants, their
dependence on merchants and money lenders and the operation of
many farms without any security of tenure (cf. p. 19). In those
circumstances, the rapid development of Indian agriculture requires
the overcoming of the institutional obstacles by government policy
which reduce the dependence of peasants on money-lenders and
introduce security of tenure.

In general, the development of agriculture requires government
intervention to overcome institutional obstacles. The measures by
government 'range from land reform and cheap bank credit for
peasants to improvements in the method of cultivation, small scale
irrigation and cheap fertilizers' (p. 48). 'The key . . . is the removal of
obstacles to the expansion of agriculture, such as feudal landowner-
ship and domination of peasants by money lenders and merchants'.
In general Kalecki linked together desirable social changes (e.g. shift
in power from landowners to the peasants) with increased productivity in agriculture and development. But the political and social
changes involved were likely to be considerable, and 'the overcoming of all the obstacles to economic development . . . amounts to
more than the upheaval created in the eighteenth century by the
French Revolution. Thus it is not surprising that these reforms are
not peacefully carried out' (p. 27).

The third constraint arises from a lack of foreign exchange, and difficulty in producing and selling sufficient exports. Kalecki often analysed growth under the assumption of either a close economy or balanced foreign trade. But this was in part for analytical convenience (by taking one problem at a time, leaving other problems on one side) and to stress the nature of the domestic constraints facing an economy. Further, the next stage of the analysis can then be to look at the ways in which foreign trade can be balanced, or at least the way in which any deficit is to be financed. Foreign trade and the import of capital equipment is an important source for overcoming bottlenecks in production and the associated inflationary pressures. There are, however, severe limitations on the export possibilities for paying for these imports (which Kalecki explored in more detail under his analysis of growth in socialist countries, cf. pp. 251–2 of the next chapter).

Whilst recognising the advantages of importing capital equipment Kalecki argued that the financing of those imports through various forms of borrowing presented substantial, if not insuperable, problems. He considered the three forms of financing a perpetual balance of trade deficit of foreign government grants, commercial loans and direct investment by foreign firms.

Actual grants (from foreign governments, international agencies) do not create the problems of future repayment and interest charges which the other forms of financing a deficit have. But 'some political strings would usually be attached to such grants as would be available on a large scale, and this may adversely affect the whole course of development' (p. 56). The provision of loans on interest free or interest reduced basis would face similar problems for the developing country.

Commercial loans may not present the specific political problems which the other two forms do, but clearly do have the economic problems of high interest rates and the difficulties of obtaining such loans. The problem arising from high interest rates and from failure of exports to grow in the hoped for manner are vividly illustrated by the financial difficulties of many indebted developing countries in the mid-1980s. Although Kalecki did not mention this, the problem of paying interest charges can be seen as worsened by variable interest rates on loans, particularly when high interest rate policies are being followed by some major developed countries.

Kalecki did not accept the frequently advocated advantages of direct investment by foreign firms. He thought (e.g. p. 56) that direct investment would often be directed towards certain areas of the economy such as production of raw materials, which may bias economic and social development in those directions and away from a balanced development of the economy. Further, the large multinational firms making the direct investment would acquire political influence, which could further influence the course of economic development in a harmful manner. Further, direct investment may well yield high rates of profit, leading to a high rate of transfer of dividends abroad. In that case, the financial flows out of the developing country may well be as high for direct investment as for loans.

Kalecki further argued that a partial substitute for the inflow of finance to cover a trade deficit would be the reduction of outflows of finance. Since a major way in which funds can be transferred from one country to another include through the use of transfer pricing, the remission of dividends and royalty payments, it is likely that seeking to reduce financial outflows would involve control over transfer pricing, dividend and royalty payments. In turn, substantial control by central government over foreign business would be required.

Much of the emphasis of Kalecki's writings on development, and particularly the case studies contained in Kalecki (1976) (on Israel, India, Cuba), was on identifying and then *planning* to remove the relevant binding constraints. Of significance here is the stress of planning and government intervention. The market mechanism is seen as unable to generate the right level and mix of investment for development purposes and to favour the rich over the poor. Thus Kalecki's advocacy of government intervention was based on the inadequacy of market mechanisms, the need for the social control of investment and development and the redistribution of income towards a more egalitarian distribution.

However, Kalecki 'was always suspicious of too sweeping formulations and excessive reliance on one single "miracle" solution. He would always emphasise the importance of analysing concrete solutions and bringing into the picture all relevant factors be they economic or not. Only in this way could the limitations of the particular case under scrutiny be unveiled, the constraints to action clearly perceived, the bottlenecks identified and a set of consistent policies and measures eventually arrived at' (Sachs, 1977).

Political Constraints

'At no time would Kalecki indulge in what might be called pure economics. The adjective "political" weighed high in his brand of political economy' (Sachs, 1977). Thus the preceding analysis of economic constraints must not be taken out of the political context. As can be envisaged from the discussion in Chapter 7, Kalecki was well aware that government planning was subject to much political resistance.

The constraints on development posed by the existing social and political order were seen as particularly severe in the rural agricultural sectors. Kalecki argued that even if all the required material resources for the development of agriculture were available, nevertheless there would still be a variety of social and political limitations. Kalecki viewed the semi-feudal relations of land tenure and the domination of merchants and money lenders as powerful restrictions on development, which would have to be removed for that development to occur. But, 'it is perfectly clear that overcoming the resistance to such institutional changes by the privileged classes is a much more difficult proposition than the financial trick which solves the problem of effective demand crucial for the developed economies' (p. 26).

Similarly, an increase in the level of investment has to be financed and requires the injection of resources. Kalecki often argued in a variety of circumstances against the resources for investment being obtained by the reduction of the consumption of necessities by workers (i.e. real wages being maintained). Hence any shift of domestic resources into investment would have to come by the reduction of luxury consumption of the rich. The taxation of the rich was one means towards that objective, which would reduce their consumption and provide the state with the finance for investment. But this was again subject to political and social constraints.

Finally, there arises the problem of adequate taxation of the rich and well to do to make room for higher investment. Here again serious obstacles are encountered. Tax collection in under-developed countries is very difficult and tax evasion is rampant, even when the respective laws are passed. This is also used as an argument against introduction of the taxes in question by the vested interests concerned. As a result not much progress is usually made in this matter (p. 26).

With Kalecki's commitment to various economic measures which shifted the balance of economic welfare towards the poor, but with his recognition of the political constraints, it is not surprising that 'he hardly ever saw a positive correlation between the advice dispensed by him and the line of conduct adopted by the government'. In the specific case of advice drawn up for the Israeli government, 'the guarded thanks of the Minister of Finance of Israel show that Kalecki's home truths were sometimes painful and the policies he commended too strenuous to be popular' (Robinson, 1976a).

One of the strongest statements on these political constraints comes at the end of an address on the difference between the crucial economic problems of developed and underdeveloped non-socialist countries which it may be interesting to note, in light of recent developments, to the reunion of Latin American schools of economics. Kalecki concluded that the political problems arising from the

> intervention of the government in the sphere of investment with the aim of securing its planned volume and structure, the overcoming of the institutional barriers to rapid development of agriculture, and adequate taxation of the rich and well-to-do – clearly present a formidable problem. In theory, most people will approve of the economic necessity of undertaking the measures in question, even including many representatives of the ruling classes. But when it comes to their implementation, affecting all sorts of vested interests, the situation changes radically and a formidable counteraction develops in a variety of ways. . . . Thus it is not surprising that these reforms are not peacefully carried out (p. 27).

In developed economies, the problem of the adequacy of aggregate demand is a major one, but one which can be 'solved by a sort of financial trick' (p. 21), i.e. the manipulation of aggregate demand by government. This is undertaken against a background of plentiful capital equipment in the sense that the equipment is adequate to provide employment for the whole labour force (provided that the demand is forthcoming). But in developing economies (and Kalecki was particularly writing here of non-socialist economies), 'resources have to be built and this requires far-reaching reforms amounting to revolutionary changes. This simple fact explains the difference in the economic and political situations in these two groups of countries and, in a sense, determined the present phase of history' (p. 27).

Intermediate Regimes

In seeking to understand the nature of the political and social structure and constraints in a range of underdeveloped countries, Kalecki advanced the concept of an 'intermedite regime'.[1] Countries in this category were generally countries which achieved independence after the Second World War, in which the power and influence of foreign interests had been restricted. In these countries, there had been agrarian reform and whilst seeking economic development with government involvement, could not be considered socialist, but had diverged from being strictly capitalist. These intermediate regimes are 'the proverbial clever calves that suck two cows, each [political power] bloc gives them financial aid competing with the other' (p. 35).

The nature of the government of these intermediate regimes is that they represent the interests of lower middle class, rich peasants and managers in the state sector. The lower middle classes were seen as having gained a strong political position in these intermediate regimes. The political importance of the feudal elements of the upper-class can be much reduced by successful land reform which redistributes land and power away from those elements. But the political importance of big business can vary considerably between countries, and it is the extent of that importance which is seen as having considerable effect on the economic and other policies pursued within a country.

At the other end of the class scale, the poorest strata of society are seen as not constituting a threat to the regime, for they are unorganised and lack any power. Kalecki saw this as the reason why there is repression against communists and other leftist groups since 'the communists are simply at least potential spokesmen for the rural and urban paupers and the lower-middle class is quite rightly afraid of the political activisation of the latter' (p. 35). In a postscript to his paper on intermediate regimes Kalecki discussed the anti-communist terror in Indonesia in 1965 in terms of an intermediate regime with a large communist party which represented a considerable threat to 'the reactionary middle classes' and the army.

One of the questions which Kalecki posed was whether there were specific conditions which favoured the emergence of governments which represented the interests of the lower middle class (e.g. p. 30). One of the conditions which Kalecki saw as favouring this development was the numerical superiority of the lower middle class as compared with big business, especially when big business had been predominantly foreign-controlled at the time of independence from colonial rule. He argued that

> in the process of political emancipation [from imperial occupation] . . . representatives of the lower-middle class rise in a way naturally to power. To keep power they must:
>
> (a) achieve not only political but also economic emancipation, i.e. gain a measure of independence from foreign capital;
> (b) carry out a land reform;
> (c) assure continuous economic growth (p. 31).

The land reform which is carried through would be expected to benefit the lower middle classes, with some limitations on the pace and nature of land reform arising from the residual power of feudal landlords and others. '[L]and reform, which is not preceded by an agrarian revolution, is conducted in such a way that the middle class which directly exploits the poor peasants – i.e. the money lenders and merchants – maintains its position, while the rich peasantry achieves considerable gains in the process' (p. 33). But land reform will bring a lower-middle class government into conflict with the feudal landlords. This conflict 'helped us to see better the limitations of land reforms carried out in Egypt and India . . .' (Sachs, 1977).

The growth of state capitalism and involvement in the economies of intermediate regimes can be seen in part as arising from conditions (a) and (c) listed above from Kalecki as necessary for the maintenance of power by the middle class. Kalecki argued that the native upper class was unable to operate as dynamic entrepreneurs on a sufficiently large scale to generate development. This prevents the emergence of local big business to which the interests of the middle class are submitted. But if Kalecki was right, it would mean that 'spontaneous' local development would not occur. Investment by foreign business on a large scale might be thought a possible means of development. But the pre-independence involvement of foreign busines and the desire to limit foreign influence are seen as restricting any encouragement of foreign business investment. Further, foreign business is likely to be most interested in particular forms of investment (e.g. exploitation of natural resources) which may not fit into the pattern of development desired.

The growth of state capitalism and attempts at planning could then be seen, in part, as a response to the lack of acceptable alternatives. But further

> State capitalism concentrates investment on the expansion of the productive potential of the country. Thus there is no danger of forcing the small firms out of business, which is a characteristic feature of the early stage of industrialisation under *laissez-faire*. Next, the rapid development of state enterprises creates executive and technical openings for ambitious young men of the numerous ruling class (p. 33).

The growth of managerial functions helps to satisfy the demand for employment by the middle class, as well as helping to add to the numbers of the middle class.

The development of state capitalism and associated planning arise from an internal situation but is subject to various external pressures. The internal financing of investment may be achieved through a government saving, although subject to various constraints. But any external borrowing that is required to help finance development imposes constraints. These have been to some degree discussed above. Kalecki here drew attention to the dislike of state activities leading to capitalist countries placing conditions on the granting of credits and loans. These conditions would not be merely on the rate of interest, term of loans, etc., but also conditions on how loans are to be used, government policy to be pursued etc. The degree to which capitalist countries impose conditions was seen as depending on the availability of credits and loans from communist countries.

Sachs (1977) argues that the concept of intermediate regimes 'was an attempt at understanding the specificity of the situation as it arose in the 'sixties and was a clear departure from the traditional Marxist standpoint that would reject the possibility of a durable class coalition based on the hegemony of the lower middle class'. It is clear that in Kalecki's concept of an intermediate regime, the capitalist class was weakened but without the working class having taken power. Indeed, Kalecki saw the working class as powerless in an intermediate regime. Joan Robinson wrote that 'some Marxists objected to Professor Raj's article [which applied the concept of intermediate regime to India] but Kalecki and Raj after him, were attempting to use Marx's own method of analysis on problems that have come up since his day' (Robinson, 1976a). This can be seen in that Kalecki moved away from a two class dichotomy (workers and capitalists) towards a three class (capitalist, middle class and workers) structure. It retained the general notion of the importance of class and seeking to understand the operation of economy and society in terms of relative strengths and interests of classes. Finally, we note that Joan Robinson also argued that Kalecki 'foresaw that the intermediate regime is not likely to be a permanent system, but he was too optimistic in supposing that it might give birth to a viable socialist alternative' (Robinson, 1976a).

Foreign Aid and the Financing of Development

Foreign aid is a financial flow, which enables a country to import more goods and services than otherwise, and thereby places more resources at a country's disposal. Kalecki argued that not all inflows of foreign capital should be counted as aid. Only those inflows which allowed a country to improve its growth rate and development should count as aid. Those inflows which were only secured as loans carrying commercial or higher rates of interest were to be excluded, as was any inflow which was effectively used to finance the consumption of luxuries (even though the exclusion of such inflows from measures of aid would be difficult in practice). An important aspect of aid is to enable a higher level of imports, and an important role of imports is to relieve various bottlenecks of supply.

Kalecki argued (p. 69) that the evaluation of foreign aid should pay regard to two functions of aid. First, there was the question of the extent to which foreign aid improved a country's balance of payments position, and then how that improvement had been used in terms of increased supply of capital goods, luxuries or intermediate goods. Second, there was the question of whether the additional financial resources actually raised investment above the level of domestic savings, or whether those savings had been diverted into consumption.

Kalecki continued by indicating that in his view (joint paper with Sachs) aid can be considered to be appropriately used if it adds to investment (apart from in the production of luxuries) or to the consumption of essentials and the social services.

Kalecki showed a strong preference for aid from public sector rather than private sector. He based his first on the ground that public sector funds were generally more flexible in the sense that they could be used for either public or private sector use in the recipient country, whereas private sector funds were usually tied to a specific firm, and not available for use in the public sector nor to fit in with the development plan. Second, foreign direct investment (which Kalecki argued should not be regarded as part of aid) involved relative high rates of profit and the transfer of substantial profits abroad at some stage. He also argued that for 'minimum conditions, which form the recipient's country's point of view should be respected in order to make the inflow of foreign private capital useful, if not part of aid'. He advocated conditions which would control the type of investments allowed and the repatriation of profits from developing countries. But, Kalecki 'doubt(ed) whether much new direct foreign investment would be available under these regulations' (p. 84), so he could be seen to place the gains of increased usefulness of direct investment and the retention of sovereignty resulting from the controls as offsetting the lower level of direct investment.

Kalecki (pp. 85–8) also discussed the role of 'aid through trade'. He had previously noted that in the decade up to the mid-1960s (when that chapter was written) the inflow of long-term capital had been largely offset by the burden of debt and changes in the terms of trade (p. 67). He began his discussion of aid through trade by stressing the important role of foreign aid was to add to the import capacity of developing countries. The improvement of export trade services is a similar purpose and is in any event required to avoid growing dependency on foreign aid.

Kalecki considered the role of 'aid through trade' (which meant improvement of the terms of trade in favour of developing countries and the creation of additional markets) as increasing the capacity of developing countries to import (since real value of exports rise) and thereby to reach a higher rate of growth. Besides advocating multilateral schemes to assist the trade of developing countries, he also advocated some bilateral measures. Such measures could include bilateral long-term export contracts which help introduce an element of price stability (which in turn would help with planning) and would also serve as a way of testing out stabilisation schemes on a bilateral basis, with the possibility of extending the successful on to multilateral basis. Another proposal advanced by Kalecki was the development of 'industrial branch agreements', which would be bilateral long term agreements between developed and a developing country which establish

> over a given period of time a changing pattern of mutual supplies, not necessarily balanced, including raw materials, intermediate goods, final products and equipment, with a final aim of implanting in the developing countries new industries, partly or wholly export oriented, and at the same time creating complementarity of economies based on specialisation and partial division of labour (p. 88).

Conclusion

Development economics emerged during the 1950s and 1960s as a distinct area of study within economics. It was a subject, rather like macroeconomics, where policy and theory were closely linked. The claim of development economics to be a distinct area of study was underpinned by the notion that economic theory appropriate for developed countries (particularly if that theory was taken as neoclassical economics) was not the relevant theory for developing countries. Sen (1983) argues that

> in terms of policy the following have been among the major strategic themes pursued [by development economics] since the beginning of the subject: (1) industralisation, (2) rapid capital accumulation, (3) mobilisation of underemployed manpower, and (4) planning and an economically active state. . . . These themes . . . are closely linked to criticism of the traditional neoclassical models as applied to developing countries.

The general idea that developing countries differ significantly from developed countries can be seen above to have influenced Kalecki's writings as can the idea of planning and an economically active state. The three other themes identified by Sen can also be seen as arising to some degree in Kalecki's writings, as well as the rejection of neo-classical economics (both for developing and developed countries). In addition, Kalecki stressed the political and social constraints on the implementation of those types of policies. Indeed, it is probably in these writings on development that the interdependence between economics and politics in Kalecki's work is most clearly evident.

The bulk of the writings of Kalecki which we have drawn on above were written in the 1960s. We have observed before that Kalecki's theoretical work rests on assumptions chosen to reflect the important ingredients of a problem. Some parts of Kalecki's analysis reflect the circumstances of the 1960s and hence would need to be amended for the 1980s.

Note to Chapter 10

1. Sachs (1977) indicates that Kalecki wrote his essay on intermediate regimes (which is reprinted as Kalecki (1976), Chapter 4) to 'generalise the findings of an empirical study on Nasser's Egypt . . .' Other countries to which the concept of 'intermediate regime' was applied by Kalecki include Bolivia (Kalecki, 1976, Chapter 11), Indonesia and India.

11
Kalecki and the Economics of Socialism

Introduction

Kalecki's writings on the economics of socialism were undertaken only after his return to Poland in December 1954.[1] The first two years of Kalecki's return to Poland coincided with the growth of overt political opposition to the government, the Poznań workers' uprising in June 1956 and the spread of strikes across Poland, and the spontaneous setting up of workers' councils in October 1956 (the 'Polish October' as it is often called). Gomulka was restored to power in that October after having been in disgrace since 1949 (including a $3\frac{1}{2}$ year period under house arrest).[2] After the Stalinist era (so far as Eastern European countries were concerned) of the period 1949–53, there had been 'a thaw' following the death of Stalin in early 1953, with the famous denunciation of Stalin by Krushchev in February 1956. The first Six Year Plan in Poland, covering the years 1950 to 1956, had followed the Soviet pattern, with an emphasis on rapid and heavy industrialisation, the promotion of investment over consumption, collectivisation and centralisation. Whilst the Six Year Plan was officially declared to have been 'over-fulfilled', there was widespread dissatisfaction with its results, exemplified by the Poznań uprising and strikes.[3] Zielinski (1973) a Polish observer of these events has described

> [t]he characteristic feature of Polish 6-year plan strategy [for 1950–6 as] ... its lack of balance between investment and consumption ... Generally speaking, the Polish 6-year plan was too

taut. It assumed a too high rate of growth and favoured not only investment at the expense of consumption but also investment in heavy industry at the expense of investment in consumer goods industry.

Thus, the background against which Kalecki began work on the economics of socialism was then one of liberalisation after the Stalin years and of dissatisfaction with the results of central planning.[4]

Kalecki was directly involved it many of the debates in the mid-1950s on the development and organisation of the Polish economy. He was head of the perspective plan division of the Planning Commission, where he was in charge of drawing up the fifteen-year perspective plan to cover the years 1961–75. The authorities heavily criticised the plan. Those criticisms are discussed below since conflict over the perspective plan can illustrate some of the differences between Kalecki's approach to planning and the Soviet/Eastern Europe orthodoxy.

Kalecki was also one of the vice-chairmen of the Economic Council, which was an advisory body to the Council of Ministers, from February, 1957 until it was disbanded in 1963.[5] Zielinski (1973) (p. 49) described this Economic Council as including 'many eminent Polish economists – together with several economic administrators – and for one or two years (1957–8) it was the main driving force behind Polish economic reform proposals'.

After 1960, Kalecki's activities were centred on academic work, and though he continued in an advisory role with the government, his influence was much reduced. He again came into sharp conflict with the authorities in 1964 over his alternative proposals for the 1966–70 Five Year Plan, which led to his removal from any advisory capacity.[6] 'In 1968, in the wake of Czechoslovak Spring and the Polish March events, the blow was directed against Kalecki's theories and his school of economics' (Brus, 1977a). Many of Kalecki's colleagues were sacked from their university posts and Kalecki resigned in protest.[7]

The discussion of Kalecki's approach to the economics of socialism is divided into seven parts. In the first part, the general position taken by Kalecki on the major issues relating to the organisation of a socialist economy (e.g. the extent of centralisation, the appropriateness of the use of markets) is outlined. His discussion on these issues has not, in the main, been translated into English and much of the relevant material is contained in relatively short papers in Polish prepared in the 1950s.[8] In the second part, Kalecki's views on the development of socialist economies (particularly on the relative shares of consumption and investment) are outlined. His views on the appropriate rate of investment, and on the 'realism' of plans were one of the main factors which brought Kalecki into conflict with the authorities.

In the third part, the differences which Kalecki saw between the operation of capitalist economies and socialist economies are outlined. The fourth and fifth parts deal with Kalecki's theory of growth of socialist economies. This was the major thrust of his theoretical work, but he still regarded it as an introductory stage. It is also notable that this theoretical work strongly reflects his involvement with planning in Poland, and the issues which he saw as important in that context, particularly the relationship between consumption and investment and the foreign trade constraint. Kalecki saw the decisions over investment share of total output and growth rate of the economy as two of the key decisions to be taken by central planners, and his theoretical work can be seen as seeking to bring out the type of choices in those directions facing the central planners. In the sixth section we briefly look at Kalecki's approach to technical progress.

The final part considers Kalecki's work on investment decisions, rules and ways in which investment decisions could be decentralised such that the overall outcome fitted in with the overall plan.

Kalecki on Questions of Socialist Organisation

In this section, we outline the nature of Kalecki's views on the organisation of a socialist economy. These views emerged in the context of debates over the 'shape' of the Polish economy in the late 1950s and are therefore likely to reflect the issues raised in those debates and the experience of Poland and other Eastern European economies.

The debates over the organisation of a socialist economy usually involve questions of the degree of centralisation, the appropriate use of markets, the implementation of decisions and the relationship between the centre and the productive enterprises (amongst other questions). In this part we outline Kalecki's attitudes to these issues.

Kalecki's general approach is well summarised by Lipiński (1977).[9]

> While defending central planning against the attacks of the extreme decentralizers, he took a very active part at the same time, in the work of the Economic Council and the Planning Commission on producing a new model for the economy which would be a departure from the old system of bureaucratic centralism. He was very eager to ensure that the conditions of decentralisation should mean an increase in self-management for the workers' collective as well. For this reason, amongst others, he felt that workers' councils should be installed as high as the level of the group of enterprises. Perhaps he saw the conflict between Workers' Councils and central planning more clearly than any of us. This is what he wrote about the synthesis model of workers' councils combined with central planning which was foreshadowed at the time. 'We ought not to delude ourselves that a system of this kind is free of contradictions and will be easy to run. On the one hand there will be the danger that the Workers' Councils will be weakened and the whole system of management bureaucratized. On the other it could happen that the Workers' Councils will exert such pressure that it will become necessary to slow up the tempo of development, or to make maintenance of the growth rate dependent on aid from abroad, or again that there will be a period of chaos, after which things will be tidied up with the aid of a return to the system of bureaucratic centralism' (Lipiński, 1977, quoting from Kalecki, 1956b).[10]

There are many aspects of this quote which we seek to highlight. The first aspect is that Kalecki supported the notion that central planning should be used to determine the main lines of development of a socialist economy. 'He did not . . . oppose the idea of utilizing the market-mechanism, but considered it a subordinate element in the running of an economy which should be planned centrally as far as the main lines of development were concerned' (Brus, 1977a).[11,12] In his work on economic growth of socialist economies, discussed below, Kalecki introduced the notion of a government decision curve as between the rate of productive accumulation (roughly share of investment in national income) and the rate of growth of output. Kalecki clearly saw those decisions as taken by a central body. Whilst it is not certain from that work whether Kalecki regarded this central decision-making as desirable, there is little to suggest that he thought that decisions on the overall rate of investment and growth should not be taken by the central authorities. In his outline of a method of constructing a perspective plan (Kalecki, 1962c), he argued that the particular plan variant

> finally adopted *should* be distinguished by the highest possible rate of growth at which there is a realistic possibility of balancing foreign trade and at which the relative share of productive investment plus the increase in inventories in the national income is considered tolerable by the authorities from the point of view or the impact upon consumption and unproductive investment in the short-run (italics added).

Further, there is the evidence from his work on investment decision rules as well as the comments from his colleagues that he thought that such decisions should be taken centrally.

The second aspect, which is only implicit in the quote given above from Lipiński, was the rejection of the unfettered use of the market mechanism in a socialist economy. He saw it as having a subordinate role but not a dominant role. In particular,

> Kalecki was never attracted by theories which defended the economic rationality of socialism by trying to prove that full fledged market operations can be introduced or imitated by it, or by those who claimed that the superiority of socialism over capitalism was to be sought in the fact that it was better equipped to create and safeguard the cherished textbook conditions of perfect competition and general equilibrium (Brus, 1977a).[13]

We have seen above that Kalecki was not anyway favourably disposed towards the model of perfect competition in general equilibrium as a realistic analysis of capitalism. But, further, his general hostility to the use of markets and his view that markets often malfunction also carried over from the analysis of capitalism into the analysis of socialism.

A number of writers have indicated the nature of Kalecki's views on the use of the market mechanism under socialism. 'Authoritative students have expressed their scepticism, therefore, as to the ability of the market forces – in these circumstances [of a centralised physical allocation of resources] – to channel the supply of manpower to the most needy sectors of the economy, in accordance with demand (as determined by the planners' social priorities)' (Zauberman, 1964). In a footnote, Zauberman refers only to Kalecki (1956b) as an example of authoritative students. Toporowski (1982) remarks that 'Kalecki himself was opposed to the autonomous operation of markets in production because of the degree of slack that would be necessary in the labour market and in the markets for other inputs, in order to maintain equilibrium. Furthermore, he was sceptical about the responsiveness of enterprises to parametric finetuning . . .' (p. 109, fn. 21).

However, and this is the third aspect of Kalecki's approach, the above remarks should not be taken as implying support for the highly centralised planning of the form practised in Poland during the first Six Year Plan, and in the Soviet Union in their five year plans. There are three parts to Kalecki's disagreements with these practices. The first part relates to the use of 'taut' planning, and the preference for heavy industrial investment over other forms of investment and particularly consumption. This is discussed more fully below.

The second and third parts related to the decision-making at the enterprise level and to the form in which the decisions of the central planners were transmitted to the enterprises. These are summarised by Brus (1977a), when he wrote that '[i]n the early autumn of 1956 he [Kalecki] became vice-chairman (in practice chairman) of a special commission charged with drafting of three basic laws – the Workers' Councils Act, the Enterprise Fund Act (profit-sharing) and the Government Order . . . reducing quite radically the number of targets enterprises had to meet' (Brus, 1977b). In Kalecki (1956b)

he stressed that it was the 'extension of the rights of the enterprises which created for the workers' councils the possibility of showing initiative in the organisation of production'. On the other hand, the system of workers' councils combined with central planning seemed to him to provide the proper blend of factors indispensible for avoiding past degeneration in the economic mechanism and for creating the necessary conditions for the development of socialist democracy (Brus, 1977a).[14]

The powers embodied in the Workers' Councils Act were never implemented.[15] By 1958, 'the workers' councils were reduced to the role of debating societies' (Dziewanowski, 1959, p. 288). They continued in formal existence but without any effective decision making powers. However, Kalecki 'was one of those members of the Economic Council who demanded extension of the workers representation to the levels above the enterprise (industrial associations); he took up this position at the time when the party leadership was already backpedalling on the whole issue of workers' self-management'. (Brus, 1977b).

Zauberman (1964) has described the system of incentives proposed by Kalecki as

a 'new system of stimuli and command' based on four 'elements': value added as the principal index of a firm's activities; its wage bill component; the rate of increase of profits as a basis for premium type remuneration; and non-repayable interest-bearing investment credits. A proportion of amortization allowance would also remain with the firm. Mechanisms actually devised have borrowed a good deal from this scheme – in varying degrees and different combinations in individual countries.

Kalecki

devoted considerable time and effort to finding theoretical and practical solutions for: a reasonable devolution of economic decisions; curtailment of the number of obligatory plan-indicators and elimination of obviously harmful ones (like the discredited gross-output target); the introduction of economic incentives linked to profitability and the active use of prices, credit policy and interest rates (Brus, 1977a).

The final aspect of the quote from Lipiński given above is some acknowledgement of contradictions and conflicts within a socialist economy. This can also be contrasted with 'Soviet, and later, Eastern European official texts [which] have more explicitly claimed the correspondence of production relations and productive forces under socialism, i.e. the end of conflicts and dialectical contradictions' (Nuti, 1979). Brus (1977a) indicated that for Kalecki 'socialism ... was never a conflictless utopia' and makes the comparison with 'institutional Marxist(s) [who were] refusing to submit socialism to Marxist dialectical scrutiny of contradictions'.

Kalecki and Socialist Development

Kalecki's major disagreement with Polish (and Soviet) economic planning policies, was probably that

> against the so-called official 'law of faster development of department I', which produced producer goods as an allegedly absolute condition for sustained growth. This dogma had just been re-established in the USSR after the fall of Malenkov in 1955. Kalecki chose this topic for his paper to the Second Congress of Polish economists in June 1956 (Brus, 1977a).

The challenge of Kalecki to the prevailing orthodoxy in this report can be seen as leading to his eventual loss of influence, as will be outlined shortly. The topic of his paper in 1956 (Kalecki, 1956a) can be seen as running through most of his work in the economics of growth under socialism, which we discuss in some detail below. Before coming to those issues, we can outline the two ways in which Kalecki came into conflict with the 'law of faster development of department I'.

The first way could be seen as Kalecki arguing that the theory underlining that law was either wrong or inapplicable. For example, Nove and Nuti (1972) state that in the 1920s

> Fel'dman formalised the main features of the Soviet investment strategy in a two-sector model of acceleration of growth ... The

assumptions of the model – capital equipment as the limiting factor, plentiful labour, a closed economy, technical rigidities – correspond closely to the Soviet conditions in the period between the Wars, and Fel'dman seems to vindicate the principle 'priority for heavy industry' that characterized socialist investment policy. However, this policy continued to be implemented when the fundamental assumptions of the model ceased to be satisfied – when reserves of labour had long been exhausted, with international trade and balance of payments problems – and was imitated by other socialist countries whose economic reality did not correspond to these assumptions. The Polish economic school, under the guidance of Kalecki, were the first to reformulate the theory of socialist accumulation to take the new conditions into account.

The other aspect of this line of argument is the simple conclusion which Kalecki drew that after a period of raising the rate of accumulation (investment share) the rate of growth will drop back to its previous level. Thus to keep raising (temporarily) the rate of growth requires further and further rises in the share of investment in national income, with the counterpart of reductions in the share of consumption.

The second argument against orthodox policies was that the actual attempts at implementation of a 'taut' overambitious plan would lead to numerous problems. These would include the sacrifice of consumption for investment when the overall plan could not be implemented, and investment projects would be left uncompleted and therefore virtually useless.

Zielinski (1973) described actual experience in these terms.

It is well known that during the Stalinist period Eastern European economic plans were excessively 'taut' and the CPB (Central Planning Body) preferences were strongly biased in favour of heavy industry and military objectives. When difficulties of plan fulfilment arose, the targets of the consumer goods sector were the first to be negatively affected (pp. 35–6).

Further, 'the CPB treats personal consumption as a *cost* of growth rather than the ultimate goal of growth. There is abundant implicit proof of this thesis ... The overinvestment policy may also be the result of a misguided effort of planners to forestall the declining growth rate of socialist countries *vis-à-vis* their capitalist adversaries' (p. 43).

In terms of long-term planning, 'Kalecki's fundamental principles ... [were] that the plan should be realistic, internally balanced, and it should protect the current interests of the consumer' (Osiatyński, 1982). This stands in contrast with the official approach described above by Zielinski. Clearly, when the protection of the current interests of consumers is stressed, there are substantial limits on the extent to which current consumption can be sacrificed for investment (particularly for heavy industrial investment which yields extra consumption with only a long time lag). Thus plans which incorporate ideas of great leaps forward, an investment rush, catching up with capitalist countries as objectives in their own right, would usually run counter to the ideas of Kalecki.[16]

There were two particular occasions where Kalecki came into sharp conflict with the prevailing orthodoxy. The first one arose from the construction of the fifteen year perspective plan (for 1969–75), and the second over the five-year plan for the years 1966–70.

The long-term plans were 'a formulation of a long term programme of economic development, intended to facilitate reasonable solutions of current problems of detailed planning in shorter periods' (Kalecki, 1959). The long run plans 'can be conceived as a moving plan which after fulfilment of each five year plan is shifted by five years' (Kalecki, 1959). The conflict between Kalecki and the authorities arose in part from the overlap between the perspective plan for 1961–75 and the five year plan for 1961 to 1965. Essentially, Kalecki and his co-workers were postulating a lower growth rate of output and lower share of investment in the perspective plan for the first five years as compared with the figures in the five year plan covering the same period. Over the fifteen-year period, the growth rates being postulated were regarded as too low.

The most heated controversies were evoked by the growth rate of national income and social product. Many participants in the discussion pointed out that the rate of grwoth adopted in the perspective plan was lower than that in the 1961–5 plan. This led them to the conclusion that the authors of the long-term plan allowed themselves to be guided by the principle of the 'damped curve' of development. Kalecki categorically refuted this charge (Osiatyński, 1982).

Further, 'at the discussion some economists called for a rise in productive investment. Kalecki explained that such investment must not constitute an end in itself. The basic end of socialist production was to raise the standard of living in all its respects' (Osiatyński, 1982).

The second major conflict arose over the construction of the 1965–70 five year plan in 1964. At this stage, Kalecki was an adviser to the Planning Commission. He was critical of the proposed plan, and drew up his alternative plan. The quantitative differences between the official plan and Kalecki's alternative one were relatively small, at least in respect of consumption, with Kalecki postulating a 5.5 per cent annual increase during the period as compared with a 4.8 per cent annual figure in the official plan. But there were major qualitative differences, particularly over the structure and size of investment. Kalecki's approach sought to place consumption as centrally important such that if the plan had to be amended part way through its time horizon, adjustments would not fall mainly on consumption. Further, he argued that in a number of areas, the authorities should opt for less capital-intensive, more labour-intensive production techniques, and seek to generate some of the planned growth from more intensive and efficient use of existing capital equipment. Kalecki's alternative proposals are discussed in Feiwell (1975), Chapter 19. It can be seen that Kalecki's alternative proposals were, in his view, 'realistic', but in a number of important respects (consumption versus investment, capital intensity versus labour intensive production techniques) this involved going against the prevailing and deeply embedded orthodoxy.

Differences Between Economics of Capitalism and Economics of Socialism

Much of Kalecki's writings on socialist growth, particularly the equations which he derived may appear at first sight to be similar to writings on capitalist growth. He confronted this type of argument in Kalecki (1970), which we have already made reference to in Chapter 3. It is convenient to summarise his argument with reference to his equation for the rate of growth of output:

$$r = (1/m)(I/Y) - a + u \tag{11.1}$$

where r is the rate of growth of output, m the productive effect of gross investment, which is labelled I, a is loss of production due to depreciation, etc., and u the change in utilisation of productive capacity. This equation is effectively (with suitable definitions of m, a, and u) an identity. The differences of significance between economics of capitalism and of socialism here were seen to be:

(a) Capitalist economies were seen as generally demand-constrained in their operations in the sense that the levels of output, employment, etc. were set by aggregate demand considerations rather than supply consideration. Thus capitalist economies were seen as generally characterised by excess capacity and unemployment. In contrast, socialist economies were seen as generally supply (or resource) constrained. The degree to which such an economy did not operate at full employment (of labour and capital equipment) would arise not through a lack of aggregate demand but through mismatch of resources and supply bottlenecks. In terms of equation (11.1), this would mean that for capitalist economies the determination of u on a year-to-year basis would be dominated by changes in the level of aggregate demand which lead to changes in capacity utilisation. 'It is only in the socialist economy, where utilisation of productive capacity is safeguarded by the plan (first and foremost by fixing an appropriate relation between prices and wages) that the coefficient u begins to reflect solely the effect of organisational and technical improvements which do not require significant capital outlays' (Kalecki, 1972a, p. 12).

(b) Decisions over savings and investment are in the hands of the private sector (usually the capitalists) in a capitalist economy, and are undertaken in the pursuit of private profits. In a socialist economy, the savings and investment decisions are in the hands of the planning authority (unless these decisions have been decentralised, but such decisions are often amongst the last to be decentralised). Thus the analysis of the decision-making over savings and investment must be different for the two systems. Under socialism there is at least the possibility that these decisions will be undertaken in the social interest. Further, if planning is undertaken efficiently there should be less possibility of a serious discrepancy between planned savings and planned investment.

(c) There may be greater flexibility under socialism than under capitalism. In the latter, as seen above, Kalecki saw price–cost margins are set by firms at a level dependent upon the degree of monopoly. If that degree of monopoly is relatively inflexible, then so will be the price–cost margin. Thus there would be a lack of price flexibility, which would rule out those theories (e.g. neo-classical monetarism) which rely on price flexibility to ensure continuous full employment. Further, price rigidities are a feature of both the short-run (business cycle) and the long-run. Kalecki also considered that under socialism, the problem of effective demand is solved by price flexibility since the planning authorities could fix prices, relative to wages, to ensure full employment (cf. Kalecki, 1970). And so, 'it is ... paradoxical that, while the apologists of capitalism usually consider the "price mechanism" to be the great advantage of the capitalist system, price flexibility proves to be a characteristic feature of the socialist economy' (Kalecki, 1971a, p. 97).

It is clear that Kalecki's views on the relative degrees of price flexibility arise from his general views on capitalism (dominated by oligopolies) and socialism (central planners able to take effective price decisions). A full evaluation of this proposition of price flexibility would probably be very difficult. It could, however, be noted that there were seen to be limits on price flexibility by the authorities in Poland where that flexibility was geared to reductions in real consumption and real wages. Indeed, Kalecki often stressed the limits on trying to reduce consumption. However, as we have seen above (p. 117), Kalecki saw a rise in real wages (and consequent rise in consumer demand) as a solution to a lack of effective demand. Similarly, if there were a lack of investment (rather unlikely), then that could be resolved either by a planned increase in investment or by a rise in real wages and consumer demand.

The ideas suggested by Kalecki developed from equation (11.1) above listed under heading (a) above were developed by his colleagues Brus and Łaski (1964), which provides a discussion of the meaning of full employment in those circumstances and the impact which these ideas have on the theory of growth. These ideas were independently developed (and much more extensively) by Kornai and his associates in Hungary.[17] Kornai (1979), for example, is entitled 'resource-constrained versus demand-constrained systems', and he argues that 'in understanding the problems of a socialist economy, the problem of shortage plays a role similar to the problem of unemployment in the description of capitalism. . . . socialist economy is, in its 'classical' form, a resource-constrained economy . . . [in which] shortage and slack are not mutually exclusive phenomena . . .'.

Kalecki and Socialist Growth

The bulk of Kalecki's writings on socialism which have been translated into English are concerned with long-term growth, with particular emphasis on the relevance of the labour supply, foreign trade constraints and the relationship between consumption and investment (accumulation). These writings are largely brought together in Kalecki (1972a), and we draw heavily on the essays in that collection in this chapter. Quotes and page references given without further details are from and relate to Kalecki (1972a).

We begin briefly by noting the definitions which Kalecki used. National income is 'the value of *goods produced* in that year after deducting the value of raw materials and semi-manufacturers used in the process of production' (p. 1, italics added). Thus the production of services is excluded, partly on the grounds that 'in the study of economic dynamics the treatment of national income as production of goods offers appreciable advantages' (p. 2), mainly in terms of measurement problems. National income is measured gross of depreciation and at factory rather than market prices (with the difference between them in socialist countries being largely accounted for by turnover tax). Investment in fixed capital is defined in terms of the volume of new capital delivered in a given period, with increases in work-in-progress (including production of machines, buildings, etc.) included as increase in inventories. This enables a direct link to be forged between investment increases in output in the next period.

Kalecki began by considering a closed economy. The real national income in a given year is denoted by Y, productive investment by I, and the increase in inventories by IN and consumption in a broad sense (collective consumption, individual consumption, 'non-productive' investment) by C, and then $Y = C + I + IN$.[18, 19] In this part, productive investment is restricted to investment coming on stream to have an impact on current production, with the effect of raising output by I/m, where m is the incremental capital–output ratio. The depreciation of existing equipment (after repairs and maintenance) is taken to reduce output by $a.Y$, where a is the 'parameter of depreciation'. Improvements in the utilisation of equipment, derived largely from improvements in the organisation of work, the use of materials, etc., contributing an amount $u.Y$ to output. Bringing those factors together leads to the equation for growth which we reported above of:

$$\Delta Y/Y = (1/m)\,(I/Y) - a + u \qquad\qquad (11.1)$$

The main point of interest in this equation is that the u-term is interpreted as arising predominantly from improvements in efficiency of production, and not from changes in aggregate demand.

The increase in inventories (which would include stocks and uncompleted investment in equipment) is taken as proportional to changes in income (i.e. $IN = \mu\Delta Y$). With $r = \Delta Y/Y$, $i = (I + IN)/Y$, $k = m + \mu$, $C/Y = 1 - i$, equation (11.1) can be written as:

$$r = (i/k) - m(a - u)/k \qquad\qquad (11.2)$$

This simple equation forms the basis of much of Kalecki's discussion of growth, with various extensions to allow for foreign trade, employment situation etc.[20] It can be used to highlight the trade off between growth and (immediate) consumption, for it can be seen from (11.2) that to increase the rate of growth, r, requires a rise in the investment share, i, and hence a decrease in consumption share. Further, it can be seen that the impact of a higher investment share on the growth rate will depend on how the other parameters respond to a change in i. If the increased investment is providing capital equipment to employ previously unemployed labour, capital intensity may remain constant, yielding a higher rate of growth. But in circumstances of full employment that option is not available, so that either capital intensity rises or idle capital equipment is created. In both cases, the ratio of output to capital falls, nullifying eventually the effect of a rise in *i* on the rate of growth.

Kalecki showed (Chapter 3) that the capital stock of the economy will grow at the same rate as income provided that the lifespan of the capital equipment is also constant. He also noted (Chapter 11) that the value of the parameter *m* would depend on the sectorial composition of growth. In particular, a policy of raising the growth rate would involve investment in consumer goods industries, since the latter industries rely on the output of investment goods industries. The incremental labour ratios may be quite different as between investment-goods industries and consumer-goods industries, leading to a varying value of *m*.

It is useful to summarise Kalecki's method of modelling capital equipment. He sought to measure investment in real terms, and discussed the problems which that involved in Chapter 1. Depreciation is measured in terms of its impact of production, summarised in the depreciation of parameter *a* above. But this depreciation is seen as largely the result of the scrapping of old equipment, and not through the deterioration of equipment remaining in existence. Maintenance is assumed to be carried out on existing equipment to help maintain its productive potential, and the cost of that maintenance is included as part of the current costs of production. There is no attempt (nor need there be) for a socialist economy to measure the 'value of the capital stock', a problem which has dogged neoclassical economics when applied to capitalist economies. For in the latter context, the rate of profit is equated to the marginal productivity of 'capital', and a theory of distribution based on marginal productivity theory requires a measure of 'capital' independent of the rate of profit itself. In the context of socialist economies, income distribution does not rest on marginal productivity considerations, and a measure of the stock of capital equipment is relevant only in terms of production and employment potential. Thus, the capital stock is defined by Kalecki as the sum of investments (at constant prices) undertaken in the past, which have not been scrapped. In most of his analysis, Kalecki assumed a centrally determined scrapping rule – e.g. equipment of a particular type is used for, say, ten years. But Kalecki did not make any allowance for mistakes in investment decisions such that the resulting capital equipment has to be scrapped earlier than intended.

The measure of capital stock does not play a key role in Kalecki's analysis. In particular, although Kalecki added together (p. 17) investments of different vintages, nevertheless he did assume that different vintages would have different levels of productivity. It can also be noted that much of Kalecki's analysis related to decision-making by central planners and to changes in the capital stock (investments of particular vintage), and the historically given level of the capital stock is not very relevant to that analysis.

In much of his discussion of growth, Kalecki adopted the vintage, fixed-factor proportion assumptions for the relationship between inputs and output. Thus machinery produced at different times will have different technologies incorporated and give different levels of productivity. The productivity on capital equipment may improve as the equipment ages as a result of improvements in organisation, new ideas and 'learning by doing' effects. The ratio of employment to capital equipment for a particular vintage of capital equipment is taken as given at a particular point in time (though it may change over time due to the forces listed in the previous sentence). In his analysis of growth, the capital–output and capital–employment ratios for new equipment are seen as centrally determined, and then later Kalecki discussed how those ratios could be decided upon. Once the equipment is installed, then the ratios between capital, output and labour are seen as set technologically.

When there is full employment of the labour force, then the growth of the economy is effectively constrained by the growth of the labour force plus technical progress. This growth rate, which is designated r_0 is equal to $p+n$, where p is the growth of productivity (arising from technical progress) and n the growth rate of the labour force. The rate r_0 corresponds to the rate of growth described as the natural rate of growth in neo-classical growth theory. In circumstances of full employment, the equality of the growth rate given by (11.2) and by r_0 requires that:

$$p + n = (i/k) - m(a - u)/k \qquad (11.3)$$

This equation (11.3) means that in the circumstances of full employment with the rate of technical progress given, the growth rate of the economy becomes labour supply-constrained. This constraint can be seen as more important under socialist economies (since they are seen as supply-constrained and operating at full employment) than the corresponding constraint under capitalism which would be seen as demand-constrained and often not operating at full employment.

Development of the Basic Approach

The further analysis of growth (derived from equation (11.2)) requires some further specification of the binding constraints on the rate of growth (e.g. by r_0 in circumstances of full employment) and/ or by discussion of the choice of growth rates amongst those available. Kalecki's theoretical discussion clearly reflects his evaluation of the constraints facing Polish economic growth. In his discussion on perspective planning, Kalecki argued that 'the obstacles to a very high rate of growth ... are the high capital outlay required both directly and as a result of the difficulties in equilibrating the balance of foreign trade and possibly also of the shortage of labour'. In fact the difficulties in foreign trade may make it virtually impossible to exceed a certain level of the rate of growth. It will be seen that Kalecki often incorporated the constraint of balanced foreign trade, and no foreign borrowing. This again reflects the general Polish policy during the 1950s and 1960s.[21]

Kalecki considered a number of different situations, particularly distinguishing between the case of unlimited supply of labour, which can be thought of in terms of developing countries where there is a large pool of unemployed or partially employed labour such that growth in unlikely to be restricted by the labour supply for, say, twenty to thirty years ahead, and the case of a limited labour supply.

Unlimited labour supply

We begin with the unlimited labour supply case, then equation (11.3) is not a binding constraint. The government or planning authorities are then able to vary the rate of growth by varying the key parameters. Consider, first, a closed economy. For equation (11.2), it can be seen that there is a trade-off between growth (and thereby future consumption) and current consumption since an increase in r requires *ceteris paribus* a rise in i and hence a fall in the consumption to income ratio. Kalecki stressed this trade-off, and particularly argued that there were severe difficulties involved in lowering current consumption (even with the promise of higher consumption in the future). Hence, planners were not in a position to choose very high growth rates which would involve high values of the investment/income ratio (and hence low consumption/income ratios).

The relationship between the growth rate r and the investment--output ratio i given in equation (11.2) is a linear one, and to raise the growth rate by Δr requires raising i by Δi equal to $k\Delta r$, with present income of Y_0, this means raising investment by $\Delta i Y_0$ and lowering capacity by the same amount, and proportionately by $\Delta i/(1-i)$ (since consumption is $(1-i)Y_0$).

Kalecki introduced the notion of $w(i)$, a coefficient which is higher the stronger are the objections against reducing consumption on the short-run. The coefficient $w(i)$ depends on i (the proportion of income devoted to accumulation) with the first derivative of w being positive. The net gain or loss from raising the growth rate is given by $\Delta r - w(i).\Delta i/(1-i)$, where the first term indicates the gain in consumption from a faster rate of growth, whilst the second term indicates the perceived loss from a reduction in consumption share resulting from higher investment. From usual considerations, it is then seen to be worthwhile to increase the investment ratio when the above expression is positive, i.e. up to the point when the expression becomes zero, which is when:

$$\Delta r/\Delta i = w(i)/(1-i) \tag{11.4}$$

It might be thought that the coefficient w has some links with the social rate of time discount. But Kalecki would not have argued in those terms, rather viewing the decision on w as a crucial political decision, and also incorporating constraints on reducing consumption in the short run. This is reflected in Kalecki's idea of a government decision curve, which is drawn in Figure 11.1. The horizontal line AB reflects the technical relationship between i and r

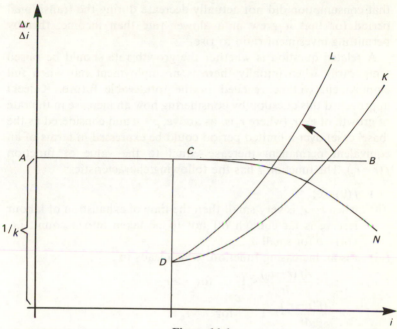

Figure 11.1

given by equation (11.2), expressed in change-form, with m, a and u constant, as $\Delta r = \Delta i/k$. Thus growth of output and investment share change together in a linear fashion (constant returns to scale assumption). The DK line is the line of $w(i)/(1-i)$, and is labeled the 'government decision curve' by Kalecki. It serves, but not in any precise fashion, 'only to illustrate the attitude of the government towards "sacrificing the present for the future"' (p. 35). Further, the decision curve may have a steep upward slope reflecting the idea that a substantial increase in i would 'lead to a prohibitive deterioration in current consumption and consequently in real wages'. It is not clear from the context as to in whose view the reduction in consumption would be a 'prohibitive deterioration', but it clearly carries the overtone of resistance by workers (actual or in the view of the government) to any reduction in current living standards.

This led Kalecki to suggest that the movement to a higher growth rate should be undertaken gradually and subject to the restriction that consumption did not actually decrease during the transitional period (or that it grew at a slower rate than income, thereby permitting investment ratio to rise).

A related question is whether the growth rate should be raised temporarily when initially there is unemployment but when full employment will be reached in the foreseeable future. Kalecki approached this question by considering how an increase in the rate of growth of $r - r_0$ (where r_0 is, as above, $p + n$ and considered as the 'base' case) over a limited period could be expressed in terms of an equivalent permanent increase equal to the value of function $f(r - r_0)$. The function f has the following characteristics:

(i) $f(0) = 0$;
(ii) when $r - r_0$ is very small then the time of exhaustion of labour reserve is far enough off not to be taken into account. i.e. $f(\delta) = \delta$ for small δ;
(iii) f is an increasing function, which leads to

$$0 < \frac{\Delta f(r - r_0)}{\Delta r} < 1 \qquad \text{for } r > r_0$$

$$\frac{\Delta f(r - r_0)}{\Delta r} = 1 \qquad \text{for } r = r_0$$

This leads to the condition for determining the rate of growth to be:

$$\frac{\Delta r}{\Delta i} = \frac{w(i)}{(1 - i) \dfrac{\Delta f(r - r_0)}{\Delta r}}$$

In terms of Figure 11.1, this leads to a decision curve DL which has the indicated relationship with the decision curve arising in the unlimited labour supply case, that is DK. Thus the chosen investment/income ratio is seen (from the intersections of DK and DL with AB) to be lower in the limited labour supply case as compared with the unlimited case.

The next consideration is the introduction of an open economy and foreign trade considerations. Kalecki paid particular attention to the case where foreign trade is planned to balance (exports = - imports) under the assumption that such an economy either cannot or does not wish to receive foreign credits or grants. The analysis would be little changed if there were some fixed amount of foreign credits available. The case which is ruled out is deliberately incurring foreign debt over the period of the plan. In his discussions on development and elsewhere, Kalecki often exhibited a strong fear of the problems, particularly over issues such as loss of sovereignty, which would arise from foreign borrowing. Thus the balanced foreign trade assumption can be seen as reflection of Polish economic policy in the 1950s and 1960s and of Kalecki's distrust of foreign debts. Kalecki, as has been seen above, placed considerable emphasis on the constraints imposed on a country by its foreign trade position. Nevertheless he saw imports as an important means of overcoming bottlenecks and of gaining from international specialisation.

During the course of economic development, the demand for imports increases, generating the need for exports to rise alongside. The higher rate of growth and the need to promote exports and restrain imports would be associated with some reduction in export prices (to stimulate demand), a shift into less profitable markets and the export of less profitable goods. The constraints on imports lead to home-made substitutes. The impact of these considerations is that the output obtained for a given increase of labour and capital as inputs gradually decline. Thus 'efforts to maintain the rate of growth at a higher level will reduce the increment in the national income corresponding to given outlays and this reduction is greater the higher the level attained'.

Because of these difficulties in foreign trade the rate r cannot exceed a certain level. In previous discussion, Kalecki had adopted the view that output would expand in line with the capital stock (as would employment). Thus there were no technical difficulties to expansion by replication. But foreign trade considerations mean that such expansion of output in line with capital equipment is no longer possible. There are the limitations on the expansion of exports (which would be needed to finance an increase in imports as output expanded) since price reductions and/or movement into less profitable lines of exports would be required at some stage. There are also limitations on the possibility of import substitution.

At this point, Kalecki also introduced the technological and organisational constraints arising with faster growth, although such constraints would apply to a closed economy as much as to an open one. These constraints include failures to complete projects when many are attempted, limited availability (or rate of expansion) of natural resources (with coal often mentioned), the time required for people to master new skills, etc.

The impact of foreign trade consideration can be seen in terms of the diagrams used above. The relationship between r and i is no longer a linear one, but incorporating the difficulties of faster growth of exports, etc. leads to a curve which displays a declining relationship between changes in the growth rate and changes in investment share, as that share is increased. This is portrayed by a curve such as *ACN* in Figure 11.1, leading to the choice of a lower investment share. In the case of unlimited labour supply, the effect of considering the constraints from foreign trade is to reduce the apparent benefits of faster growth (as compared with a no trade case). However foreign trade, for reasons explored below, may permit a higher initial growth rate. But in the foreign trade case, it is seen that a reduction of consumption (raising i) raises the growth rate by less than in the no trade case. In the limited labour case, the growth rate is constrained to the rate $r_o = p + n$ in any event.

Kalecki also argued that calculations of the possibility of raising exports, reducing imports, etc. are very hypothetical in nature, and that this uncertainty leads to pessimistic estimates of foreign possibilities (i.e. the line *ACN* tends to be estimated as lower than it 'really' is). He then argued that 'the elimination of uncertainty by long term trade agreements, such as are concluded within the socialist camp favours a higher rate of growth of national income. Obviously, such agreements do not solve the problems of placing the increased exports. . . . But the results of the agreements are facts, rather than tentative forecasts; thus they need not be treated as cautiously as expectations concerning the future prospects of foreign trade' (p. 50).

At the end of his discussion on foreign trade and growth, Kalecki argued against adopting a self-sufficiency approach, since imports were useful in overcoming bottlenecks, that the absence of foreign trade would hamper development, and that in many cases the production of domestic substitutes for the scarce goods would be much less favourable than the expansion of exports.

Limited labour supply

When there is full employment, then equation (11.3) comes into play, which for convenience we repeat:

$$r_0 = p + n = (i/k) - m(a - u)/k \qquad (11.3)$$

The obvious, but often overlooked, point about his equation is that the maximum rate of growth of the economy is determined by $p + n$, which means that debates over raising the growth rate of an economy should focus on raising p (growth of productivity). But frequently, in both Western and Eastern debates on growth, much emphasis is given to the role of investment. It is often suggested that raising investment is the means to faster growth. The point to be made here is that under conditions of unemployment of labour through a lack of capital equipment, then raising investment will permit faster growth (as well as adding to the level of aggregate demand). But under conditions of full employment, then raising investment share may temporarily raise the growth rate, but not on a permanent basis, as can be seen by reference to equation (11.3).

Kalecki (1972a), Chapters 7 to 9 discusses the impact on growth of raising the capital–output ratio (m, which is a part also of k) and of shortening the lifespan of equipment (which is equivalent to increasing the rate of scrapping, i.e. a in equation (11.3)). Once the binding constraint of r_0 on the growth rate is perceived it might be thought that discussion on the impact of, for example, changes in the capital–output ratio on the growth rate is superfluous. But the frequency with which the idea of increased investment to raise the rate of growth is advanced without specifying the conditions under which such an increase in the rate of growth would be forthcoming suggests that such discussion is needed.[22]

The purpose of Kalecki's discussion could be seen as twofold. First, to emphasise the point that whilst policies of increased capital-intensity and of shortening the lifespan of equipment would have some temporary effect on the rate of growth (through raising the recorded rate of growth of productivity), there would not be a permanent effect. The increase in capital intensity, raises capital--output and presumably output–labour ratios, whilst the shortening of lifespan raises the average productivity of equipment in operation (since newer equipment is more productive than older equipment). Second, there would be a higher level of output at the end of a period of raising capital-intensity or of reducing the lifespan of equipment even though the growth rate will have resumed its initial level. The benefits of this higher level of output have to be offset against the costs. There are the short-term costs associated in moving from one growth path to another. For example, an increase in capital-intensity has the effect of increasing the investment ratio, both in the short-run and in the long-run. In the short-run, an increase in the investment ratio means a reduction in consumption below what it would have been, and possibility below what it has been (depending on how sharp the increase in investment is). In the long-run, the share of consumption is lower, though the level may well be higher than it would have been.

> [T]he problem of what capital–output ratio secures, in a uniformly expanding system, the highest real wage, while full employment is maintained, may be of small practical importance; for if the initial capital–output ratio is less, the 'retooling' of the stock of capital in order to achieve this paradise means a long period of higher investment, in the early part of which the real wage would fare *worse* than if no change in capital–output ratio were attempted. We have here a typical case of 'sacrificing the present for the future' which I believe to be a political problem of first rank in the socialist economy. But the basis for political decisions on problems of this nature is a thorough economic enquiry into the *transition* from one curve of growth to another (Kalecki, 1970).[23]

For the discussion on the effect on growth of raising capital-intensity and shortening the lifespan of equipment, Kalecki introduced the 'production curve', an example of which is drawn in Figure 11.2. The curve indicates different combinations of increases in labour employment (labour outlays) and in capital equipment (investment outlays) would generate a desired increase in output. The production curve is drawn for the particular increase in output, and is essentially a decision trade-off curve facing central planners in their pursuit of that increase. The curve is drawn for the particular decision rules governing investment. The one considered is: minimise $(J/T) + W$, where J is total investment outlay, W total current costs (per period, assumed constant here) and T is the centrally determined recoupment period over which any new investment costs must be recouped. Various modifications and complications to this decision rule are considered below, and it is used to correspond with Eastern European practice (p. 113). Kalecki in the

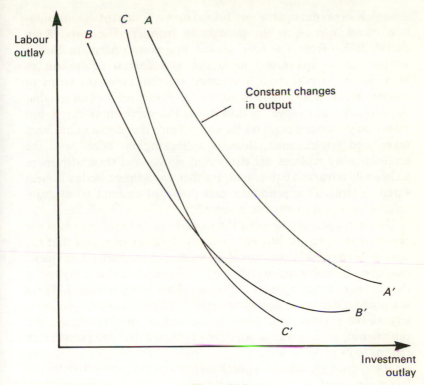

Figure 11.2

Appendix to Part I shows that this decision rule would generate a production curve of the shape indicated in Figure 11.2.

The production curve in Figure 11.2 may look at first sight rather like a neo-classical isoquant. But it does differ significantly from such an isoquant. It is an aggregate curve, drawn for a specified increase in the mix of goods and services. It has some common features with the idea a set of blueprints from which an economy is able to choose, in the sense that this 'production curve' is taken to represent the possibilities open to central planners. Inferior alternatives (e.g. those using more labour with the same investment outlay for the same production) have been eliminated. At this level of discussion, full information is assumed on production possibilities though Kalecki did discuss (see below) how a system of decentralisation could help reach the production frontier. The 'production curve' differs from the neo-classical isoquant concept in that it relates outlays (increases) in labour and capital equipment to increases in output, from a specified starting point (in terms of equipment, etc.). But, more importantly, there is no implication that the economy can move up and down the production curve, but rather may choose a point on the curve. Once that decision has been taken and implemented, there is a 'locking in' effect, and the economy only replaces old equipment slowly and then with more technically advanced equipment. Further, investment outlay is measured in terms of expenditure, and does not attempt to measure 'capital' involved in any other sense.

The discussion of changing the capital–output ratio involves the notion that there are different vintages of equipment, and that the impact of changes in the capital–output ratio are only felt on 'new' machines. Labour productivity rises on average, since it is higher on the machines being brought in than on those being scrapped. There is a gradual rise in the aggregate capital–output ratio and productivity as the process continues. At the end of this 'recasting', the capital–output ratio and productivity is higher. But the growth rate returns to its previous level, since the impact of the higher value of m on the rate of growth (cf. equation (11.3)), is exactly offset by the larger depreciation involved such that more machines have to be replaced each year. The rate of growth then falls back to $r_0 = p + n$. In this context, n is the rate of technical progress, when technical progress is deemed 'neutral', as discussed below.

The effect of shortening the lifespan of equipment (raising rate of depreciation) is to raise the average productivity of labour since equipment is on average younger and incorporates higher productivity. The effect of the 'rejuvenation' of capital equipment through increasing the speed of scrapping productive capacity is rather similar to the 'recasting' discussed above. There is a higher growth of productivity during the period of rejuvenation, but productivity growth drops back to its old level when that period comes to an end. Another complication which Kalecki dealt with (Chapter 11) is the fact that some investment is devoted to the investment goods sector. The production of investment goods may involve a different degree of capital-intensity as compared with the production of other goods.

Further, the production of investment goods has to proceed in time with the expansion of the production of other goods. These relatively simple remarks have two important implications for the previous discussion. First, the value of *m* during a period when investment share is being expanded (and hence concentrated on the investment in the production of investment goods) may well differ from the value of *m* during a period of steady growth. Second, the length of time between raising investment share and the increased consumption derived from the larger capital stock which eventually results in longer than might be indicated by the previous discussion. The details of how Kalecki's analysis was amended for this complication are given in his Chapter 11.

Kalecki became involved in a debate with Dobb and Sen (Dobb, 1960; Sen, 1960; Kalecki, 1972a, Chapter 10) over the choice of technique (of production), or equivalently the capital–output ratio. We do not intend to review that debate here, but we can indicate the question debated. This was whether it was reasonable for a government (or central planning authority) to raise the capital–output ratio (i.e. to opt for a more capital-intensive production technique) to promote growth in an economy with an unlimited labour supply and unemployment, when the reduction of real wages is not feasible. The relevance of that debate here is that it illustrates Kalecki's interest in deriving decision-rules for central-planners and the emphasis on the trade-offs between consumption and investment.

Technical Progress

Technical progress was largely viewed here by Kalecki in terms of the enhancement of labour productivity. Thus technical progress is described in terms of its power to reduce labour input per unit of output. Kalecki's approach can be formalised as $l(t) = f(k) . e^{-a(k)t}$, where $l(t)$ is the labour–output ratio (at time t), k is the capital–output ratio, f is a function describing the technical conditions of production and the function $a(k)$ indicates the effect which capital intensity has on the rate of technical progress. Kalecki described technical progress as neutral when the rate of increase of labour productivity is not affected by capital intensity. Thus, in terms of the formalisation given above, $a(k)$ is constant.

Neutral technical progress is a uniform 'shrinkage' of the 'production curve'. In terms of Figure 11.2, neutral technical progress in Kalecki's sense would be illustrated by a shift in curves from AA' to BB', so that technical progress does not then encourage either a move to a labour intensive or to a more capital intensive scheme of production. Kalecki's notion of 'neutral' technical progress provides a dividing line between technical progress which encourages capital intensity and that which discourages capital intensity (pp. 53–5). A shift from AA' to CC' in Figure 11.2 would be described as a capital-encouraging in the sense that the 'gap' between AA' and CC' is greater for larger investment outlays, indicating faster technical progress with more capital intensive production. Thus in order to raise the rate of technical progress, planners would be encouraged to use some capital-intensive techniques.

Kalecki's definition of neutral technical progress can be compared with the definitions used in neo-classical growth theory. There is one aspect which simultaneously illustrates both similarities and differences. Harrod-neutral technical progress is defined such that when technical progress is of that form the marginal productivity of capital remains constant provided that the capital—output ratio remains constant over time as technical progress proceeds. Thus, under conditions of perfect competition and profit maximisation, a constant real rate of interest would lead to a constant marginal productivity of capital and hence to a constant capital—output ratio. Kalecki's definition of neutral technical progress similarly sees that form of technical progress as generating under certain circumstances a constant (incremental) capital—output ratio, although 'in the case of neutral technical progress there is no necessity for m (the capital—output ratio) to remain constant' (p. 56). The difference is, of course, that the decision-makers and the factors influencing their decisions are quite different (capitalists versus central planners, pursuit of profits versus dictates of the central plan).

When a production function of the form $Q = F(L, K, t)$, exhibiting constant returns to scale, can be written as $Q = F(Le^{mt}, K)$, then technical progress will be Harrod-neutral at the rate m. It can be shown (e.g. Łaski, 1972, pp. 88–90) that the definitions of neutral technical progress given by Harrod and by Kalecki are algebraically equivalent. However, there is 'the not unimportant point that Kalecki's curve of production was, in his view, applicable only to a socialist economy' (Łaski, 1972).

There are a number of other contrasts to be made in this context. Clearly, the definitions used in neo-classical theory relate to production functions, are generally cast in terms of marginal productivities, and for consistency in the area of income distribution requires the assumption of constant returns to scale.[23] The coherence of the neo-classical approach with an emphasis on balanced growth paths requires that technical progress be Harrod-neutral.[24] Kalecki's approach does not make use of production functions nor marginal productivity concepts (particularly for factors payments). Whilst the assumption of Kalecki-neutral technical progress eases the algebra, the coherence of the approach does not rely on that assumption.[25] Further, there is no requirement for constant returns to scale to be assumed in Kalecki's approach.

Now we interpret Figure 11.2 with the axes normalised to represent the labour outlay and investment outlay required for a one unit decrease in output, i.e. the axes now read DL/DQ and DK/DQ (changes in labour relative to changes in output, and changes in capital equipment relative to changes in output, with no marginal productivity implications). With neutral technical progress as defined by Kalecki, when the (incremental) capital–output ratio is constant, then the labour–output ratio falls at the constant rate of technical progress, and labour productivity grows at a constant rate which we label p. The growth of employment ε is then given by the equation $(1 + \varepsilon) = (1 + r)/(1 + p)$ and this result was used in equation (11.3) above.

Efficiency and Investment Decisions

Kalecki had relatively little to say on efficiency in terms of input-output efficiency. At the level of the enterprise, whilst he did not make the conventional neo-classical assumptions of technical efficiency, nevertheless he took as given for the purpose of analysis the degree of technical efficiency and of the intensity of labour in his theories of capitalist economies. In the context of socialist economies, Kalecki paid relatively little attention to the problems of achieving technical efficiency at the enterprise level and to the role of incentives.

A distinction has been drawn between extensive and intensive stages of development growth (under socialism), whereby the former relates to growth of output through the expansion of inputs (drawing workers into employment from unemployment or partial employment, increasing the capital stock rapidly) and the latter relates to growth of output through increases in output/input ratio (productivity rises) and technical innovation. It has been argued that central planning is much better equipped to generate extensive growth rather than intensive growth. In the extensive growth stage, central planning and direction are seen as necessary to overcome the obstacles to industrialisation and provide the necessary capital investment. In many of the countries of Eastern Europe, and particularly the Soviet Union, central planning was used for the purpose amongst others of industrialising a mainly agricultural economy. The difficulties for central planners are much increased, it is argued, in the intensive growth stage where improvements in efficiency, introduction of new products and methods of production, higher quality goods are required, and where there are more decisions to be made.

The approach of Kalecki disagreed with the emphasis on high and increasing rates of investment in the context of Poland in the postwar era. Nevertheless, Kalecki's approach fits in with the general notion of central planners determining the growth rate, pattern of consumption and investment etc. Kalecki did not deal very much in his writings with the questions which the intensive stage of growth are seen to raise, e.g. questions of efficiency, high quality goods, new products etc.

The theories on economic growth under socialism and particularly Kalecki's debates with Dobb and Sen over the choice of techniques, can be seen as relating to macroeconomics questions on the choice of growth rates, consumption/investment shares, appropriate capital-intensity of techniques, etc. Those writings and concerns of Kalecki clearly involve questions of allocative efficiency, particularly as between current and future consumption. It was seen above that Kalecki regarded decisions on that allocation as particularly important but at the same time a major political decision. Thus Kalecki did not discuss those allocation decisions in terms of individual utility maximisation and a Paretian framework, but rather saw key decisions such as consumption/investment as major social decisions rather than individual decisions.

The other aspect of allocative efficiency discussed by Kalecki relates to investment decisions. This is discussed in two stages: first, can rules be devised for taking aggregate investment decisions? Second, can decentralised rules be devised such that if those rules are applied at the enterprise level, the overall desired result will be achieved? This provides a good example of Kalecki's concern with the importance of central decision making and the ways in which those central decisions can be implemented.

Kalecki and Rakowski (1959) discussed the 'generalised formula of the efficiency of investment', within the context of the use of a recoupment period rather than of a rate of discount. Nuti in an editorial note to Kalecki (1972a, p. 113 footnote) describes

> the 'recoupment period' [as] a parameter fixed by the Planning Commission in instructions issued to enterprises and project making organizations. It is defined as the number of years over which the *additional* investment expenditure associated with the project selected – in comparison with the immediately less invest-ment-intensive project available to reach the same planned target – must be 'recouped' by means of lower yearly operating costs.

Kalecki and Rakowski considered first the simplest case of formula for the efficiency of investment, where equipment and factories are built instantaneously, have the same length of life and all have an even distribution of costs and output over their life. Their purpose is to relax gradually these assumptions to provide a generalised formula. The simple formula from which they begin is that the choice between alternatives depends on minimising $J/T + K$ (when the alternatives produce the same output), where J is invest-ment outlay, K is the reduction in operation costs and T the (maximum) recoupment period.

The relaxation of the assumptions indicated above leads them to the formula:

$$E = \frac{J(1/T)\ (1 + q_z n_z) + K_c Y_n}{P_c . Z_n}$$

where J is investment, T the recoupment period, q_z is the 'net national product generated per unit of investment resource per annum, n_z is the length of the period for which the investment outlay is on average 'frozen' before production (so that if the investment outlay is uniform over the period of construction as length t_b, then $n_z = t_b/2$), K_c is the equivalent reduction of operating costs and P_c the equivalent increase in output (with allowance for the variability of costs and output over time). Y_n and Z_n are adjustment factors to costs and output respectively to allow for differences in the length of life of equipment. Space precludes anything like a full discussion of this formula. The relevance to our discussion is threefold. First, it is indicative of Kalecki's approach to begin with the very simplest case, and then seek to allow for various complications. Second, it clearly illustrates his desire to develop operational rules for decision-making. Third, these decision rules are developed within the context of a recoupment period (which is akin to the pay-off period which is often postulated as a decision rule actually used by capitalist enterprises) without any direct reference to discount rates. Kalecki and Rakowski specifically argue against 'suggestions . . . to discount investment outlays, outputs and current costs at a rate equal to the average rate of growth of the economy. . . . They have no theoretical justification; moreover, they dissociate the problem of the reduction of current costs through higher capital outlays from that of the balance of labour force'.

Kalecki (1972a), Chapters 12 and 13 presented a related alternative. This has two features. First, the decision rule above based on a recoupment period is replaced by 'the index of efficiency of investment',

$$E = e.i. \frac{r+a}{r} + \left(c.\frac{r+a}{r} - \frac{x.a}{r} \right)$$

where e is a positive parameter (discussed below), i the investment intensity of output, c the labour intensity on new equipment, r the growth of production planned, a the rate of depreciation and x the labour intensity of equipment being scrapped. This formula is a linear function of investment and labour requirements per unit increase of production. The growth of output at a rate r requires investment of $i.Y(r+a)$, where the term $i.Y$ converts output into investment requirements, which are required to cover growth (r) and depreciation (a). The labour 'released' by scrapping old equipment is $x.a.Y$ (since output lost thereby is equivalent to $a.Y$, and each unit of output there had required x units of labour), and the labour required to operate new equipment is $c.(r+a)/Y$. The net increase in labour per unit increase is then $(c.(r+a) - x.a)Y/rY$. The coefficient c will be less than x reflecting technical progress.

The parameter e is used to reflect the relative weights placed on investment and labour. In the recoupment period approach, the parameter *e* would be closely related to $1/T$, where T is the recoupment period. The parameter *e*, once determined by the central planners, can be used for the decentralisation of decision-making on investment. Thus enterprises can be instructed to decide on investment according to whether *E* calculated for a particular investment is positive or negative. The central planners may also intervene by setting growth rates (*r*), scrapping rules (reflected in *a*).

The investment decision rules considered in this section reflect Kalecki's interest in the decisions on investment to be made by central planners, as well as some concern as to how appropriate guidelines could be devised for firms and industries such that their decisions conform to the requirements of the central planners.

Conclusions

This chapter has sought to provide a relatively brief introduction to Kalecki's writings on socialist economies. It can be seen that again his theorising is closely related to the important issues of the time and place to which they relate. The theorising is undertaken to provide answers to current questions, and the assumptions of the theorising is informed by the crucial elements of the current circumstances.

Notes to Chapter 11

1. Kalecki's colleague, Włodzimierz Brus, indicates that

   [b]eing aware of his rather special brand of Marxism, Kalecki came back to Poland in December 1954 with a firm intention to stay away from the economics of socialism which was still fettered by theological dogmas that we had only just started to discard. The situation changed with unexpected speed during the period preceding the Polish October 1956, and from spring 1956 onwards Kalecki became deeply involved both in most challenging theoretical debates on the economics of socialism and in tracing new policies and institutional reforms (Brus, 1977a).

2. For a biography of Gomulka, see Bethell (1969).
3. See Mieczkowski (1978) for an attempt to link political upheaval in Poland with the growth-rate of consumption.

4. Zielinski (1973), Chapter 1 provides some statistical background; and that book also contains a glossary of the main political events in Poland 1956–71 compiled by Dr Zbigniew Pelczynski. Brus (1975), Chapter 3 provide a broad ranging discussion and analysis of changes in the post-Stalin period in Eastern European countries with emphasis on Poland.

5. Oscar Lange was chairman of the Economic Council, and Wlodzimierz Brus was another of the vice-chairmen besides Kalecki.

6. 'In another case – the so-called general national discussion on the draft plan for 1966–70 before the IV Congress of the PUPW – Michal Kalecki's attempt to submit his own constructive proposals produced a reaction which forced the author to give up his position of scientific adviser in the Planning Commission. From then on the government did without independent expert advice, being content with the most obviously servile paens of praise for every single policy' (Brus, 1975, p. 145). The PUPW is the ruling Polish United Workers Party. Brus (1977a) (and also Brus, 1973, p. 107) argues that it was the adoption of the unamended five year plan for 1966–70 which finally sparked off the workers' revolt of December 1970, through setting consumption plans (particularly for meat) too low and investment plans too high. On a slightly different but closely related point, in connection with the fifteen-year perspective plan, Osiatyński argues that the problem was not an heavy investment programme crowding out consumption, but rather declining efficiency which required more investment per unit of consumption (Osiatyński, 1982).

7. These include Włodzimierz Brus (who initially was demoted to a research post at the Housing Institute, but later came to Britain), Kazimierz Łaski (now at the University of Linz, Austria), Stanislaw Gomulka (now at the London School of Economics, London).

8. The papers are mainly in the third volume of Kalecki's *Collected Works*, edited by Jerzy Osiatyński on *Socialism: Functioning and Long-Term Planning* currently only available in Polish. A relatively small selection of these papers are to be published in English in Toporowski (1985).

9. Professor Edward Lipiński was a senior Polish economist, who was directing the Institute of Research and Business Cycles and Prices where Kalecki obtained his first economics job in 1929. In the post-war period he became Professor at the Central School of Planning and Statistics in Warsaw. In 1975 he was a leading organiser of the 'Manifesto of the 59' which addressed political complaints and demands for civil liberty to Parliament (Nuti, 1981).

10. Lipiński's paper was first published in Poland in 1971. Many of the dangers foreseen by Kalecki in 1956 could be said to have come to pass. The dangers foreseen in the last sentence of the quote in the text fit in with the experience of the 1970s, with the exception that it was not pressure from Workers' Councils (which were emasculated) but pressures from workers uprisings in 1968 and 1970. After 1970, a policy of foreign borrowing to finance industrialisation and consumption was adopted (Nuti, 1981, p. 115; Pravda (1982)), following the replacement of Gomulka by Gierck. It could be argued that at different times all

three of the possible dangers identified by Kalecki in 1956 have occurred in Poland.

11. Brzeski (1976, 1977), presents a somewhat different picture of Kalecki (to which Brus, 1977b is a response). But apart from associating Kalecki with the Stalinist 'economic boss' of Poland, Hilary Minc, the main differences between the views of Brzeski and Brus appear to be modes of expression, reflecting differences of attitude to Kalecki as a person, and to the desirability of decentralisation. Brzeski was involved in the Planning Commission in Poland in the 1950s, and is now in the United States. For example, '. . . Kalecki's orientation: a bias towards centralisation and interventionism and, no less, a lack of interest in microeconomics'; 'in his, Kalecki's opinion, targets including product mix had to be determined at the centre, and preferably transmitted by command; incentives were ancillary'. But '. . . in the midst of a global emergency [the Second World War], Kalecki saw the indispensability of economic incentives; he seems to have concluded that patriotic enthusiasm alone would never do' (Brzeski, 1976).

12. Sire (1969) wrote that in the debates of 1956

> the Polish economists were divided amongst themselves into at least three groups: the conservative orthodox group, which wishes to preserve all the elements of planning and administrative control in the new 'economic model' including government price fixing at average cost; a pragmatic group wanting to couple planning and marginal cost pricing with more independence for enterprises; and finally a small liberal group plumping straight for the use of markets.

Whilst Kalecki does not fit exactly, the second group would be the closest approximation for his position.

13. The last part of this quote would apply to, for example, Lange (1937), in which he argued that a socialist economy could use a price mechanism to help allocate resources. This refuted the charge of Mises (1935) that economic calculation were not possible under socialism, although 'Lange never looked upon his model of market socialism as a blueprint for a socialist state' (Wellisz, 1968). Lange (1937) also argued that the competitive model might be more applicable to a socialist economy than to a capitalist economy (with oligopolies, advertising and a maldistribution of income).

Oscar Lange had, like Kalecki, left Poland in the later 1930s (initially also financed by a Rockefeller Fellowship), and he returned to Poland in 1945. He was, *inter alia*, Polish ambassador to the USA and delegate to the Security Council of the United Nations (1945–7), and Chairman of the Economic Council in Poland (1957–62). He was politically active in Poland, being member of Parliament and of the Council of State (deputy chairman for part of the time). Lange also maintained a considerable flow of academic work. 'His activity on behalf of socialist democratization is closely connected with his other aspiration: to found economic planning and management on scientific grounds' (Kowalik,

266   *The Economics of Michał Kalecki*

1965). For a biography of Lange, see Kowalik (1965) and *International Encyclopedia for the Social Sciences*, Vol. 8 (Stanislaw Wellisz (1968)).

14. 'In December 1956, Kalecki published an article "Workers' Councils and Central Planning", showing the fundamental importance of industrial democracy under socialism' (Brus, 1977b). The same author (Brus, 1975, p. 177, fn. 47) also wrote that 'some economists attached greater weight to this element of reform (workers' councils) than to decentralisation and new forms of material incentives', which is followed by a reference to Kalecki (1956b).

15. Horvat, Markovic and Supek (1975), pp. 244–5 provides an English translation of the *Law on Workers' Councils*, 1956.

16. We say usually here since if there were clearly a strong preference by workers for, say, future consumption over current consumption this would lead to an emphasis on accumulation over consumption.

17. Kornai (1979) makes an acknowledgement to Kalecki (1970) and to Goldman and Kouba (1969) as developing similar ideas.

18. 'Non-productive' investment is outlays on new fixed assets which do not contribute to the production of goods – e.g. houses, schools, hospitals, parks.

19. The notation used by Kalecki (1972a) has been adhered to as far as possible. However, I have made changes to avoid using in this chapter, symbols which have been widely used elsewhere in the book with a different meaning. In this equation, *IN* has been used for inventories whereas Kalecki used *S*.

20. For papers which work within this approach and seek to develop it, see, for example, Łaski (1972), Brus and Łaski (1964, 1965a, b).

21. 'After Gomulka's basically autarkic policy [during the 1960s], Gierek's growth strategy [in the 1970s] envisaged opening the Polish economy to foreign trade and capital. Borrowing on a large scale from Western countries would enable Poland to modernise its industrial structure . . .' (Nuti, 1981, texts in brackets added). The Polish trade deficit with the West was a cumulative 303 million dollars during the years 1961–70, but *averaged* 2.6 billion dollars in the years 1975–8. See also Blazyca (1980).

22. From equations (11.2) and (11.3), it can be seen that one set of circumstances when an increase investment will raise the growth rate is when there is unemployed labour, and a shortage of capital equipment for labour to be employed on. An increase in investment in those circumstances would help provide equipment and in the short term add to demand. But when the equipment is available, the demand for the output may not be – in a sense Kalecki's paradox of investment referred to in Chapter 9 (p. 156). These circumstances are ruled out in a neoclassical analysis, in part because that approach postulates full employment and partly because of the assumed flexibility in capital labour ratios.

23. In the neo-classical analysis applied to capitalist economies the discussion on maximising consumption per head (which is close to maximising real wages since only members of the labour force are included in the 'heads' over which consumption is maximised) is under the heading of

the 'golden rule' (see, e.g., Dixit, 1976). In those discussions little regard is paid to problems of movement between one growth path and another.

24. Harrod-neutral technical progress is often defined in terms of a constant marginal product of capital for any constant capital output–ratio whilst Hicks-neutral technical progress relates to the ratio of marginal product of labour to the marginal product of capital remaining constant for each capital–labour ratio. Payments to factors according to marginal productivity will only exactly add up to the product available when there are constant returns to scale.

25. When technical progress is Harrod-neutral, it can be represented as labour-augmenting. Balanced growth at full employment is then mathematically possible with output, capital stock and 'efficiency' units of labour all growing at the same uniform rate.

12
Kaleckian Macroeconomics: Speculations on Future Developments

Introduction

In this final chapter, we return to the analysis by Kalecki of capitalist economies presented in Chapters 2 and 7 above. Although readers will no doubt form their own judgements, the view underlying this chapter is that Kalecki's approach provides a coherent foundation for macroeconomic analysis (broadly conceived). The analysis of Kalecki is seen as consistent with a broad range of evidence (as argued in, for example, Sawyer (1982a), Chapter 7). Klein (1964) has noted that the main features of Kalecki's analysis have found their way into many macroeconometric models, and that point was elaborated on in Chapter 9 (pp. 204–7). This chapter has two major purposes. The first purpose is to discuss those elements of Kalecki's approach which require, in my view, further work. The second purpose is to outline those aspects of modern capitalist economies which have become important in, say, the past twenty years and which are at most only partially reflected in Kalecki's analysis.

There are at least three reasons for seeking to develop and extend Kalecki's analysis. The first is that, at the present time, macroeconomics has a surfeit of competing paradigms including monetarism (of various forms), Keynesian (again of various forms), post-Keynesian, new classical, etc. An approach based on the work of Kalecki has many common elements with post-Keynesian approaches. For those seeking a macroeconomic analysis which offers some elements of realism (with its basis in an oligopolistic view of the world) and a break from equilibrium analysis, Kalecki certainly offers a possible way forward. The contrast with the unrealism and equilibrium approach of the new classical school could not be sharper.[1]

The second reason is that Kalecki had little regard for those who slavishly followed the work of others in an uncritical manner (cf. p. 3 above). Thus, to put Kalecki's work on a pedestal without critical appraisal would be counter to his general philosophy. The third is that since Kalecki viewed economy (and society) as evolving through time, then the precise content of economic analysis must change to reflect changing circumstances and institutions. There are a number of post-war developments (e.g. growth of international trade and of multinational enterprises) which are likely to change some of the elements of the analysis, even if they do not change the thrust of the analysis.

It is, of course, very much a matter of personal opinion which aspects of Kalecki's work are in need of refinement and what are the major post-war developments which need to be incorporated into Kalecki's analysis. This chapter is particularly speculative and idiosyncratic and certainly makes no claim to indicate what Kalecki would have done or what Kalecki really meant.[2]

Kalecki's Macroeconomics Methodology

In Chapters 1 and 9, we have touched on some elements of Kalecki's methodology and general approach. In this section, we present some general aspects which are relevant for the discussion of an approach to macroeconomics.

Within the neo-classical tradition, macroeconomics is often seen as little more than simplified general equilibrium theory (through dealing with only a few different types of agents, e.g. the representative firm). Drazen (1980), for example, argues that the 'explanation of macroeconomic phenomena will be complete only when such explanations are consistent with microeconomic choice theoretic behaviour and can be phrased in the language of general equilibrium theory'.[3]

The approach of Kalecki could be seen as rejecting that view of macroeconomics in four important respects. First, Kalecki did not make use of choice theoretic behaviour as a basis for analysis, and specifically did not use the tools of utility analysis. Further, much of the analysis of Kalecki (and also of Marx and many others) does not place much weight on individual choices but rather on the constraints on those decisions.

Second, and to some degree related to the first point, there are aggregate or system level relationships which do not have micro-level analogies. Pasinetti (1974) describes the approach which he used as

> not 'macro-economic' in the sense of representing a first simplifed rough step towards a more detailed and disaggregated analysis. It is macro-economic because it could not be otherwise. Only problems have been discussed which are of a macro-economic nature; an accurate investigation of them has nothing to do with disaggregation. They would remain the same – i.e. they would still arise at a macro-economic level – even if we were to break down the model into a disaggregated analysis.

Pasinetti wrote this in the context of investigating the relationship between the rate of profit and the rate of growth. This view means, *inter alia*, that a primacy of macroeconomic level over microeconomic level in the sense that the relationships being considered are macroeconomic level ones which impinge at the microeconomic level.[4] Some of the alternative explanations of unemployment can be used to illustrate this. The neo-classical approach would build up from the individual household and firm level to derive demand and supply of labour schedules, and their intersection would determine the equilibrium level of unemployment. Thus the macroeconomic variable of unemployment level is determined solely by interaction of micro-level relationships. A Ricardian–Marxian explanation such as the level of unemployment tends to a level which maintains the growth of real wages in line with growth of labour productivity is more clearly a macro-level explanation. It is derived from a macro- (or system) level requirement that real wages rise in line with productivity (equivalent to a constant share of profits in national income). It impinges on individuals, by making some of them unemployed and by influencing the behaviour of others. Individual choices may enter to some degree to determine who is unemployed and who is employed, but not to influence the overall level.

Third, Kalecki's rejection of equilibrium analysis would include rejection of a general equilibrium approach. He saw capitalist economies as subject to fluctuations, crisis, growth and change, and these do not sit easily with any equilibrium analysis which is intended to help understand an actual operating economy.[5]

Fourth, Kalecki explicitly rejected the usefulness of perfect competition. Although the term general equilibrium is used in a number of senses, it is reasonable to take it that in this context general equilibrium includes the assumption of perfect competition. It is reasonable in that the discussion of the micro-foundations of macroeconomics based on the work of Clower (1965), Leijonhufvud (1968), Barro and Grossman (1971), Muellbauer and Portes (1978), etc. assume an industrial structure of perfect competition (in sense of dealing with small firms) and examine the consequences of markets to clear in the absence of a price-setting auctioneer.

One final remark here is on the old question of the realism of assumptions and how assumptions are to be chosen. Kalecki's methodology in this respect could be seen as encompassing the following. There are problems for which the use of 'thought experiments' are useful in highlighting key features. Kalecki used this technique in his discussions of, for example, the effect of reducing money wages on the level of employment (Kalecki, 1939, Chapter 3) and in tracing the effects of a rise in investment on employment and output (Kalecki, 1971a, Chapter 3). But in most of his theorising, Kalecki had a clear objective in mind (e.g. explanation of unemployment, causes of business cycles), and whilst the assumptions would be attuned to the purpose at hand they were also based on observations of the real world. Thus assumptions are specifically chosen for their apparent relevance and importance.

The discussion below looks at refinements and developments of Kalecki's approach to macroeconomics under eleven headings. There is some inevitable overlap between these subject areas. The first four headings deal largely with refinements to Kalecki's approach, which reflect weaknesses (in our view) in Kalecki's approach. The final seven headings deal mainly with the way in which Kalecki's approach could be developed to recognise some of the major changes which have occurred in post-war capitalism.

The Degree of Monopoly Approach

The first topic which we deal with is the degree of monopoly approach, which was discussed and defended against a number of criticisms in Chapter 2. There are, however, in our view some aspects of the degree of monopoly approach which require some attention.[6] The first aspect is the question of which costs are to be counted as prime (or direct) costs by the firm, and hence marked up by the firm, and which costs are to be counted as fixed costs by the firm and hence not marked up but are a deduction from profits.

We begin this discussion by considering which labour payments are to be regarded as part of prime (direct) costs. Kalecki worked with wages as part of prime costs whilst salaries were part of overheads (fixed costs). In British statistical usage, salaries are payments to administrative, technical and clerical workers, whilst wages are payments to operatives. In empirical work relating to the degree of monopoly approach, Kalecki used figures for the UK and the USA on wage share, thereby linking his concept of wages with the statistical definition of wages.

The division between wages and salaries could be seen to reflect a narrow economic division based on which labour inputs are variable in the short run and those which are not. Another view would be that there are significant social status differences between wage-earners and salary-earners. Before we explore this in more detail, we note that there have been substantial changes in the relative proportion of wage-earners and salary-earners during this century. In the UK, for example, salary-earners increased from around 10 per cent of the civilian working population to nearly 28 per cent in 1961, whilst wage-earners decreased from over 77 per cent in 1911 to 65 per cent in 1961.[7] Recent overall data are not available, but in manufacturing industries, operatives (manual workers) declined from 79 per cent of employees in 1960 to 71 per cent in 1983. This would suggest that the economic and social significance of wages relative to salaries is likely to have changed. Salary-earners are now more likely to be unionised than previously, and the social status of a typical salary-earner is now rather from such status in, say, the interwar period. Further, which labour payments are prime costs may now be different.

Kalecki (1939) argued that whilst 'from the social point of view it would be more interesting to consider the share of labour as a whole; ... it is the relative share of manual labour which is suitable for theoretical analysis' (p. 13). This suitability would appear to be based on the inclusion of wages (of manual workers) in variable costs (for which average and marginal are approximately equal) and the inclusion of salaries as part of overheads (for which the marginal costs are virtually zero). However, other passages in Kalecki's writings suggest some modifications. In his analysis of the effects of money wage cuts (Kalecki, 1939, Chapter 3), argued that

> we divide the salary earners into two categories, which we shall typify as 'clerks' and 'managers'. We assume that the salary rates of the first group move proportionately to wage rates, and that both manual workers and 'clerks' do not save. . . . However, we do allow for 'managers' savings, and suppose their salaries to change in the same direction as capitalists' income but in a lesser proportion (p. 86).

This is closely related to the remark that 'in salaries are included those of higher business executives which are rather akin to profits'. It can also be noted that Kalecki argued that trade unions could influence money wages (and to a limited extent real wages). Since the growth of trade unions in UK in recent years has been heavily concentrated on non-manual workers, this would suggest that perhaps the term wages should be interpreted more widely than earnings of manual workers.[8]

Recent changes in the relative roles of wages and salaries would suggest the need to reappraise the details of Kalecki's approach. But the reappraisal is also undertaken to bring out some of the difficulties in Kalecki's approach, and to suggest ways of resolving them.

There would appear to be two basic approaches to the division of labour payments as between variable/marked up costs and overheads/non-marked-up costs. The first approach is reflected in the standard presentation of Kalecki's approach, namely on the grounds of which costs vary and which do not within the price decision period. Even if that approach is accepted, it does not follow that the statistical division into wages and salaries is the appropriate one for the theory. The second approach is the division into the labour income of the controllers/managers of the firm and 'other' labour income (probably all wages, and most salaries especially of 'clerks').

The first approach was linked with profit-maximisation and the formal presentation of Kalecki's approach. Under profit maximisation, the (first order) condition is that firms seek to equate marginal revenue and marginal costs, which leads to price expressed as a mark-up over marginal cost. Clearly, in Kalecki's case, that mark-up depends on the degree of monopoly, and it is assumed that marginal costs are approximately constant. The general view of price as a mark up over marginal cost is deceptively precise, especially with regard to what are regarded as marginal costs. The problems with marginal costs are well illustrated in the nationalised industry pricing literature with the frequent recommendation of pricing in line with marginal costs.[9] The obvious problem which arises is the definition of marginal costs. The actual size of marginal costs depends on the time period considered and which inputs are believed to be capable of being varied. Their size also depends on the perceptions of the decision makers, and this is particularly important in the pricing case where prices are announced ahead of production. Further, marginal costs are defined as the difference in costs associated with a small difference in output. But, at any time, only one level of output is actually produced, and what the costs would have been if the level of output had been slightly different can never be known with certainty (though reasonable estimates may be possible).

The estimated marginal costs associated with meeting a rise in demand are likely to depend on whether that rise in demand is viewed as permanent or temporary. In the first case, the firm may take on extra labour whereas in the second case it may meet the surge in demand out of stocks or by labour working overtime. The marginal costs are likely to differ in the two cases. These remarks apply, of course, quite generally to any short-run profit maximising approach to price determination. Kalecki's 'solution' was the assertion that variable costs were manual labour costs plus material costs and that average variable costs were constant. The constant average variable costs assumption mainly simplified the analysis, though it is the one which has been focused upon. But the former assumption is rather more questionable, but has not been much discussed.[10]

It could also be noted here that Kalecki argued as though output and employment (of manual workers) moved together over the course of the trade-cycle. This means that the problems raised in the previous paragraph are overlooked, as is the cyclical movement in measured labour productivity.

One way to answer the question of which labour costs are marked-up, which might fit in with Kalecki's general approach, would be to adopt a pragmatic approach in which we sought to discover how firms arrive at their pricing decisions, and observe which costs are calculated and to which a mark-up is applied. Studies of pricing behaviour from Hall and Hitch (1939) onwards would form an important part of this line of approach.

The second line of approach would be to stress the division of those who work for a firm into the 'controllers' (e.g. 'top' managers, directors) and the rest. This approach would stress the social differences between different employees. It would also draw on the distinction which Kalecki made between 'managers' and 'clerks', where we are interpreting 'managers' in the narrow sense in which it is used in, for example, the managerial theories of firm literature (e.g. Baumol, 1959; Marris, 1964) to refer to 'top' managers who are effective decision makers. Kalecki also saw the salaries of 'clerks' rather like wages, in the sense that those salaries were taken to move in line with wages and were largely spent. Similarly, the salaries of 'managers' were seen to move in line with profits and a significant proportion saved. The idea of the importance of the internal organisation of firms (especially large ones) is taken up below.

The next part of our assessment of Kalecki's degree of monopoly approach is the influence of overheads on the degree of monopoly and thereby on the mark-up of price over costs. Kalecki (1971a, p. 44) stated that 'it will be assumed that the actual level of overheads does not directly influence the determination of price since the total overhead costs remain roughly stable as output varies'. In one sense, this is a statement of the conventional proposition that fixed costs do not affect prices set under short run profit maximisation. However, Kalecki proceeded to state that 'the level of overheads may have an indirect influence upon price formation'. The way in which Kalecki dealt with the influence of overheads on price formation reflects two features of the general approach. First, if, say, capital intensity increases (so that overhead costs increase relative to output) then if prices rise (relative to direct costs) this is seen to occur not automatically but only as a consequence of a rise in the degree of monopoly. If firms continue to compete and accept the same profit margins as in the past then obviously no such rise in price–cost margin will occur. Second, whilst the price–cost margin reflects profit-seeking by firms, the historical and industrial factors influence the extent and form of tacit agreement amongst firms. Thus in terms of the discussion in

Chapter 2, it would be possible to list many factors which influence the a_i-term (the degree of effective collusion) including the history on agreements between firms concentration and degree of capital intensity.

There are two aspects of the aggregation from firm to industry and then to economy level of the price equation which have not been fully explored. The first aspect here has been briefly discussed in Chapter 2, namely the algebraic problem of adding together disparate industries and allowing for differences in the degree of vertical integration. The idea used there was that if starting with a price equation for a final consumption good as a mark-up over labour costs and material input costs, the input costs can be traced back to the prices of supplying industries. Those prices can in turn be broken down into labour costs, material input costs and the degrees of monopoly in those industries. Ultimately, the price of consumption goods is broken down into labour costs, imported input costs and degrees of monopoly. This process of breaking down prices may be endless with the final breakdown as indicated in the previous sentence never reached. However, the approach indicated in the Appendix to Chapter 8, using an input–output framework would permit that obstacle to be overcome.

The second aspect relates to the relationship between the degree of monopoly in one industry and the degrees of monopoly elsewhere. This aspect has two sides. First, the degree of monopoly in one industry (and thereby the price–cost margin) is likely to be influenced by the degrees of monopoly amongst competing industries. This inter-industry rivalry is overlooked in the usual presentation of the degree of monopoly approach. This would require amendment to allow for some interdependence between degrees of monopoly.

Second, the degree of monopoly in one industry may be influenced by the degree of monopoly in supplying industries and in purchasing industries. Consider a vertical integrated industry for which there is a price–cost margin which would maximise profits. When there are several stages of production, the question arises as to how the various stages of production share out the profits, and whether the ratio of final price to labour costs and imported input costs is above or below that which would maximise profits overall. Waterson (1984), Chapter 5 provides a review of recent work in this direction.

The final aspect of Kalecki's degree of monopoly approach on which we comment relates to the balance of competition and rivalry on the one hand and of monopoly and collusion on the other. This does not necessarily detract from the general notion that, at a particular moment in time, the extent to which prices exceed prime costs depends on factors such as concentration, collusion, etc. Instead, it suggests rather more rivalry is conveyed by the term degree of monopoly. In Chapter 2, we remarked on the extensive operation of cartels in interwar Poland and Kalecki's studies of international cartels. More generally, the 1930s was a favourable environment for cartels with governments fostering cartelisation (e.g. under the New Deal in the USA). The post-war period has generally been less favourable for cartels. Governments have tended towards a relatively hostile attitude to cartels (e.g. in the UK the *Restrictive Practices Act*, 1956). Although governments have not been consistent in this respect and policies may not have achieved their declared objective, nevertheless there is probably less collusion in Western European economies in the 1980s as compared with the 1930s.[11] The growth of international trade and of multinational companies is also relevant here, though we consider those changes further below.

The effect of the separation of price decision making and investment decisions which is evident in Kalecki's work has the unfortunate result that the interaction between prices and investment is lost sight of. There is the link running from degree of monopoly to price –cost margin and through profits to investment decisions. But the reverse flow is neglected in the sense of investigation of the impact which investment has on unit costs and thereby on price and competitive position of firms. Thus the element of competition to achieve lower costs, improved products and market shares through investment is largely overlooked.

Business Cycles

Kalecki's work emphasised the cyclical nature of capitalist economies. The relevance of undertaking an analysis of the business cycle is reinforced by the arguments of Blatt (1983) to the effect that equilibrium analysis is a poor guide to the quantitative impact of, for example, government expenditure changes if the economy is actually cyclical. Further, the impact of, say, government expenditure changes may depend on the points in the cycle when they are made.

A persistent problem in the development of business cycle theories has been the question of whether it is possible to develop theories and associated mathematical equations which are 'self-contained' in the sense that the theories do no rely on either some particular specified relationship between the parameters to hold or on random shocks to ensure cycles which do not die away over time. It was seen in Chapter 3 that Kalecki initially used the first of those possibilities to generate continuing cycles, but in most of his work on the business cycle used the latter idea. However the work of Goodwin (1982), Blatt (1983) and others point to the relevance here of non-linear equations which generate limit cycles. This then holds out the prospect of continuing (limit) cycles without the requirement of random shocks or a particular relationship between parameters (though random shocks may be relevant).

The two important aspects of Kalecki's approach to the business cycle which should be reiterated here are the focus on investment and the notion of the 'top' of the cycle often not involving full employment. Experience of business cycles since the mid-1970s reinforces the practical relevance of the second point. The particular focus on investment as the major cause of economic fluctuations may need to be modified. Government activity and to some extent consumer expenditure are likely to be now rather more important ingredients in the business cycle than they were in the pre-war period. Further, the growth of multinational enterprises means that investment in one country may be only loosely related to the demand conditions in that country. Multinational enterprises are making location of investment decisions as well as volume of investment decisions. It is also the case that Kalecki drew on the identity of savings and investment in a private sector closed economy, and the relationship between savings and investment is weakened when an open economy with an important government sector is considered.

Three other additions which would be helpful in the analysis of business cycles are the discussion of expectations, monetary factors and the role of government activity. These are considered more generally below.

Money and Finance

Kalecki recognised the importance of the expansion of credit to finance investment expansion, and saw the monetary sector as adapting rather passively to the real sectors, as seen in Chapters 5 and 9. Although the views of Kalecki on the financial sectors were never expressed at length (partly reflecting his laconic style), his views could be seen as fitting into the general post-Keynesian view of money as largely credit money endogenous to the private sector which usually expands to accommodate an increased demand for money (e.g. Moore, 1979; Kaldor, 1981). For the purpose of analysing in terms of a thought experiment the consequences of, say, an increase in demand for investment (as in Kalecki, 1971a, Chapter 3), then such an approach may be sufficient. But as an aid to understanding the actual operation of capitalist economies, it could be expanded in three respects. In doing so, the work of post-Keynesian and some monetary economists can be drawn upon.

The first respect arises from treating the economy as moving through time, and hence with 'hang-overs' from the past. Thus, the creation of money in one period, and the discrepancy between investment demand and intended savings in that period have consequences for the behaviour of the economy in subsequent periods (pp. 93–96 above).

The second respect is that there may be certain times when banks are constrained in lending activities. This may arise from specific government intervention (perhaps in the belief that control of the money supply is possible and desirable). But more relevant here would be occasions when banks were constrained by their liquidity ratios, level of deposits or pessimism from further lending. Kalecki briefly indicated that banks could, by hoisting interest rates in response to a rise in the demand for loans, thereby reduce investment demand. But this was introduced as a possibility, rather than any indication of when banks would hold back on loans. A related aspect of this point is the degree to which any single bank is limited in its ability to expand faster (or much faster) than the other banks.

The third respect is consideration of the particular nature of banks and other financial institutions which simultaneously take in deposits, make loans and purchase assets (including financial assets). Further, there is 'pyramiding' whereby liabilities of one institution are the assets of other institutions. These aspects of financial institutions lay them open to confidence crises (with the removal of deposits from the financial institutions and the consequent calling in of loans), of loan defaults (especially in times of depression) and of cumulative problems arising from 'pyramiding'. These are clearly occasions when the financial sector may have a strong impact on the real sector. Minsky (1976, 1978) has particularly emphasised these aspects of the financial sector.

Expectations

Many recent debates in macroeconomics have involved expectations formation with the idea of 'rational expectations', making much of the running. Kalecki's work on macroeconomics reflects the time when it was written and does not explicitly discuss the role and nature of expectations. However, it is possible to outline his views on these matters. Throughout Kalecki adopted a view of expectation formation which could be labelled generalised adaptive expectations. The expectations are adaptive in the sense that they do adapt to circumstances. When prices have been rising rapidly, people tend to believe that they will continue to rise rapidly (Kalecki, 1962b). In business up-swings, rising output and profits generate an air of optimism, whilst in the down-swing an air of pessimism prevails. But the term adaptive expectations usually means a mechanism by which currently held expectations (on, say, price changes) are a weighted average of previously held expectations and past occurrences. Whilst there are elements of that view in Kalecki's work, it is not so rigidly applied and there is recognition that a wide range of events may influence expectations on, say, price changes. In sum, it could be said that in Kalecki's work expectations on future events were strongly influenced by current and recent events.

Another question which arises in connection with expectations and macroeconomics is that for which variables are expectations formed. Much recent work, especially that of the 'new classical' school, has related to expectations of future prices and price changes in the context of competitive markets. In that context, prices are 'given' for economic agents (households, firms). Economic agents make decisions in response to expectations on future prices, and mistakes occur when expectations are faulty.[12]

In developing the work of Kalecki, it can be argued that expectations on relative prices are rather unimportant. For oligopolists able to set and adjust prices can react to actual cost and price changes as they occur, rather than on the basis of expected cost and prices changes. Price expectations become more important when considering wage bargaining since it is observed that such bargaining takes place infrequently (say annually). The expectations held by one oligopolist on how others in the same industry would react to its moves in terms of price, output, advertising, etc. are likely to be important in the determination of price cost margins, as could be seen from the analysis in Chapter 2.

In Kalecki's approach, expectations on the level of demand and of profits are more important than price expectations. When it is recognised that production takes a significant period of time, then the determination of the scale of output will be strongly influenced by the expected level of demand. Further, investment decisions are strongly conditioned by expectations on future demand and profitability.

The refinements in the area of expectations could be threefold. First, it may be necessary to spell out more clearly than Kalecki did where expectations about the future are relevant. Second, whilst Kalecki stressed the importance of expectations in investment demand, he did not do so in the area of output determination. Effectively, he assumed that any change in demand would quickly be reflected in changes in output. But when stocks of finished goods can be held and when changes in the level of output take some time to effect, expectations on future demand and the level of stocks are important in the determination of output decisions. Third, and this applies more generally, it is necessary to discover how relevant expectations are formulated. To date, economists have largely made more or less plausible assumptions about how expectations are formulated with little or no attempt to see whether these assumptions match up with how expectations are actually formed.

Workers' Savings

Through out his writings, Kalecki considered workers savings to be unimportant (e.g. Kalecki, 1971b). In one sense the assumption that workers do not save can be seen as a simplification of the more general proposition that the savings ratio of workers is substantially lower than the savings ratio of capitalists. Indeed, in a number of places this is how Kalecki appears to have treated that assumption (cf. Kalecki, 1971a, Chapter 7).

The point raised in Kaldor's theory of income distribution

(Kaldor, 1955) by Pasinetti (1962) is relevant here.[13] This point was that when workers save, they become owners (directly or indirectly) of part of the capital stock and hence entitled to part of the flow of profits. Pasinetti (1962) argued in effect that the difference in savings behaviour was between workers and capitalists rather than between those made out of wages and those out of profits. Thus the differential savings proposition relates to differences between social classes rather than to types of income. But, it can be argued that profits are subject to 'double-savings', with savings directly out of profit and indirectly out of dividends, with in both cases relatively high propensities to save observed. For that reason, it is reasonable to maintain the notion of differential savings out of profits and out of wages.[14]

However, it is relevant to consider the effect of changes in the pattern of and volume of savings in the post-war era. Savings by the personal sector in the UK have risen substantially (relative to disposable income) from below 2 per cent of personal disposable income in the late 1940s/early 1950s to figures generally in the range 10 to 15 per cent in the 1970s and early 1980s.[15] An evaluation of this type of trend cannot be comprehensively treated here, but the following points appear relevant.

First, the personal sector covers households (which include the self-employed) and non-profitmaking institutions, and thus income figures cover much more than just labour income. Savings are effectively money income minus consumer expenditure. The figures on savings take no account of the depreciation in real terms of financial assets with value fixed in nominal terms during a period of inflation nor do they take account of capital appreciation (e.g. on houses). Estimates by the Bank of England (e.g. *Bank of England Quarterly Bulletin*, June 1984) suggest that during most of the 1970s 'real savings' by personal sector (making allowance for effects of inflation) was generally negative at a time when the nominal savings ratio was reaching all time high levels. Their estimates indicate that 'real' savings by personal sector was positive in the 1980s but much below the figure suggested by nominal savings. Similarly, the income concept is not adjusted for the impact of inflation.

Second, it can be noted that savings are calculated 'before providing for depreciation, stock appreciation and additions to tax reserves', which are of significance for the savings of the self-employed which are included in the personal sector. In 1982, net savings were around 65 per cent of gross savings for the personal sector.

Third, the institutional arrangements for pension provision and the way in which these are treated in the national income accounts are highly significant. Contributions made towards pensions made by employers and employees are generally compulsory (at least at the individual level), as part of the contract of employment and encouraged by legislation. Employers' contributions for pensions are considered as part of employment income, and since those contributions cannot be directly spent are also part of savings.[16] The receipts by life assurance and superannuation schemes are included as part of income of the personal sector. The net acquisition of financial assets in life assurance companies and superannuation funds (after administrative costs, payments of pension, etc.) amounted to £12,803 million in 1982, which was equivalent to 63 per cent of the savings of the personal sector.

The important aspects of these pension arrangements are:

(i) Much of the savings is compulsory, and a large part of the voluntary savings is of a long-term contractual nature;

(ii) Pension schemes are 'self-liquidating' for the individual over a life-time with savings during working life and dissaving during retirement;

(iii) The assets which are acquired by workers are rights to future pension. The assets held by the pension funds to finance those pension rights mean that the immediate ownership of financial assets, shares, property, etc. lies in the hands of the pension funds and not the workers.

Fourth, another major outlet of savings is house purchase. The gross domestic fixed capital formation in new dwellings and the net purchase of land and existing buildings by the personal sector fluctutates from year to year but generally have amounted to around 30 per cent of savings. These figures include self-employed purchases, and would be influenced by, e.g. sales of houses by property companies and by local authorities.

The important elements of these forms of savings (pensions rights, housing) are:

(i) They do not provide any direct control for workers over the means of production;

(ii)   The immediate ownership of companies has tended to pass from the personal sector into the hands of financial institutions;

(iii) Demise of private landlords.

Money Wage Determination

Kalecki was writing against a background in which, outside of wartime and immediate post-war periods, prices and wages did not rise continuously. Whilst wages and prices varied, this was often around a trend of virtual price and wage stability. This meant that factors such as inflationary expectations and the difficulties of making calculations in inflation-adjusted terms (i.e. problems of inflation accounting) could be overlooked (though Kalecki did consider inflationary expectations in his discussion of hyperinflation). Some aspects of this arise in the next section. In the context of money wages, Kalecki and Keynes could be said to have adopted a common approach in the sense of conducting part of their analysis with a given (for the purposes of the analysis) money wage, and then consider what would happen when money wages change as a complicating factor and for which time lags in the adjustment of prices to wage change could be important. In both cases, the effect of money wage changes was in the nature of a 'thought experiment', with nothing said about the actual determination of money wages in the economy. This partly reflected their concern to defuse the arguments favouring the reduction of money wages as a cure for employment. But it does leave a large gap for macroeconomic models, etc. to try to fill.

My own advocacy of a target real wage approach to the determination of money wages has been advanced elsewhere (Henry *et al.*, 1976; Sawyer, 1982a, 1983), and I will not repeat the full set argument here. The three features of that approach which we highlight here are:

(i)   Money wages are the outcome of collective (or similar) bargaining over an important range of the economy;

(ii)   Workers have a notion of acceptable real wages for which they strive;

(iii) Money wage increases will be strongly influenced by actual and expected price increases and to some degree by level and change in unemployment and other factors influencing trade union power/pressure.

This, at least in its general form, would appear to be broadly consistent with Kalecki's approach in the sense that it stresses the role of collective bargaining, and that it recognises the importance of social and historical factors in the determination of wages (through the notion of an acceptable real wage target).

Inflation

As we argued above in Chapter 6, the inflation of the 1970s and 1980s does not easily fit into the various types of inflation which Kalecki analysed. However, the view of inflation often described as a 'conflict theory of inflation' (e.g. Rowthorn, 1977; Sawyer, 1983, Chapter 1) could be seen as a development of Kalecki's ideas (although generally that theory has many roots). The three key elements of the conflict theory would be:

(i) The power of economic institutions (firms, unions, government) to be able to raise their prices to offset any cost increases which they face, e.g. firms raise prices to offset cost increases, unions raise money wages to offset cost of living increases;

(ii) An 'elastic' money supply which can expand relatively easily in response to price and wage increases;

(iii) At certain times, a conflict between social classes and within social classes over income shares. These conflicts lead to wage and price increases, and the conflict may be temporarily relieved by those increases.

These features would again appear to be generally consistent with Kalecki's approach. The element (iii) fits in with Kalecki's general view of a class society with conflict of interests between classes, and serves as a trigger which can set off an inflationary process. The second element would appear to fit in with the view of the money supply created by the banks which was part of Kalecki's approach (cf. Chapter 5 above). The accommodating money supply is an ingredient of the inflationary process which permits prices and wages to continue to rise. The other element is that as money wages and other costs rise, firms find that the costs of their work in progress and stocks rise, and the finance has to be found. One mechanism is through bank lending, etc. The first element arises in Kalecki (1971a), Chapter 14, where firms are seen as being about to largely offset wage increases by price increases, and workers respond by further raising money wages. However, in that paper Kalecki saw that process as eventually coming to an end when firms accepted a reduction in the degree of monopoly (and hence a higher wage share). The conflict approach would see the process as possibly continuing for a long period of time.

This last point does lead on to the question of why rates of inflation sometimes decline. We can here pick up some suggestions in Kalecki's writings. An upsurge of inflation would arise from some initiating sector(s) which seek to increase their share of national income. This leads to some price rises, followed by further price rises as other sectors seek to offset the gains of the initiating sector. Inflation does not proceed at a uniform rate either through time or across sectors. As it proceeds, there are gainers and losers (and the membership of these groups may well change over time). Applying the idea of Kalecki on hyperinflation to the 'stagflation' situation, it could be said generally that attempts will be made to bring inflation down (or to a halt) when the powerful groups in society either have initially gained from an upsurge of inflation but whose gains are threatened by further inflation or come to find the losses imposed on them from inflation 'intolerable'. Pressures for an emphasis on the reduction of inflation may be linked with other demands, e.g. reduction of public sector, control over trade unions.

Enterprises and the Intensity of Labour

For the purposes of his macroeconomic analysis, Kalecki effectively made two crucial assumptions. First, he treated the firm as largely synonymous with the entrepreneur, and thus did not consider the internal organisation of the firm, problems of internal control, etc. Second, he took 'the intensity of labour' as given. It is quite reasonable to seek to deal with problems one step at a time, and for the purposes of macroeconomic analysis hold a range of factors constant. In this sub-section, we seek to see whether these assumptions can be 'opened up', and the implications for macroeconomic analysis.

Over the past century and more the size of large firms has generally increased substantially, as a consequence of increased concentration and of firms operating in several industries. This increased size has generated a large literature concerned with, e.g. divorce between ownership and control, and treating firms as large organisations. For the purposes of our discussion here, we can highlight two features. First, increased size will generally involve some loss of effective control by the owners and managers. The divorce between ownership and control suggested by Berle and Means (1932) and many others focused on the difficulties of owners maintaining control in large firms. Further, managers may find difficulty in ensuring implementation of their decisions. However, some of these difficulties may be overcome by technical advances in information gathering, monitoring of the implementation of decisions, etc.

Second, the conflict of interests between owners and managers may be reflected in how the surplus available to an enterprise is divided between reported profits and managerial salaries, and the division of profits into dividends and retained profits.

These two features are developed by Cowling (1982) and, since his starting point is based on the work of Kalecki, his work can be seen as developing Kalecki's ideas to take account of the evolution of large firms. Cowling argues that

> [m]anagerialism is usually portrayed in terms of a conflict between managers and stockholders. . . . (W)e seek to identify two basic struggles involving managers and stockholders, one between big capital and small capital, with big capital occupying a normally dominant position *within* the corporation, and the other between high level and lower-level management, where high-level management includes the important representatives of big capital.

Further, he argues that

> while it is safer to assume that managers will follow their own interests wherever possible, rather than behaving as if to maximise the welfare of external holders of stock, it does not follow that

they will want to abandon profit-maximising price-output rules implicit in the oligopoly equilibrium [similar to that described in Chapter 2 above]. It seems reasonable to assume that in any short run situation management will want to maximise the excess of revenue over variable costs, for any given interfirm arrangement. Having picked the profit-maximising price or output for any degree of collusion which it appears possible to sustain, the problem becomes one of distributing this flow of income between stockholders and management.

In terms of the discussion in Chapter 2, payment to management will appear as part of overheads. Thus the approach of Cowling means that the controllers of the firm would seek to maximise the excess of revenue over variable costs and then there is the share-out of that excess between profits, managerial salaries and other overheads to be determined.

Kalecki's macroeconomic analysis included the assumption that the intensity of labour and labour productivity were held constant. But this was clearly a case where an assumption was made for the purpose of focusing on other effects, but did not imply that the intensity of labour would actually be constant nor that the topic of the intensity of labour was unimportant. However, Kalecki did not extent his analysis to incorporate factors influencing the intensity of labour. But when questions such as the effects of unemployment, trade union legislation, etc., on labour productivity are discussed or when attempts are made to explain differences between countries in levels and growth rates in labour productivity, then the assumption of constant labour intensity would no longer be at all appropriate. (See Hodgson (1982) for a survey and extensive bibliography.)

Internationalisation

The international scene in the 1980s can be compared with, say, 1930s and 1940s in the following respects (though some elements were already emerging in 1930s and 1940s):

(a) International trade is generally much more significant – i.e. imports and exports to national income ratios are much higher;
(b) There has been a spread of operation by multinational enterprises;

(c) There has been considerable integration between national finance markets, and a much greater flow of funds across international borders;
(d) Flexible or quasi-flexible exchange rates in place of largely fixed exchange rates.

These differences are clearly only a sketch, but we would argue that the macroeconomic analysis of Kalecki was largely based on the implied view of the 1930s and 1940s contained in that list – i.e. some international trade, no regard to multinational companies, insulated domestic financial markets and fixed exchange rates. The importance of international trade, multinational enterprises and the constraints which they imposed on domestic economies can be seen from Kalecki's writings on developing economies and on socialist economies (Chapters 10 and 11 above).

The first two points above can be taken together. The recognition of an open economy and government sector means that the simple condition which Kalecki often dealt with, namely: gross profits = gross investment plus capitalists' consumption has to be amended. This was done by Kalecki (as in Kalecki, 1971a, Chapter 7) to read gross profits = gross investment + gross surplus + budget deficit − workers savings + capitalist consumption. At one level this is seen as merely a complication to the original analysis. But it has two consequences. The first has been dealt with above (pp. 77–9), where it was indicated that as far as gross profits were concerned, the impact on them of investment, export surplus and budget deficit are analogous, which as was seen there leads to the view that the search of markets overseas (raising the export surplus) and the government deficit (particularly when related to expenditure such as on armaments) are related to the drive for profits. The second consequence is that the simple equality between savings and investment, which Kalecki invoked in his investment theories would no longer hold. This would only be important if there was some tendency for changes in investment to provoke changes in export surplus and/or government deficit.

The next consideration arising from points (a) and (b) is the impact on market power, degree of monopoly and thereby on price–cost margins. The conventional view is that the growth of international trade means an effective increase in competition, as 'foreign' firms invade 'domestic' markets. This is reflected for example in the view that the calculation of concentration amongst domestic firms is of very limited significance because of international trade and the lowering of trade barriers. A full assessment of this line of argument is difficult, but the following would need to be considered. It is implicitly assumed in the 'conventional' view that there is competition and rivalry between 'domestic' and 'foreign' firms. Whilst this may often be the case, there are also cases where there has been international collusion (tacit or otherwise) and where 'foreign' firms have accepted 'domestic' firms as market price leaders. Cowling (1982) explores this in detail (Chapter 6). It could also be noted that the eventual impact of international competition is that 'domestic' firms are wiped out as happened in, e.g., the UK motorcycle industry. Thus, after some time, the amount of competition may be little changed although instead of domestically owned firms contesting the domestic market it is 'foreign' firms that contest the domestic market.

The third point above requires rather more amendments to be made to the Kaleckian framework. In that approach, the short-term rate of interest was determined by the interaction of the money supply and the transactions demand for money, and the longer term rate was linked closely to the short term rate. Further, Kalecki argued that the government would be able to manipulate interest rates by a suitable monetary policy. The significant aspect of that here is that interest rates are a domestic monetary phenomenon with no effect seen from international interest rates.

Technical Progress

There are two interesting possibilities which arise out of Kalecki's approach to investment which is relevant for discussion of technical progress. The first is the idea that there is a stimulus to investment arising from inventions and innovations. It was seen above (pp. 60–3) that a reduction in the underlying pace of invention and innovation lead to a fall in the incentive to investment and thereby to a fall in investment and in capacity utilisation. The interesting part of this approach is that low levels of capacity utilisation arise from slow technical progress.

A popular view is that unemployment arises from faster technical progress, and the basis of that view is the assumption that technical progress tends to be labour-replacing. Kalecki's approach also tends to treat technical progress (Kalecki, 1941a) as generally labour-replacing. Bringing the two elements together would suggest that technical progress is seen to have two offsetting properties of lowering unemployment (through enhancing aggregate demand) and of increasing unemployment (through being labour-replacing).

The second aspect is that the 'additional stimulus to investment which is a direct outcome of innovations' depends 'on past economic, social and technological developments' (Kalecki, 1971a, pp. 173–4). Although Kalecki did not explore this aspect, it clearly opens up the way for the exploration of the wide range of factors which influence the rate of technical progress. Here we mention three factors. First, it could be anticipated that there are periods of history when recent discoveries give much greater impetus to investment than at other times. This could lead to some bunching of significant new ideas, products, etc. which trigger off an investment boom. Ideas such as this are associated with Schumpeter (1939), Mensch (1975), and briefly surveyed by Delebeke (1983).

Second, there are 'past economic developments', notably past levels of research and development (private and public, domestic and foreign) and the general willingness of people to accept new ideas, products and methods of production. Of particular relevance in macroeconomics is likely to be the idea that current levels of demand, profits, etc. influence current expenditure on research and development which in turn influences future growth.

Third, there is the proposition advanced by Kalecki that the rate of innovation will be adversely affected by monopolisation. This proposition was discussed in some detail by Steindl (1952), can, in part, be seen as a reflection of the general view that the rate of technical progress is influenced by social and institutional factors. It could also be seen as fitting in with many of the debates in industrial economics on the question of what influence industrial structure has on invention and innovation.[17]

Government Economic Policy: Causes and Consequences

A vast amount has been written on government economic policies in capitalist economies from a variety of political and economic positions. In this section we seek to give some indications of how Kalecki's general approaches relate to the debates over economic policy. Inevitably, a full treatment of this complex subject cannot be attempted in the space available. We can pick out two key aspects in Kalecki's writings which relate to the topic of government economic policy.

First, a significant level of unemployment is seen as a frequent occurrence under conditions of *laissez-faire* capitalism, and hence prolonged full employment would require substantial government intervention. This was fully discussed above in Chapter 7. It can be seen from there that there are two types of precondition for prolonged full employment advanced by Kalecki. The first is the adoption of the relevant fiscal and monetary policies by government, which will often involve a long term budget deficit to help maintain an appropriate level of demand for full employment, and the development of suitable international agreements to avoid world-wide deflation. The second is the development of institutional changes, particularly reflecting the enhanced power of labour in periods of full employment, needed for the maintenance of full employment. In terms of both of these preconditions, it can be argued that the post-war Keynesian/social democrat consensus failed to develop the necessary arguments and institutions to be able to maintain full employment on a permanent basis.[18, 19] During the 1950s and 1960s it would appear that government deficits on current account were not required on a long term basis to maintain full employment, even if the belief that governments would act to maintain full employment engendered the optimism needed to underpin investment sufficient to generate full employment and leave the actions by government unnecessary. In the 1970s and 1980s, when government deficits have grown there has been a marked reluctance to tolerate the deficits necessary for full employment.[20] There would be severe doubts as to whether the financial sector would be willing to supply the required finance to cover a government deficit on terms acceptable to the government.[21]

In conventional Keynesian economics, using the IS–LM curve framework, a higher level in government expenditure would be represented as a shift in the IS-curve which would generally be seen to lead to increases in income level and in the rate of interest. A suitable increase in the money supply, reflected in an outward shift in the LM curve, would be able to offset the rise in interest rate, if required, and reinforcing the rise in income level. This view can be seen to overlook two key elements. First, it is now recognised (especially since Christ, 1968; Blinder and Solow, 1973) that fiscal and monetary policy are not independent since a government deficit or surplus will generally involve changes in the money supply. But within the equilibrium condition incorporated in the IS curve there are continuing financial flows between the private and public sectors. The analyses of Blinder and Solow and others have included the long term requirement of a balanced government budget, with the consequence that the equality of government expenditure and taxation is the key long-run relationship. But what is overlooked in the equilibrium analyses is that the expansion of the economy requires an increase in, say, government expenditure ahead of a rise in taxation and savings, as detailed above (pp. 91–6). The reactions of financial markets to the necessary increase in the money supply may make such an expansion untenable.

Second, the LM-curve relates to a stock equilibrium between the demand for and the supply of money when bonds are the alternative asset. An increased level of income involves a higher transactions demand for money which has to be offset by a lower 'speculative' demand for money and hence a higher rate of interest. Within the LM approach, there is no element of financial institutions being unwilling to lend to governments through mistrust (rightly or wrongly) of their policies. The other aspect of IS–LM is the omission of alternative financial assets (e.g. equities). Thus a demand management policy involving government deficits requires a degree of both public and financial market approval if they are to be used successfully.

The maintenance of full employment under capitalism also requires institutional and socio-political reforms, which may be so great that a suitably reformed capitalism would not be capitalism at all. The problems involved in continuous full employment as compared with frequent periods of unemployment are succinctly stated in the concluding essay in Oxford University Institute of Statistics (1944) (to which all the authors of the volume including Kalecki subscribed):

> In this sense, unemployment is the most powerful of all economic controls. If there is pressure on the balance of payments, deflation and unemployment will relieve it; with unemployment there is no danger that pressure for money wage increases will create an inflationary spiral: instead of controlling the location of industry,

unemployment forces the workers to move to wherever an employer chooses to establish his factory. All the 'controls' directly associated with full employment are, in fact, required to take over the trade previously performed by unemployment and the trade cycle.

In Chapter 7 (p. 141), we have given a quote from Kalecki in which he argued that fundamental reforms would be required if capitalism were to adjust to full employment. Whilst Kalecki did not spell out what these reforms would have to be, there are strong hints in his writings. The reforms would have to take account of the increased power of trade unions and workers which would result from continuous full employment. The account taken would not be a negative one of legal controls, but the positive one of involvement in decision-making. At least in the context of Poland in the 1950s, Kalecki clearly involved workers' in decision-making and the development of Workers' Councils. The preceding paragraph would also suggest that ways of controlling inflation, regional development, correcting balance of payments difficulties, etc. would have to be found to replace unemployment as the control or correction mechanism.

The second aspect on which we touch is the view of the nature of the State and the explanation of why certain policies are adopted. The discussion above on hyperinflation (pp. 122–3), full employment (Chapter 7) and developing economies (Chapter 10) would strongly suggest that Kalecki did not see the State as adopting some 'neutral' role, or operating in the 'social interest' (as would be generally implicit in the Keynesian approach). Instead, he saw the State as subject to many pressures, and the policies adopted as reflecting those pressures. Thus, in the context of developing economies, Kalecki's idea of intermediate regimes indicate a State largely acting in the interests of the middle class, though subject to pressures from landlords, local big business, etc. His view of the political business cycle (pp. 140–1 above) suggests a changing balance of power between workers and capitalists, which is reflected in changing government policies.

The general idea of seeking to explain changes in economic policy in terms of the changing balance of power between classes and changing perceptions of their interests surfaces in a few places in Kalecki's writings. Before giving some examples, it should be noted that Kalecki's analysis was not always in terms of a two-class (workers versus capitalists) conflict, involving on occasions conflicts within the capitalist class and, in the idea of intermediate regimes, the idea of three basic social classes. Bhaduri and Steindl (1983), drawing on the reminiscences of Steindl, wrote that

> Kalecki used to interpret the events in Britain around 1931–2 in terms of a shift of power from the City to industry. The interest of the City was overruled by abandoning the Gold Standard, adopting a floating exchange rate and establishing the Exchange Equalization Account. Industry got protection again and free trade was rejected in a major turn about of British economic policy. This change was connected with a decline in the international status of the City as the financial centre of the world.

Bhaduri and Steindl then continue to develop an explanation of the 'rise of monetarism as a social doctrine' (their title) in rather similar terms in the sense of seeking an explanation in terms of the interests and power of the financial sector.

Kalecki (1972b), Chapters 2 (written in 1956), 3 (written in 1964) and 4 (written in 1967) discussed certain aspects of post-war American economic and political developments. In the first of those, he saw the post-war prosperity as founded on increased government expenditure, which rested heavily on armaments expenditure, which helped with its political acceptance. The second and third of those papers discussed political developments in the mid-1960s, particularly the significance of the candidature of Goldwater for President in 1964. This discussion may well have some contemporary relevance as 'Reaganism, as is well known, grew out of the movement led by Senator Barry Goldwater that in 1964 temporarily took control of the Republican Party' (Reichley, 1981). Kalecki saw

> the oil interests in Texas, the armament industries of the West, and the Bank of America, also very active there, are some of the main groups [backing Goldwater]. All are 'young' dynamic concerns. They are not particularly worried about slumps because they think that not only will they survive them but that they will increase their possessions at the expense of 'old' capitalist groups (Kalecki, 1972b, pp. 102–3).

Kalecki highlighted the opposition of Goldwater and his supporters, to social security, government intervention and trade unions and their support for heightening the Cold War and increased armaments expenditure.

We could summarise Kalecki's general approach as often viewing changes in policy as arising from shifting balances within the capitalist class.

Conclusions

It is our view that the type of extensions and developments discussed immediately above are consistent with the broad thrust of Kalecki's work. It should be a tribute to his work that the framework laid down fifty years ago maintains the ability to absorb and incorporate recent developments. Further, whilst there are clearly loose ends left, the Kalecki approach provides a framework within which important issues can be discussed. The contrast can be drawn with neo-classical monetarism. It is difficult within that monetarist framework to discuss the causes of unemployment since the model denies any substantial unemployment. Neo-classical models have portrayed growth as a steady process at a rate determined by growth of the labour force and technical change. It permits an indication that a change in the rate of technical progress will change the balanced growth rate (though that is rather a trivial conclusion), but it does not permit discussion of problems of moving from one path to another, to why the rate of technical progress changes, etc.

Notes to Chapter 12

1. The discussion with new classical economists and their opponents reported in Klamer (1984) are of relevance here. Sargent (p. 79) argues as a new classical economist that '(i)t is true that these assumptions are unrealistic, but what is equally true is, if you take any macro-model the assumptions are unrealistic ... The test for whether they're realistic or not is in the econometrics'. Tobin (pp. 105–6) argues that 'we are not so good at testing typotheses so that we can give up any information we have at whatever stage of the argument. The realism of assumptions does matter. Any evidence you have on that, either casual or empirical, is relevant'.
2. However, little debate has been generated over the question of what Kalecki really meant. Johansen (1978) argued that this was because of Kalecki's clarity. 'As is witnessed every day, there is very much

controversy about what Keynes "actually meant to say"'. But that does not arise in the case of Kalecki. 'In most of his writing he is terse and to the point. He is near to the optimum from the point of view of communicating his ideas clearly and efficiently. There will, therefore, hardly ever arise any great controversy about what Kalecki actually meant . . .'.

3. Weintraub (1979) suggests that '[t]here appears to be only one *legitimate* macroeconomic mode of discourse when conformity with general equilibrium theory is presupposed. Alternative macroeconomic theories, like those of the post-Keynesians, fall outside the pale of *legitimate* discourse' (italics added). However, Weintraub concludes that 'there should be little argument about the proposition that some sort of revivified, reconstituted general equilibrium theory is the only logically possible general link between microeconomics and macroeconomics'.

Fitoussi (1983a) argues that there are two implicit axioms in this approach, namely:

Axiom 1 'The existence of a metalanguage': macroeconomic relations *must* have microeconomic foundations. This proposition establishes from the outset the subordination of the macro to the micro approach, and at the same time it ranks economic arguments in implicitly acknowledging that microeconomics itself is well founded. Yet it is not clear that macroeconomic relations can be derived in this fashion . . .

Axiom 2 'The existence of a metatheory': there exists a class of models that yield macroeconomic propositions while rendering explicit their microeconomic foundations: namely, general equilibrium theory, which by virtue of this axiom is given the status of a metatheory, a common structure within which all other theories must be expressed. In this framework the 'no bridge' problem is spurious, for it is theoretically possible to represent a system at as detailed a level as one wants. The level of aggregation chosen depends on the problem one is given to analyse.

The arguments that follow in the text can be seen as a rejection of the validity of these axioms (whilst accepting that these axioms do lie behind the type of views expressed by Drazen and Weintraub). Skott (1983) in discussion of Keynes and general equilibrium theory quotes from Weintraub (1979) that general equilibrium theory 'is a metatheory, or an investigative logic, which is . . . used to construct *all* economic theories' and that it is 'rooted . . . in the very structural unities of science itself' (italics added). Skott, then states that 'I find Weintraub's statements absolutely false. If one wants to analyse dynamic questions – and what economic questions of interest are not inherently dynamic? – then strict adherence to a GE [general equilibrium] framework will inevitably impede progress' (text in brackets added). It should be clear that Kalecki's approach would be ruled out from consideration if Weintraub's statement were accepted, and we are in agreement with Skott's position.

4. This can clearly be contrasted with the primacy of microeconomics over macroeconomics which pervades much of conventional theory as indicated in the previous note.

5. Equilibrium analysis could be viewed in two other ways. First, it could be seen as used to simplify analysis in the belief that such a simplification would not upset the basis of the analysis and would enable certain factors to be highlighted. The approach of Sraffa and neo-Ricardians could be seen in this light as focusing on the relationship between wages, profits and prices of production (under the assumption of an equilised rate of profit). Second, equilibrium analysis could be used to indicate the considerable difficulties there would be in the achievement of equilibrium (or of the smooth operation of the economy). Marx's use of the three department schema can be seen in this light.

6. Fine and Murfin (1985) develop many criticisms of Kalecki's degree of monopoly approach, generally from a Marxian perspective.

7. Employers and self-employed make up the remainder of the civilian working population. The figures for 1911 include Southern Ireland, and hence are not exactly comparable with the figures for 1961. Source of figures is Feinstein (1972).

8. For discussion on non-manual workers and unionisation, see, for example, Hyman and Price (1983); figures relevant to the UK are given on p. 151 of that book.

9. See, for example, Webb (1976) on the application of marginal cost pricing in nationalised industries. But see also Wiseman (1959) for a strong critique of the usefulness of marginal cost pricing rules. Many of his criticisms on the lack of precision on what constitutes marginal cost would also apply to the use of prices as a mark-up over marginal costs by private firms.

10. It is tempting to suggest that the questioning of the constant average direct cost assumption arises from the idea that acceptance of that assumption would be fairly destructive for perfect competition theory (e.g. how could price be equated to a constant marginal cost? what restricts the size of a firm?) The successful questioning of the notion of marginal costs would clearly be destructive of the neo-classical approach to economics.

11. See, for example, Sawyer (1981), Chapter 16.

12. This is usually discussed under the heading of the 'surprise supply function': for a critique see Sawyer (1985).

13. Pasinetti (1962) set off a debate between Samuelson and Modigliani, Robinson, Kaldor and Pasinetti in the *Review of Economic Studies*, vol. 33.

14. It should be noted that Pasinetti's analysis relates to long-run equilibrium, whereas Kalecki would not be concerned with such equilibrium analysis.

15. Figures for the earlier period are taken from *Economic Trends*, Annual Supplement 1982. The lowest savings ratio was recorded for 1948 at 0.1 per cent. Figures for the latter period are taken from 1983 edition of *National Income Accounts*. The statistics on the savings ratio have been

subject to frequent and substantial revisions. In the source used, the highest ratio was reached in 1980 at 14.8 per cent.

16. It could be the case that the existence of employers' contributions (and hence enhanced pension provision) leads workers to reduce their own savings to offset those contributions. If there was complete offset than the volume of savings would be unaffected, but the form of savings would be changed. However, Green (1981) states 'the main conclusion from these two UK tests is that pension saving does not substitute with other types of saving, and that this concurs with the US results of Cagan and others'. In 1982, employers' contributions accounted for nearly 6 per cent of personal disposable income, and employees' contributions $1\frac{3}{4}$ per cent. This indicates the scale by which other savings would have to be reduced or dissaving incurred if the 'no-effect' hypothesis were to hold.

17. See, for example, Kamien and Schwartz (1982) for a survey of the empirical work on the relationship between industrial structure and technical advance.

18. Tomlinson (1981, 1984) particularly has argued that there never was a Keynesian 'revolution' in macroeconomic policy; for a critique of his position, see Schott (1982), Booth (1983, 1984). As might be expected some of this debate turns on what is meant by Keynesian.

19. Keynesians are often left in a difficult position in explaining the rise of monetarism (as I argued elsewhere in Sawyer (1982b, pp. 9–10)) to the extent to which they accept the view of Keynes on the importance of ideas and the importance of 'vested interests'. Hodgson (1984) put it as follows:

Traditionally, Keynesians have tended to view Thatcherism (and Reaganomics) as products of misjudgement or blinkered vision, resulting from 'some academic scribbler of a few years back' (Keynes, 1936, p. 383). . . . As Donald Moggridge has written: 'Keynes always believed that "a little clear thinking" or "more lucidity" could solve almost any problem . . . Reform was achieved by the discussions of intelligent people' (Moggridge, 1976, pp. 37–8). Yet there are many highly intelligent people in the Cabinet, at the Treasury, within the Confederation of British Industry, and even, perhaps in 10 Downing Street. If the Keynesian view of the workings of the advanced capitalist economy is valid, then there must be more the erroneous policies of Thatcherism than a failure of the powers of reason.

20. In conventional accounting terms, it is clear that governments ran a substantial deficit from the mid-1970s onwards. In periods of high inflation, the government deficit is pushed up by the payment of high nominal rates of interest, but without account being taken of the gains to government of the reduction in the real value of outstanding debt which inflation causes. Thus historically high (for peacetime) government deficits are combined with falling ratios of national debt to GDP, see Boltho (1982), p. 318; OECD *Economic Outlook* (e.g. July 1984)

provides data on government deficits relative to GDP for developed countries over the past decade.

21. 'With this tarnishing of the international image of the City, the centre of gravity of British economic policy shifted to the home-front in favour of domestic industries. This provided the necessary socio-political base for the acceptance of Keynesian policies'. A footnote to the last sentence begins 'Or, in particular, that aspect of Keynesian policy which argued for the economic autonomy of the state in managing demand through public works to provide a sufficient market for domestic industries so as to maintain full employment' (Bhaduri and Steindl, 1983).

List of Kalecki's Publications Referred to in the Text

Only these publications referred to in the text are listed here; a comprehensive list of publications can be found in Feiwel (1975). Those references followed by (a) were reprinted in Oxford University Institute of Statistics (1947).

(1933) *Proba teorii koniunktury*, Warsaw: Institute of Research on Business Cycles and Prices (translated as Kalecki (1966), Chapter 1 and reprinted in Kalecki (1971a, Chapter 1).

(1935a) 'Essai d'une théorie du mouvement cyclique des affaires', *Revue d'economie politique*, vol. 2.

(1935b) 'A Macrodynamic Theory of Business Cycles', *Econometrica*, vol. 3.

(1935c) 'Istota poprawy koniunkturalnej', *Polska Gospodarcza*, no. 43.

(1935d) 'Koniunktura a bilans platniczy', *Polska Gospodarcza*, no. 45.

(1936) 'Pare uwag o teorii Keynesa', *Ekinomista*, no. 3.

(1937a) 'A Theory of the Business Cycle', *Review of Economic Studies*, vol. 4.

(1937b) 'A Theory of Commodity, Income and Capital Taxation', *Economic Journal*, vol. 47 (reprinted as Kalecki, 1971a, Chapter 4).

(1937c) 'Principle of Increasing Risk', *Economica*, vol. 3 (revised version is Kalecki, 1971a, Chapter 9).

(1938a) 'The Determinants of Distribution of the National Income', *Econometrica*, vol. 6.

(1938b) 'The Lesson of the Blum Experiment', *Economic Journal*, vol. 48.

(1939) *Essays in the Theory of Economic Fluctuations* (Allen & Unwin).

(1940) 'The Supply Curve of an Industry under Imperfect Competition', *Review of Economic Studies*, vol. 7.

(1941a) 'A Theorem on Technical Progress', *Review of Economic Studies*, vol. 8.

(1941b) 'The Short term Rate of Interest and the Velocity of Cash Circulation', *Review of Economics and Statistics*, vol. 23.

(1941c) 'The Theory of Long Run Distribution of the Product of Industry', *Oxford Economic Papers*, no. 5.

(1941d) 'What is Inflation?', *Bulletin of the Oxford University Institute of Statistics*, vol. 3. (a)

(1941e) 'Inflation, Wages and Rationing', *The Banker*, October 1941. (a)

(1942a) 'A Theory of Profits', *Economic Journal*, vol. 52.

(1942b) 'Mr. Whitman on the Concept of "Degree of Monopoly"', *Economic Journal*, vol. 32.

(1943a) *Studies in Economic Dynamics* (Allen & Unwin)

(1943b) 'Political Aspects of Full Employment', *Political Quarterly,* vol. 14 (Reprinted in E. K. Hunt and J. G. Schwartz (eds) *A Critique of Economic Theory* (Penguin, Harmondsworth, 1972) and in a slightly amended version as Kalecki, 1971, Chapter 12).

(1943c) 'Economic Implications of the Beveridge Plan', *Bulletin of the Oxford University Institute of Statistics*, vol. 5, Supplement no. 4. (a)

(1943d) 'The Burden of the National Debt', *Bulletin of the Oxford University Institute of Statistics*, vol. 5. (a)

(1944a) 'Professor Pigou on "The Classical Stationary State": A Comment', *Economic Journal*, vol. 54.

(1944b) 'Three Ways to Full Employment', in Oxford University Institute of Statistics (1944).

(1944c) 'Rationing and Price Control', *Bulletin of the Oxford University of Institute of Statistics*, vol. 6. (a)

(1944d) 'The White Paper on Employment Policy', *Bulletin of the Oxford University Institute of Statistics*, vol. 6.

(1945a) 'Full Employment by Stimulating Private Investment?', *Oxford Economic Papers*, no. 7.

(1945b) 'The Maintenance of Full Employment after the Transition Period', *International Labour Review*, vol. 52.

(1946a) 'Multilateralism and Full Employment', *Canadian Journal of Economics, and Political Science*, vol. .

(1946b) 'A Comment on "Monetary Policy"', *Review of Economics and Statistics*, vol. 28.

(1947) 'The Maintenance of Full Employment after the Transition Period: A rejoinder to Mr. Wytinsky's Note', *American Economic Review*, vol. 37.

(1954) *Theory of Economic Dynamics* (Allen & Unwin) (Revised second edition, 1965).

(1956a) 'The Dynamics of Investment and National Income' (in Polish), *Economista*, no. 5, 1956.

(1956b) 'Workers Councils and Central Planning' (in Polish), *Nowe Drogi*, no. 12, 1956.

(1959) 'The 1961–1975 Long Run Economic Plan', *Polish Perspectives*, no. 3, 1959.

(1962a) 'Observations on the Theory of Growth', *Economic Journal*, vol. 72.

(1962b) 'A Model of Hyperinflation', *Manchester School*, vol. 32.

(1962c) 'Outline of Method of Constructing a Perspective Plan', *Teaching Materials*, vol. 8 (reprinted in Nove and Nuti (1972)).

(1965) 'Econometric Model and Historical Materialism' in *On Political Economy and Econometrics: Essays in Honour of Oskar Lange.*

(1966) *Studies in the Theory of the Business Cycle: 1933–39*, (translated from Polish by Ada Kalecki) (Blackwell, Oxford).

(1968a) 'The Marxian Equations of Reproductions and Modern Economics', *Social Science Information*, vol. 7.

(1968b) 'Trend and the Business Cycle', *Economic Journal*, vol. 78.

(1970) 'Theories of Growth in Different Social Systems', *Scientia*, no. 5–6.

(1971a) *Selected Essays on the Dynamics of the Capitalist Economy* (Cambridge University Press).

(1971b) 'The Class Struggle and the Distribution of National Income', *Kyklos*, vol. 24.

(1972a) *Selected Essays on the Economic Growth of the Socialist and the Mixed Economy* (Cambridge University Press).

(1972b) *The Last Phase in the Transformation of Capitalism* (Monthly Review Press).

(1976) *Essays on Developing Economies* (Harvester, Brighton).

References

Aaronovitch, S. and Sawyer, M. (1975) *Big Business* (Macmillan).

Addison, P. (1976) *The Road to 1945: British Politics and the Second World War* (Quartet Books).

Ando, A. and Modigliani, F. (1963) 'The Life-Cycle Hypothesis of Saving: Aggregate Implications and Tests', *American Economic Review*, vol. 53.

Asimakopulos, A. (1977) 'Profits and Investment: A Kaleckian Approach', in G. C. Harcourt (ed.), *The Microeconomic Foundations of Macroeconomics* (Macmillan).

Asimakopulous, A. (1983) 'Kalecki and Keynes on Finance, Investment and Saving', *Cambridge Journal of Economics*, vol. 7.

Bain, J. (1951) 'Relation of Profit Rate to Industry Concentration in American Manufacturing, 1936–1940', *Quarterly Journal of Economics*, vol. 65.

Baran, P. (1957) *The Political Economy of Growth* (Monthly Review Press, New York).

Baran, P. and Sweezy, P. (1967) *Monopoly Capital* (Penguin, Harmondsworth).

Barro, R. and Grossman, H. (1971) 'A General Disequilibrium Model of Income and Employment', *American Economic Review*, vol. 61.

Bauer, P. (1942) 'A Note on Monopoly' *Economica*, vol. 8.

Baumol, W. J. (1952) 'The Transactions Demand for Cash: An Inventory Theoretic Approach', *Quarterly Journal of Economics*, vol. 66.

Baumol, W. (1959) *Business Behaviour, Value and Growth* (Macmillan).

Berle, A. and Means, G. C. (1932) *The Modern Corporation and Private Property* (Macmillan).

Bethell, N. (1969) *Gomulka: His Poland and His Communism* (Longmans).

Bhaduri, A. and Steindl, J. (1983) 'The Rise of Monetarism as a Social Doctrine', *Thames Papers in Political Economy*, Autumn 1983.

Bispham, J. and Boltho, A. (1982) 'Demand Management', in A. Boltho (ed.) *The European Economy: Growth and Crisis* (Oxford University Press).

Blatt, J. (1983) *Dynamic Economic Systems* (Wheatsheaf Books, Brighton).

Blazyca, G. (1980) 'Industrial Structure and the Economic Problems of Industry in a Centrally Planned Economy: The Polish Case', *Journal of Industrial Economics*, vol. 28.

Bleaney, M. (1976) *Underconsumption Theories* (Lawrence & Wishart).

Blinder, A. and Solow, R. (1973) 'Does Fiscal Policy Matter?', *Journal of Public Economics*, vol. 2.

Boltho, A. (ed.) (1982) *The European Economy: Growth and Crisis* (Oxford University Press).

Booth, A. (1983) 'The Keynesian Revolution in Economic Policy Making', *Economic History Review*, vol. 36.

Booth, A. (1984) 'Defining A Keynesian Revolution', *Economic History Review*, vol. 37.

Bradley, I. and Howard, M. (eds) (1982) *Classical and Marxian Political Economy* (Macmillan).

Bronfrenbrenner, M. (1969) (ed.) *Is the Business Cycle Obsolete?* (Wiley).

Bronfrenbrenner, M. (1971) *Income Distribution Theories* (Macmillan).

Brus, W. (1973) *The Economics and Politics of Socialism* (Routledge & Kegan Paul).

Brus, W. (1975) *Socialist Ownership and Political Systems* (Routledge & Kegan Paul).

Brus, W. (1977a) 'Kalecki's Economics of Socialism', *Oxford Bulletin of Economics and Statistics*, vol. 39.

Brus, W. (1977b) Correspondence, in *Soviet Studies*, vol. 29.

Brus, W. and Łaski, K. (1964) 'Growth and the Full Employment of Productive Forces', in *Problems of Economic Dynamics and Planning: Essays in Honour of Michal Kalecki* (PWN-Polish Scientific Publishers, Warsaw).

Brus, W. and Łaski, K. (1965a) 'The Law of Value and the Problem of Allocation in Socialism', in *On Political Economy and Econometrics: Essays in Honour of Oskar Lange* (PWN-Polish Scientific Publishers, Warsaw).

Brus, W. and Łaski, K. (1965b) 'Problems in the Theory of Growth under Socialism', in E. A. G. Robinson (ed.), *Problems of Economic Development*, (Macmillan, 1965) (abridged version published in A. Nove and D. M. Nuti (eds), *Socialist Economics*).

Brzeski, A. (1976) 'Kalecki and the Polish Economy', *Soviet Studies*, vol. 28.

Brzeski, A. (1977) Correspondence in *Soviet Studies*, vol. 29.

Cameron, J., Cole, K. and Edwards, C. (1983) *Why Economists Disagree*, (Longmans).

Chick, V.(1983) *Macro Economics After Keynes* (Philip Allan, Deddington).

Christ, C. (1968) 'A Simple Macroeconomic Model with a Government Restraint', *Journal of Political Economy*, vol. 76.

Clifton, J. (1977) 'Competition and the Evolution of the Capitalist Mode of Production', *Cambridge Journal of Economics*, vol. 1.

Clower, R. (1965) 'The Keynesian Counter-Revolution: A Theoretical Appraisal', in F. Hahn, and F. Brechling (eds), *The Theory of Interest Rates* (Macmillan).

Coddington, A. (1983) *Keynesian Economics: The Search for First Principles* (Allen & Unwin).

Coutts, K., Godley, W. and Nordhaus, W. (1978) *Industrial Pricing in the United Kingdom* (Cambridge University Press).

Cowling, K. (1982) *Monopoly Capitalism* (Macmillan).

Cowling, K. (1983) 'Excess Capacity and the Degree of Collusion: Oligopoly Behaviour in the Slump', *Manchester School*, vol. 51.

Cowling, K. and Molho, I. (1982) 'Wage Share, Concentration and Unionsim', *Manchester School*, vol. 50.

Cyert, R. and March, J. G. (1963) *A Behavioral Theory of the Firm* (Prentice-Hall).

Davidson, P. (1981) 'Post Keynesian Economics', in D. Bell and I. Kristol (eds), *The Crisis in Economic Theory* (Basic Books, New York).

Davis, E. G. (1980) 'The Correspondence between R. G. Hawtrey and J. M. Keynes on the *Treatise*: the Genesis of Output Adjustment Models', *Canadian Journal of Economics*, vol. 13.

Delebeke, J. (1983) 'Recent Long Wave Theories. A Critical Survey', in C. Freeman (ed.), *Long Waves in the World Economy* (Butterworth).

Dell, S. (1977) 'Kalecki at the United Nations', *Oxford Bulletin of Economics and Statistics*, vol. 39.

Desai, M. (1979) *Marxian Economics* (Blackwell, Oxford).

Dixit, A. (1976) *The Theory of Equilibrium Growth* (Oxford University Press).

Dobb, M. (1960) *An Essay on Economic Growth and Planning* (Routledge & Kegan Paul).

Dobb, M. (1973) *Theories of Value and Distribution since Adam Smith* (Cambridge University Press).

Drazen, A. (1980) 'Recent Developments in Macroeconomics Disequilibrium Theory', *Econometrica*, vol. 48.

Dunlop, J. (1938) 'The Movement of Real and Money Wage Rates', *Economic Journal*, vol. 48.

Dziewanowski, M. K. (1959) *The Communist Party of Poland* (Harvard University Press, Cambridge, Mass.).

Eichner, A. S. (1973) 'A Theory of the Determination of the Mark-up under Oligopoly', *Economic Journal*, vol. 83.

Eichner, A. S. (ed.) (1979) *A Guide to Post Keynesian Economics* (Macmillan).

Eichner, A. and Kregel, J. (1975) 'An Essay on Post Keynesian Theory: A New Paradigm in Economics', *Journal of Economic Literature*, vol. 13.

Eshag, E. (1977), 'Kalecki's Political Economy: A Comparison with Keynes', *Oxford Bulletin of Economics and Statistics*, vol. 39.

Feinstein, C. (1972) *National Income, Expenditure and Output of the United Kingdom 1883–1965* (Cambridge University Press).

Feiwel, G. (1972) Introduction to M. Kalecki, *The Last Phase in the Transformation of Capitalism* (Monthly Review Press).

Feiwel, G. (1975) *The Intellectual Capital of Michal Kalecki* (University of Tennessee Press, Knoxville).

Ferguson, C. E. (1969) *The Neo-classical Theory of Production and Distribution* (Cambridge University Press).

Fine, B. and Harris, L. (1979) *Rereading Capital* (Macmillan).

Fine, B. and Murfin, A. (1985) *Macroeconomics and Monopoly Capitalism* (Wheatsheaf Books, Brighton).

Fitoussi, J.-P. (1983a) 'Modern Macroeconomic Theory: An Overview', in

J.-P. Fitoussi (ed.), *Modern Macroeceonomic Theory* (Blackwell, Oxford).

Fitoussi, J.-P. (ed.) (1938b) *Modern Macroeconomic Theory* (Blackwell, Oxford).

Freeman, C. (ed.) (1983) *Long Waves in the World Economy* (Butterworth).

Friedman, M. (1956) 'The Quantity Theory – a Restatement', in M. Friedman (ed.), *Studies in the Quantity Theory of Money* (University of Chicago Press).

Friedman, M. (1969) *The Optimum Quantity of Money and Other Essays* (Aldine, Chicago).

Frisch, R. (1933) 'Propagation Problems and Impulse Problems in Dynamics', in *Economic Essays in Honour of Gustav Cassel*.

Frisch, R. and Holme, H. (1935) 'The Characteristic Solutions of a Mixed Difference and Differential Equation Occurring in Economic Dynamics', *Econometrica*, vol. 3.

Galbraith, J. K. (1971) 'How Keynes Came to America', in J. K. Galbraith, *A Contemporary Guide to Economics, Peace and Laughter* (Deutsch).

Godley, W. and Nordhaus, W. (1972) 'Pricing in the Trade Cycle', *Economic Journal*, vol. 82.

Goldman, J. and Kouba, K. (1969) *Economic Growth in Czechoslovakia* (Academia, Prague).

Goodwin, R. (1982) *Essays in Economic Dynamics* (Macmillan).

Green, F. (1981) 'The Effect of Occupational Pension Schemes on Saving in the United Kingdom: A Test of the Life Cycle Hypothesis', *Economic Journal*, vol. 91.

Gurley, J. and Shaw, E. (1960) *Money in a Theory of Finance* (Brookings Institute, Washington).

Hacche, G. (1979) *The Theory of Economic Growth: An Introduction* (Macmillan).

Hahn, F. (1973) *On the Notion of Equilibrium in Economics* (Cambridge University Press).

Hall, R. and Hitch, C. (1939) 'Price Theory and Business Behaviour', *Oxford Economic Papers*, no. 2.

Harcourt, G. C. (1972) *Some Cambridge Controversies in the Theory of Capital* (Cambridge University Press).

Harcourt, G. C. (1975a) 'Capital Theory: Much Ado about Something', *Thames Papers in Political Economy*, Autumn 1975.

Harcourt, G. C. (1975b) 'The Cambridge Controversies: The Afterglow', in J. M. Parkin and A. Nobay (eds), *Contemporary Issues in Economics* (Manchester University Press).

Harcourt, G. C. (ed.) (1977a) *The Microeconomic Foundations of Macroeconomics* (Macmillan).

Harcourt, G. C. (1977b) Review of *The Intellectural Capital of Michal Kalecki*, in *Economica*, vol. 43.

Harris, D. (1978) *Capital Accumulation and Income Distribution* (Routledge & Kegan Paul).

Harris, L. (1976) 'On Interest, Credit and Capital', *Economy and Society*, vol. 5.

Harrod, R. (1936) *The Trade Cycle* (Oxford University Press).

Harrod, R. (1951) *The Life of John Maynard Keynes* (Macmillan).

Hay, D. and Morris, D. (1979) *Industrial Economics* (Oxford University Press).

Helliwell, J. F. (1976) 'Aggregate Investment Equations: A Survey of Issues', in J. F. Helliwell (ed.), *Aggregate Investment* (Penguin, Harmondsworth).

Henry, S. G. B., Sawyer, M. and Smith, P. (1976) 'Models of Inflation in the U.K.: An Evaluation', *National Institute Economic Review*, no. 76.

Hessian, C. H. (1984) *John Maynard Keynes* (Macmillan, New York).

Hicks, J. (1936) 'Mr. Keynes's Theory of Employment', *Economic Journal*, vol. 46.

Hicks, J. (1937) 'Mr. Keynes and the Classics: A Suggested Interpretation', *Econometrica*, vol. 4.

Hicks, J. (1950) *A Contribution to the Theory of the Trade Cycle* (Oxford University Press).

Hicks, J. (1983) 'IS–LM: An Explanation', in J–P Fitoussi (ed.), *Modern Macroeconomic Theory* (Blackwell, Oxford).

Hodgson, G. (1982) 'Theoretical and Policy Implications of Variable Productivity', *Cambridge Journal of Economics*, vol. 6.

Hodgson, G. (1984) 'Thatcherism: The Miracle that Never Happened' in E. J. Nell (ed.) *Free Market Conservatism* (Allen & Unwin).

Horvat, B., Markovic, M. and Supek, R. (eds) (1975) *Self-Governing Socialism*, vol. 1 (International Arts and Sciences, Press, New York).

Howard, M. (1983) *Profits in Economic Theory* (Macmillan).

Howard, M. and King, J. E. (1975) *The Political Economy of Marx* (Longman).

Howard, M. and King, J. E. (1976) Introduction to M. Howard and J. E. King (eds), *The Economics of Marx* (Penguin Harmondsworth).

Hyman, R. and Price, R. (eds) (1983) *The New Working Class? White-Collar Workers and their Organisations* (Macmillan).

Johansen, L. (1978) Review of *The Intellectual Capital of Michal Kalecki* in *Journal of Political Economy*, vol. 86.

Johnson, H. G. (1973) *The Theory of Income Distribution* (Gray-Mills).

Johnson, H. G. (1978) 'The Shadow of Keynes', in E. Johnson and H. G. Johnson, *The Shadow of Keynes* (Blackwell, Oxford).

Johnston, J. (1960) *Statistical Cost Curves* (McGraw-Hill).

Jones, H. G. (1975) *An Introduction to Modern Theories of Economic Growth* (Nelson).

Jorgenson, D. (1967) 'The Theory of Investment', in R. Ferber (ed.), *Determinants of Investment Behavior* (National Bureau of Economic Research, New York).

Junankar, P. N. (1982) *Marx's Economics* (Philip Allan, Deddington).

Kaldor, N. (1934) 'The Equilibrium of the Firm', *Economic Journal*, vol. 44.

Kaldor, N. (1955) 'Alternative Theories of Distribution', *Review of Economic Studies*, vol. 23.

Kaldor, N. (1966) 'Marginal Productivity and the Macro-Economic Theories of Distribution', *Review of Economic Studies*, vol. 33.

Kaldor, N. (1972) 'The Irrelevance of Equilibrium Economics', *Economic Journal*, vol. 82.

Kaldor, N. (1981) *Origins of the New Monetarism* (Cardiff University Press).

Kaldor, N. (1982) *The Scourge of Monetarism* (Oxford University Press).

Kalecki, M. and Rakowski, M. (1959) 'Generalized Formula of the Efficiency of Investment', *Gospodarka Planowa*, no. 11, 1959 (in Polish): English translation in A. Zauberman (ed.), *Studies in the Theory of Reproduction and Prices* (Warsaw); extracts published in A. Nove and D. M. Nuti (eds), *Socialist Economics* (Penguin, Harmondsworth).

Kamien, N. and Schwartz, N. (1982) *Market Structure and Innovation* (Cambridge University Press).

Keynes, J. M. (1930) *A Treatise on Money* (Macmillan).

Keynes, J. M. (1936) *The General Theory of Employment, Interest and Money* (Macmillan).

Keynes, J. M. (1937a) 'The General Theory of Employment', *Quarterly Journal of Economics*, vol. 51.

Keynes, J. M. (1937b) 'Alternative Theories of the Rate of Interest', *Economic Journal*, vol. 47.

Keynes, J. M. (1937c) 'The *Ex Ante* Theory of the Rate of Interest', *Economic Journal*, vol. 47.

Keynes, J. M. (1939) 'Relative Movements of Real Wages and Output', *Economic Journal*, vol. 49.

Keynes, J. M. (1973) *The General Theory and After: Part II Defence and Development, Collected Works, vol. 14* (Macmillan).

Keynes, J. M. (1979) *The General Theory and After: A Supplement, Collected Works, vol. 29* (Macmillan).

Keynes, J. M. (1983) *Economic Articles and Correspondence: Investment and Editorial, Collected Works, vol. 12* (Macmillan).

Klamer, A. (1984) *The New Classical Macroeconomics* (Wheatsheaf Books, Brighton).

Klein, L. (1951) Review of R. Harrod, *The Life of John Maynard Keynes*, in *Journal of Political Economy*, vol. 59.

Klein, L. (1952) *The Keynesian Revolution* (Macmillan).

Klein, L. (1964) 'The Role of Econometrics in Socialist Economics', *in Problems of Economic Dynamics and Planning: Essays in Honour of Michal Kalecki* (PWN-Polish Scientific Publishers, Warsaw).

Klein, L. (1975) Introduction to G. Feiwel *The Intellectual Capital of Michal Kalecki* (University of Tennesse Press, Knoxville).

Kornai, J. (1979) 'Resource – Constrained versus Demand-Constrained Systems', *Econometrica*, vol. 47.

Kowalik, T. (1964) 'Biography of Michal Kalecki', in *Problems of Economic Dynamics and Planning: Essays in Honour of Michal Kalecki* (PWN-Polish Scientific Publishers, Warsaw).

Kowalik, T. (1965) 'Biography of Oskar Lange', in *On Political Economy and Econometrics: Essays in Honour of Oskar Lange* (PWN-Scientific Publishers, Warsaw).

Kregel, J. (1973) *The Reconstruction of Political Economy* (Macmillan).

Kregel, J. (1976) 'Economic Methodology in the Face of Uncertainty', *Economic Journal*, vol. 86.

Koutsoyiannis, A. (1980) *Modern Microeconomics* (2nd edition, Macmillan).

Lange, O. (1937) 'On the Economic Theory of Socialism', *Review of Economic Studies*, vol. 4.

Lange, O. (1939) 'Neoklasyczna szkotva w ekonomii', in *Encyklopedii Nauk Politycznych*, vol. 4 (Instytut Wydawniczy, Biblioteka Polask, Warsawa).

Łaski, K. (1972) *The Rate of Growth and the Rate of Interest in the Socialist Economy* (Springer-Verlag, Vienna and New York).

Łaski, K. (1983) 'Kalecki's Political Aspects of Full Employment-Forty Years After' (Johannes Kepler Universitat, Linz, mimeo).

Leijonhufvud, A. (1968) *On Keynesian Economics and the Economics of Keynes* (Oxford University Press).

Lekachman, R. (1977) 'The Radical Keynes', in R. Skidelsky (ed.), *The End of the Keynesian Era* (Macmillan).

Lerner, A. (1934) 'The Concept of Monopoly and the Measurement of Monopoly Power, *Review of Economic Studies*, vol. 1.

Lipiński, E. (1977) 'Michal Kalecki', *Oxford Bulletin of Economics and Statistics*, vol. 39.

Lucas, R. and Rapping, L. (1969) 'Real Wages, Employment and Inflation', *Journal of Political Economy*, vol. 77.

Mandel, E. (1976) 'Introduction' to *Capital*, vol. 1 (Penguin, Harmondsworth).

Marris, R. (1964) *The Economic Theory of 'Managerial Capitalism'* (Macmillan).

Marx, K. (1976) *Capital*, vol. 1 (Penguin, Harmondsworth).

Marx, K. (1981) *Capital*, vol. 3 (Penguin, Harmondsworth).

Matthews, R. (1968) 'Why has Britain had Full Employment Since the War?' *Economic Journal*, vol. 78.

Matthews, R. (1982a) 'Introduction', in *Slower Growth in the Western World* (Heinemann).

Matthews, R. (ed.) (1982b) *Slower Growth in the Western World* (Heinemann).

Meade, J. (1978) *The Structure of Direct Taxation: Report of a Committee* (Allen & Unwin).

Means, G. (1935) 'Industrial Pricing and their Relative Inflexibility', (US Senate Document 13, 74th Congress, 1st Session, Washington).

Meek, R. (1977) *Smith, Marx and After* (Chapman & Hall).

Mensch, G. (1975) *Das Technologische Patt* (Umschau Verlag).

Mieczkowski, B. (1978) 'The Relationship between Changes in Consumption and Politics in Poland', *Soviet Studies*, vol. 30.

Ministry of Reconstruction (1944) *Employment Policy* (Cmnd 6527, HMSO).

Minsky, H. P. (1976) *John Maynard Keynes* (Macmillan).

Minsky, H. P. (1978) 'The Financial Instability Hypothesis: A Restatement', *Thames Papers in Political Economy*, Autumn 1978.

von Mises, L. (1935) 'Economic Calculations in the Socialist Commonwealth', in F. A. von Hayek (ed.), *Collectivist Economic Planning* (Routledge & Kegan Paul).

Mitra, A. (1980) *The Share of Wages in National Income* (Oxford University Press, Calcutta).

Modigliani, F. and Miller, M. H. (1958) 'The Cost of Capital, Corporation Finance and the Theory of Investment', *American Economic Review*, vol. 48.

Modigliani, F. (1975) 'The Life Cycle Hypothesis of Saving Twenty Years Later', in J. M. Parkin and A. Nobay (eds), *Contemporary Issues in Economics* (Manchester University Press).

Moggridge, D. (1976) *Keynes* (Fontana).

Moore, B. (1968) *An Introduction to the Theory of Finance* (Free Press, New York).

Moore, B. (1979) 'Monetary Factors', in A. S. Eichner (ed.), *A Guide to Post-Keynesian Economics* (Macmillan).

Moore, B. (1983) 'Unpacking the Post Keynesian Black Box: Bank lending and the Money Supply', *Journal of Post-Keynesian Economics*, vol. 5.

Muellbauer, J. and Portes, R. (1978) 'Macro-economic Models with Quantity Rationing', *Economic Journal*, vol. 88.

National Institute of Economic and Social Research (1981) 'The British Economy in the Medium Term', *National Institute Economic Review*, no. 98.

Neild, R. (1963) *Pricing and Employment in the Business Cycle* (Cambridge University Press).

Nickell, S. (1978) *The Investment Decisions of Firms* (Nisbet, Cambridge Economic Handbooks).

Nove, A. and Nuti, D. M. (eds) (1972) *Socialist Economics* (Penguin, Harmondsworth).

Nuti, D. M. (1977) 'Discussion of Professor Asimakopulos's Paper', in G. C. Harcourt, (ed.), *The Microeconomic Foundations of Macroeconomics* (Macmillan).

Nuti, D. M. (1979) 'The Contradictions of Socialist Economies: A Marxian Interpretation', in R. Miliband and J. Savile (eds), *The Socialist Register, 1979* (Merlin Press).

Nuti, D. M. (1981) 'The Polish Crisis: Economic Factors and Constraints', in R. Miliband and J. Savile (eds), *The Socialist Register, 1981* (Merlin Press).

Okun, A. (1981) *Prices and Quantities: A Macroeconomic Analysis* (Blackwell, Oxford).

Osiatyński, J. (1982) 'Michał Kalecki's Perspective Development Plan for Poland (1960–1975)', *Oeconomica Polona*, 1982.

Oxford University Institute of Statistics (1944) *The Economics of Full Employment* (Blackwell, Oxford).

Oxford University Institute of Statistics (1947) *Studies in War Economics* (Blackwell, Oxford).

Parkin, J. M. and Nobay, A. (eds) (1975) *Contemporary Issues in Economics* (Manchester University Press).

Pasinetti, L. (1962) 'Rate of Profit and Income Distribution in Relation to the Rate of Economic Growth', *Review of Economic Studies*, vol. 29.

Pasinetti, L. (1974) *Growth and Income Distribution* (Cambridge University Press).

Pasinetti, L. (1977) *Lectures on the Theory of Production* (Macmillan).

Patinkin, D. (1982) *Anticipations of the General Theory?* (Blackwell, Oxford).

Pedone, A. (1982) 'Public Expenditure', in A. Boltho (ed.), *The European Economy: Growth and Crisis* (Oxford University Press).

Pigou, A. (1943) 'The Classical Stationary State', *Economic Journal*, vol. 53.

Pravda, A. (1982) 'Poland 1980: From "Premature Consumerism to Labour Solidarity"', *Soviet Studies*, vol. 34.

Reynolds, P. (1979) *Macroeconomic Theories of Distribution and Their Relationship with Economic Dynamics* (Unpublished Ph.D. thesis, University of Sheffield, 1979).

Reynolds, P. (1983) 'Kalecki's Degree of Monopoly', *Journal of Post Keynesian Economics*, vol. 5.

Reynolds, P. (1984) 'An Empirical Analysis of the Degree of Monopoly Theory of Distribution', *Bulletin of Economic Research*, vol. 36.

Reichley, A. J. (1981) 'A Change in Direction', in J. A. Pechman (ed.), *Setting the National Priorities: The 1982 Budget* (Brookings Institute).

Reder, M. (1959) 'Alternative Theories of Labor's Share', in M. Abramovtiz and others (ed.), *The Allocation of Economic Resources: Essays in Honour of B. F. Haley.* (Stanford University Press).

Riach, P. (1971) 'Kalecki's "Degree of Monopoly" Reconsidered', *Australian Economic Papers*, vol. 10.

Robbins, L. (1932) *An Essay on the Nature and Significance of Economic Science* (Macmillan).

Robinson, E. A. G. (1947) 'John Maynard Keynes, 1883–1946', *Economic Journal*, vol. 57.

Robinson, J. (1933) *The Economics of Imperfect Competition* (Macmillan).

Robinson, J. (1945) Review of Oxford University Institute of Statistics (1944), in *Economic Journal*, vol. 55.

Robinson, J. (1964) 'Kalecki and Keynes', in *Problems of Economic Dynamics and Planning: Essays in Honour of Michal Kalecki* (PWN-Polish Scientific Publishers, Warsaw) (reprinted in *Contributions to Modern Economics* (Blackwell, Oxford)).

Robinson, J. (1975) *Collected Economic Papers*, vol. 2 (Blackwell, Oxford).

Robinson, J. (1976a) Introduction to M. Kalecki, *Essays on Developing Economics* (Harvester, Brighton).

Robinson, J. (1976b) 'Michał Kalecki: A Neglected Prophet', *New York Review of Books*, 4 March 1976.

Robinson, J. (1977a) 'Michał Kalecki on the Economics of Capitalism', *Oxford Bulletin of Economics and Statistics*, vol. 39.

Robinson, J. (1977b) 'What are the Questions?', *Journal of Economic Literature*, vol. 15 (reprinted in *Further Contributions to Modern Economics* (Blackwell, Oxford)).

Robinson, J. (1978) *Contributions to Modern Economics* (Blackwell, Oxford)

Robinson, J. (1980) *Further Contributions to Modern Economics* (Blackwell, Oxford).

Rowthorwn, B. (1974) 'Neo-classicism, neo-Ricardianism and Marxism', *New Left Review*, No. 86 (reprinted in *Capitalism, Conflict and Inflation* (Lawrence & Wishart)).

Rowthorn, B. (1977). 'Conflict, Inflation and Money', *Cambridge Journal of Economics*, vol. 1.

Rowthorn, B. (1980) *Capitalism, Conflict and Inflation* (Lawrence & Wishart).

Rowthorn, B. (1981) Demand, Real Wages and Growth, *Thames Papers in Political Economy*, Autumn 1981.

Sachs, I. (1977) 'Kalecki and Development Planning', *Oxford Bulletin of Economics and Statistics*, vol. 39.

Samuelson, P. (1939) 'Interactions between the Multiplier Analysis and the Principle of Acceleration', *Review of Economics and Statistics*, vol. 21.

Sargent, T. (1979) *Macroeconomic Theory* (Academic Press).

Sawyer, M. (1981) *Economics of Industries and Firms* (Croom Helm).

Sawyer, M. (1982a) *Macro-economics in Question* (Wheatsheaf, Brighton).

Sawyer, M. (1982b) 'Towards a Post Kaleckian Macroeconomics', *Thames Papers in Political Economy*, Autumn 1982.

Sawyer, M. (1983) *Business Pricing and Inflation* (Macmillan).

Sawyer, M. (1985) 'The Surprise Supply Function: A Critique', *British Review of Economic Issues*, vol. 7.

Schott, K. (1982) 'The Rise of Keynesian Economics in Britain 1940–64', *Economy and Society*, vol. 11.

Schumpeter, J. (1939) *Business Cycles* (McGraw-Hill, 2 volumes).

Schumpeter, J. (1954) *History of Economic Analysis* (Allen & Unwin).

Sen, A. (1960) *Choice of Techniques* (Blackwell, Oxford).

Sen, A. (1983) 'Development: Which Way Now?', *Economic Journal*, vol. 93.

Shackle, G. (1961) 'Recent Theories Concerning the Nature and Role of Interest', *Economic Journal*, vol. 71.

Silberston, A. (1970) 'Surveys of Applied Economics: Price Behaviour of Firms', *Economic Journal*, vol. 80.

Sirc, L. (1969) *Economic Devolution in Eastern Europe* (Longmans).

Sismonde de Sismondi, J. C. L. (1819) *Nouveaux Principes d'Economie Politique* (Paris, 2 volumes).

Skidelsky, R. (1983) *John Maynard Keynes* (Macmillan).

Skott, P. (1983) 'An Essay on Keynes and General Equilibrium Theory', *Thames Papers in Political Economy*, Summer 1983.

Solow, R. (1956) 'A Contribution to the Theory of Economic Growth', *Quarterly Journal of Economics*, vol. 70.

Stafford, G. B. (1970) 'Full Employment Since the War: A Comment', *Economic Journal*, vol. 80.

Steedman, I. (1977) *Marx After Sraffa* (New Left Books).

Steedman, I. *et al.* (1981) *The Value Controversy* (Verso Books).

Steindl, J. (1952) *Maturity and Stagnation in American Capitalism* (Blackwell, Oxford); reissued with new introduction by Monthly Review Press 1976.

Swann, T. (1956) 'Economic Growth and Capital Accumulation', *Economic Record*, vol. 32.

Targetti, F. and Kinda-Hass, B. (1982) 'Kalecki's Review of Keynes' General Theory', *Australian Economic Papers*, vol. 21.

Tarling, R. and Wilkinson, F. (1977) 'The Social Contract: Post-War Incomes Policies and their Inflationary Impact', *Cambridge Journal of Economics*, vol. 1.

Tarshis, L (1939) 'Changes in Money and Real Wages', *Economic Journal*, vol. 49.

Tinbergen, J. (1935) 'Annual Survey: Suggestions on Quantitative Business Cycle Theory', *Econometrica*, vol. 3.

Tobin, J. (1956) 'The Interest-Elasticity of the Transactions Demand for Money', *Review of Economics and Statistics*, vol. 38.

Tobin, J. (1958) 'Liquidity Preference as Behaviour towards Risk', *Review of Economic Studies*, vol. 25.

Tobin, J. (1969) 'A General Equilibrium Approach to Monetary Theory', *Journal of Money, Credit and Banking*, vol. 1.

Tobin, J. (1972) 'Inflation and Unemployment', *American Economic Review*, vol. 62.

Tobin, J. (1980) 'Are the New Classical Models Plausible Enough to Guide Policy?', *Journal of Money, Credit and Banking*, vol. 12.

Tomlinson, J. (1981) 'Why was there never a "Keynesian Revolution" in Economic Policy Making?', *Economy and Society*, vol. 10.

Tomlinson, J. (1984) 'A Keynesian Revolution in Economic Policy Making?', *Economic History Review*, vol. 37.

Toporowski, J. (1982) *Sources of Disequilibrium in a Centrally Planned Economy: A Study of Planning, Fluctuations, Investment and Strategy in Polish Industry, 1950–1970* (unpublished Ph.D. thesis, University of Birmingham, 1982).

Toporowski, J. (1985) *Selected Essays of Michał Kalecki on Socialist Economic Planning* (Cambridge University Press) (forthcoming).

Waterson, M. (1984) *Economic Theory of the Industry* (Cambridge University Press).

Webb, M. (1976) *Pricing Policies for Public Enterprises* (Macmillan).

Weintraub, E. R. (1979) *Microeconomic Foundations – The Compatibility of Microeconomics and Macroeconomics* (Cambridge University Press).

Weiss, L. (1971) 'Quantitative Studies of Industrial Organisation', in M. Intriligator (ed.), *Frontiers of Economics* (North-Holland).

Wellisz, S. (1968) 'Oskar Lange', in *International Encyclopedia of the Social Sciences*, vol. 8.

Whitman, R. (1942) 'A Note on the Concept of the Degrees of Monopoly', *Economic Journal*, vol. 52.

Wiles, P. (1961) *Prices, Cost and Output* (Blackwell, 2nd edition).

Wiseman, J. (1959) 'The Theory of Public Utility Price – An Empty Box', *Oxford Economic Papers*, vol. 9.

Wood, A. (1975) *A Theory of Profits* (Cambridge University Press).

Worswick, G. (1977) 'Kalecki at Oxford, 1940–44', *Oxford Bulletin of Economics and Statistics*, vol. 39.

Woytinsky, W. S. (1946) 'The Maintenance of Full Employment after the Transition Period: Notes on Mr. Kalecki's Models', *American Economic Review*, vol. 36.

Zauberman, A. (1964) *Industrial Progress in Poland, Czechoslovakia, and East Germany, 1937–1962* (Oxford University Press).

Zielinski, J. G. (1973) *Economic Reforms in Polish Industry* (Oxford University Press).

Zwieg, F. (1944) *Poland Between Two Wars* (Secker & Warburg).

Index

There are few specific references in the index to Kalecki: his discussion of particlar topics are indexed under those topics.